Reading Drama

Reading Drama

A METHOD OF ANALYSIS
WITH SELECTIONS FOR STUDY

Fred B. Millett

Play Anthology Reprint Series

BOOKS FOR LIBRARIES PRESS
FREEPORT, NEW YORK

65186

STANDARD BOOK NUMBER:
8369-8203-7

LIBRARY OF CONGRESS CATALOG CARD NUMBER:
71-111110

PRINTED IN THE UNITED STATES OF AMERICA

CONTENTS

TO THE TEACHER

The purpose of this book is to train young people in the intensive reading of literature. I have spent all my adult life teaching English, but only within the last decade have I come to the conclusion that we, as teachers, can help young students most by training them in the technique of close reading. Most of them will learn to read rapidly without our help, although every English course should furnish some guidance to the acquisition of this important skill. But, unless we train students to read intensively, no one will, and their understanding and appreciation of literature will always be superficial.

Emphasis on the intensive reading of literature may help to keep primary the most appropriate and meaningful approach to literature, the aesthetic, the study of a work of art as a work of art and not as a footnote to biography, social or literary history, philosophy, or ethics. (See Appendix A, "The Study of Literature," for a discussion of the various possible approaches to the study of literature and a defense of the aesthetic-critical approach.) Until recent years, most introductory literature courses have favored the historical approach. If, in many colleges and universities, the introductory survey course has given way to courses in literary types or literary analysis, the reason is that teachers have come to feel that for young people the historical emphasis is less meaningful and valuable than the aesthetic.

Of the shift from the historical to the aesthetic approach, there is abundant evidence. I. A. Richards' *Principles of Literary Criticism* and *Practical Criticism* have had an enormous influence not only on critics but on teachers who keep abreast of movements in contemporary criticism. The University of Chicago English Department's stress on criticism in both undergraduate and graduate courses is another index of this change. The wide popularity of certain well-known textbooks is the result of the appeal of literary analysis to teachers and students. All this evidence points to a "return to the text."

This book is designed, as the title indicates, to set forth a method of literary analysis. To that end, it consists of three easily distinguishable and separable portions: a series of chapters outlining the technical elements essential to literary analysis; a group of selections for close study; and directions, commentaries, and questions designed to embody an analytical procedure. The book, therefore, may be used in a number of ways. You may wish to treat it simply as a collection of readings and use the theoretical chapters merely for reference, if your students show little or no interest in discussing the theory of literary technique. If, on the other hand, your students have a flair for discussing critical terms and literary processes, you may emphasize the theoretical chapters and use the readings to test your theoretical findings. With a responsive class, you may feel justified in making full use of the Directions for Analysis.

These Directions for the Analysis of imaginative literature embody an elaborate analytical procedure, and, at first, you may feel that they are not only elaborate but pedantic. They are included for two reasons: first, because they set forth the process of analysis I use in my own classes, and second, because students carry out these directions with great gusto and intelligence and with profit to them and myself. *You* will, of course, feel perfectly free to use any or all of these Directions, or to ignore them completely.

You should read Appendixes A and B before you begin work with the class. In them is defined and analyzed the frame of reference within which the book is written; in them are both the reasons for keeping the aesthetic-critical study of literature primary and the elements essential to such a study. Of the point in the course at which your students should read these appendixes, you will be the best judge. A good class might be required to read them within the first month of the course; a class of less alert or less interested students might use them as supplementary references to the earlier chapters; with a less well-prepared class, you might decide to express in your own words, instead of the author's, any ideas in it you think useful or valuable.

You will certainly find errors in this book. Of these, I should be glad to hear. You will also disagree with some of the ideas and emphases, but perhaps you may enjoy arguing with me behind my back or to my face. I have always found it more stimulating to teach a book which gave me a chance to conduct a running argument with the unseen author than to teach a book compact of gospel truth. If you feel—as you may well do—that either literary theory or technical analysis is overemphasized, the close study of the texts included will make a rich and rewarding course. After all, what matters is the literature itself.

I should have been more hesitant about offering you this method of analysis if it had not been tested again and again with students and found to produce amazing results. In 1938, the late President McConaughy of Wesleyan University asked me to take a group of students and experiment with them. At first, most of the class time was devoted to the reading and discussion of "great books"; gradually, however, as I became more and more aware of the movement "back to the text," and more and more persuaded that the study of literature as literature should be emphasized, I began developing the method of intensive analysis set forth here. If the results the students have produced are more than gratifying, the reason is not the method but the subtlety and intelligence, the curiosity and enthusiasm students bring to its application. A good class hard at work on the analysis of a piece of imaginative literature can produce coöperatively a body of insights and illuminations of which any first-rate critic would be proud. Almost every student has carried out all the Directions for Analysis with an assiduity and comprehensiveness far beyond the call of duty. The critical analyses students have made are the most valuable results of all my years of teaching.

If your students find the study of this book profitable, you may feel sure that you have given them a training that they will probably get nowhere else. They will never again read a literary work quite superficially. They will always be more observant than they would otherwise have been of at least some of the sources of a work's skill and excellence.

FRED B. MILLETT

Wesleyan University
Middletown, Connecticut

The Elements of Drama

The Nature and Substance of Drama

Drama and fiction both present a series of related actions or events, which, normally, form a pattern—the plot. They are also alike in that the elements essential to plot in drama are identical with those essential to plot in fiction. Both drama and fiction are deeply concerned with characterization, since actions take on meaning only as they are functionally related to the characters who act or are acted upon. Drama, also, like fiction and poetry, focuses on a central theme and invests that theme with a simple or complex tone. The three forms of imaginative literature further show a common concern for discovering a style that is appropriate to the material chosen for expression.

The basic—and all-important—distinction between fiction and drama is that fiction is written to be read—silently or aloud—and drama is written to be acted. In fiction, we read what the characters say and do; in the acted drama, we hear what the characters say and see what they do. Drama, of course, can be read and not heard and seen, but the effect of drama on the printed page is as remote from that of drama on the stage as the effect of a musical score of a symphony is from the performance of it in the concert hall. The printed drama is, in a certain sense, only a rough sketch of what the writer intends the acted play to be; he assumes that his play will achieve its effect not only by means of the speeches and actions indicated in his text but also through the skill

3

of the actors, the adroitness of the scene painters, and the ingenuity of the electricians.

When you read a play, you are expected to assume in turn the various personalities in the play and to conceive of the manner in which a gifted actor would speak the lines that have been written for him. The element of impersonation is one of the two basic differentiae between fiction and drama; the other is the actual, rather than the merely verbal, representation of the action. For, although drama may be acted without scenery or without artificial lighting, drama cannot be performed except by living human beings impersonating the characters and carrying out the action the author has imagined. Thus puppet plays involve human beings speaking the lines, although the characters are represented by puppets, and dramatic pantomime involves human beings who rely not on words but on gestures, to indicate what the characters are feeling and doing.

Because drama on the printed page is so different in its effect from drama on the stage, printed drama imposes a heavier responsibility on you, the reader, than does fiction. If you read a drama imaginatively, you will have to serve as actor, director, scene designer, and electrician in order to achieve from your imaginary production anything like the effect of the acted drama.

The fact that the drama is acted before an audience accounts not only for a good deal of its effectiveness but also for its subject matter. The effectiveness of action in fiction depends on your capacity for evoking clearly and vividly the images through which the action is verbalized. On the stage, you see and hear what is going on; you do not have to weave the web of action out of the threads of imagery. A violent deed persuasively simulated on the stage is almost certain to evoke a more violent reaction from you than the same deed described in words would evoke from the most skilled reader.

The element of impersonation also contributes greatly to the effectiveness of drama. The fact that a living human being is embodying the character created by the playwright adds immeasurably to the persuasiveness and the vitality of the characterization. In contrast to the two-dimensional effect of characterization in fiction, the acted drama, through the essential element of impersonation, can achieve a three-dimensional effect in characterization. The sight of a skillful simulation of suffering or joy is likely to move you more quickly to a response than a merely verbal account of suffering or joy. On the other hand, when you read a play, you are likely to consider its characterization a little thin and flat, simply because the playwright feels that he can count on talented and well-directed actors to fill in and to round out the characterization.

The essential elements of imitated action and of impersonation account for such distinction as can be made between the substance of fiction and the substance of drama. The dramatic form cries out for action that can be effectively represented, that arouses interest and suspense, and that constantly points forward to other actions that will cumulate interest and suspense. Though both drama and fiction concern themselves basically with action, drama by its very nature suffers from the minimizing or the slackening of action more than fiction does. If you do not see the talk to which you are listening leading to some exciting and absorbing action, you are likely to feel that the playwright has not fulfilled his first duty.

The playwright is concerned not only with the amount of action but with the kind of action to be represented. His decision on this point will depend on the resources of the particular theater in which he expects his play to be produced and on the conventions to which his audience adheres. The intimacy, the grandeur, or the magnitude of the action will be determined by the size and the resources of the actual theater and by the extent to which the audience is willing to accept a considerable degree of symbolization in the action. Take, for instance, actions of such physical magnitude as a chariot race or a battle. The great popular success of the play *Ben Hur* in the early twentieth century depended in very large part on the fact that a scene from a chariot race constituted the climax of the drama, and that that scene was actually represented. The audience was more than willing to overlook the fact that the horses were galloping furiously, not around an arena but on a treadmill. It eagerly accepted a symbolic action since a more exact representation of the action was impossible. Similarly, in the representation of a battle on the stage—but not, one may note, in the moving pictures—the audience accepts a half dozen soldiers as adequate symbolic representatives of an entire army in combat. So far as the amount of action represented is concerned, the playwright aims at a satisfactory compromise between the demands of the audience and the demands of the scene designers and the stage crew.

Although the playwright is theoretically free to dramatize any kind or amount of material that the fiction writer can treat, actually, he is practically limited by what can be effectively expressed in words and actions on the stage. For this reason, the playwright usually fits a subject to the type of theater for which he is working. Extremely intimate or grandiose events are likely to strain to the breaking point the resources of the stages of most theaters. On the other hand, if the writer is successful in creating strong emotional crises on the stage, he can run the risk—as did the Greek tragic writers and the neoclassic dramatists of France—of keeping off stage certain violent actions too physically difficult or aesthetically distasteful for representation and can achieve very powerful effects by having these actions narrated to persons already in a state of great emotional tension. The playwright is not, however, likely to dramatize a subject the chief interest of which is subtly psychological and essentially subjective. Extremely complicated psychological states offer considerable resistance to the objectification essential for effective drama. In *Hamlet*, the supreme example of dramatic psychological analysis, Shakespeare has seen to it that the elaborate soliloquies—the verbalization of what Hamlet is thinking—grow out of a complicated plot involving almost too many violent events.

The playwright is as concerned as the writer of fiction or the poet with shaping his subject in such a way that it will have the unmistakable unity of a living organism. This effect of unity is secured in a variety of ways almost all of which are exemplified in a successful play. The playwright may give his subject focus by concentrating on a single theme, by having one character (or at the most two) rather than several characters primarily concerned with the development of the theme, and by suffusing his treatment of the subject with a dominant mood or tone—romantic, realistic, comic, satirical, tragic—that represents his reaction to the subject and his interest in it. The playwright will achieve an effect of unity by his selection of incidents that are genuinely relevant to the development of the play's theme, by his emphasis on the character traits most significant for the relationship between plot and character, and by his choice of a style that will convey most powerfully the tone with which he wishes to invest his play.

PLOT IN DRAMA

In drama as in fiction, the essentials of a plot that has, as Aristotle said it should have, a beginning, a middle, and an end are the exposition of the situation out of which the problem of the drama arises; the development—favorable or unfavorable—of the situation; the working up of the problem to a turning point and a major climax, very probably through a series of minor crises; a second development that either complicates or simplifies the situation that results from the turn the action takes; and the denouement that settles the problem of the play in a way that is satisfactory or unsatisfactory from the point of view of the hero but that should seem aesthetically logical and satisfying to the audience.

The exposition is that part of the structure of a play that furnishes the information essential to understanding the situation out of which the problem arises. The essential information consists of facts concerning the time and place of the action, the characters, and their relationship to each other or to their environment, and the problematical element in that relationship. The exposition also suggests the tone of the play, since the tone will condition—if it does not determine—your response to the remainder of the story. Finally, exposition should be proportionate to the other elements essential to plot; it should be neither too meager nor too extended if a proper proportion is to exist among all elements of the plot. But, above all, the indispensable element in exposition is the raising of the question—the formulation of the problem—the working out of which is the burden of the rest of the play.

The second element in plot structure is the development. This may be

indicated spatially as that part of the play that lies between the statement of the problem and the turning point. The development, although
by nature transitional, is essential, because it prepares the way for the
turning point and makes it acceptable and intelligible, and because it
works out the potentialities implicit in the characters, their situation, and
their problem. The development, like the exposition, is likely to consist
of a number of incidents, and the incidents are designed to point to a
solution of the problem favorable or unfavorable to the main character
or characters concerned. The incidents that point to an unfavorable
solution may be regarded as complications of the problem; the incidents that point to a favorable solution may be regarded as simpli-
fications of the problem. Both types of incidents are usually found, and
they are frequently arranged with an effect of alternation but not of
mechanical regularity. The inclusion of incidents of both kinds is calculated to sustain your interest by arousing a feeling of fear if the incident gives the affair an unfavorable turn and a feeling of hope if
the incident gives the situation a favorable turn. In general, the effect
of the development should be to intensify your interest in the situation
central to the plot, to deepen your understanding of the characters, and
to heighten and complicate your response to the sequence of incidents
that you are experiencing.

The turning point is the incident that, at least in retrospect, points the
way toward, and prepares the way for, the solution of the problem.
The turning point may be a speech, a gesture, a momentary action, or a
full-fledged incident. It may even be so slight an occurrence as a change
in the weather. What it amounts to structurally is the shifting of the action from the direction in which a favorable solution to the problem lies
to the direction in which an unfavorable solution lies, or vice versa. If
the solution is to be satisfactory, there must be a point after which this
particular solution seems inevitable; that point is the turning point. It is
the author's problem to attempt a happy balance between obviousness
and obscurity in the treatment of the turning point. If he is too obvious,
you may feel that the solution is already in your hands, and, like the
audience in the theater that foresees the final curtain, you may stop
reading the play before it is actually concluded. If, on the other hand,
the author makes the turning point too obscure, you may feel, at the

end of the play, that you have been insufficiently prepared psychologically for the denouement which you find yourself facing.

The climax is the scene or incident that is the fruition of the accumulated suspense, and that stirs the most intense feelings or emotions. The climax, in its relation to the exposition and development, is the high point toward which they have both been building up. It is very likely to be the most elaborately presented scene in the play. A full-length play will have several big scenes, but the climax is to be distinguished from the other big scenes by its greater intensity and its structural relationship to the development and the denouement.

In some long one-act plays, you will discover the presence of a second transitional passage, a second development, so to speak, between the turning point and the denouement. This development, like the first, usually consists of a number of incidents, and these incidents, like those that constitute the first development, may give the situation either an unfavorable or a favorable turn. If the denouement is to give an unfavorable solution to the problem of the play, the second development may give a deceptively favorable turn to events and situation. If the denouement is to be a favorable solution to the problem of the play, the second development may give a deceptively unfavorable turn to events. In either case, the effect of such a development is to heighten suspense by postponing the conclusion of the play and to complicate your emotional response. In a one-act play of normal length, there may be no second development or it may be brief and simple. In some instances, denouement follows hard upon the turning point itself, and there is, therefore, practically no transition between these two important elements in the plot.

Denouement—the term used for the final essential element in the pattern of plot—is borrowed from French critical terminology and means literally "unravelling." Its use in English has become conventional, although in terms of our analysis the word "solution" might be more appropriate. The word "denouement" suggests a somewhat wider and more inclusive conception of the final element in plot than the word "solution," for the process of unravelling may begin or may at least be foreshadowed in the turning point itself. In a full-length play it is frequently possible to assign certain incidents in the falling action to denouement and certain incidents to the solution. In the one-act play, however, the denouement and the solution are frequently indistinguishable. The denouement is the phase of the final part in the plot-pattern that clarifies or simplifies the complicated situation, and the solution, the phase that gives the answer—favorable or unfavorable—to the question that the plot has presented, developed, and carried through to a conclusion.

The solution should satisfy your sense of aesthetic logic; it should seem to follow—despite purposely misleading signs that point in another direction—from everything that has preceded it in the story. Even the so-called "surprise ending"—however unprepared for it you may be —should be a plausible conclusion to whatever has preceded it. If the tone of the play is tragic, you will be aesthetically shocked by a happy ending; if the tone of the play leads you to expect a "happy ending," you will feel a sense of outrage if some sudden and unexpected circumstance brings about an unexpectedly tragic ending. The defeat or death of a tragic hero, however deeply it may move you, should appear to be the only possible conclusion to the series of experiences through which he has passed; if the defeat or death seems contrived rather than inevitable, the conclusion will not be entirely satisfactory. There are readers who insist on a happy ending at the sacrifice of aesthetic logic, but such readers treat literature as though it were a narcotic and not a means of quickening them to psychological and aesthetic awareness.

A fully worked out plot is probably more essential to drama than it is to fiction, because of the different relationships of the reader to fiction and of the audience to the drama. The relationship of the reader to a story is private and personal; the relationship of the audience to an acted drama is public, communal, and—in a sense—impersonal. If you are bored by a story, with or without a fully patterned plot, you can put the book or magazine aside or throw it across the room. If an audience is bored by a drama, with or without plot, its unfavorable reaction, because it is communal, is likely to be conspicuous and overt and to communicate itself directly to the actors and seriously hinder— if it does not actually interrupt—their attempt to do the play justice. In the commercial theater, moreover, the success of a play depends on the favorable reaction, not merely of its first audience but also of successive audiences. The playwright, aware that he is attempting to appeal to and satisfy a series of audiences, is likely to rely heavily on what is certainly the surest means of arousing and sustaining interest and of intensifying suspense, namely a full-fashioned plot that will carry its audience along with it. This circumstance is surely one of the reasons that underlie Aristotle's assertion that in drama plot is of primary importance and character secondary.

This relationship of a play not to a private reader but to a public audience also makes it desirable that the line of the plot shall be unmistakably lucid and that the relevance of the incidents shall be almost immediately apparent. Irrelevant incidents or talk may be introduced with impunity, provided that they interest or amuse or move the audience, but the playwright who indulges in irrelevancies runs the very serious risk of losing his hold on the attention of his audience and of recovering it only with very great difficulty.

Even in so brief a play as "A Farewell Supper" we can distinguish the elements essential to the formation of plot. Almost a third of the play is devoted to exposition. In this third, the time and place of the action are made clear, as is the atmosphere with which Schnitzler wants his play to be invested. Here, we meet the hero and his friend and learn of the characters of the two girls with whom the hero is involved. Structurally, the most important part of the exposition is the statement of the problem: is Anatol's plan for breaking with Mimi going to work out? With Mimi's entrance, the development begins, and it continues up to the turning point, when Mimi says, just before the play has run half its course, "I'm in love with someone else and I'm telling you straight out like you told me." This first development consists of the steps that Mimi takes to rid herself of Anatol, steps which Anatol had planned to take to get rid of *her!* Between the turning point and the climax, which comes not long before the end of the play, there is a second development. This has two phases, first, Anatol's cross-examination of Mimi as to the identity of her new lover and, second, his attempt to pay Mimi back by revealing his own plan to get rid of her. Her amusement with what she thinks is a patent trick on his part so infuriates him that he provokes the climax by hinting that his new affair has gone farther than hers: "I could have told you all that you've been telling me months ago.

And weeks ago I could have told you a good deal more." This revelation of Anatol's leads directly to the climax, which is expressed in the speeches:

MIMI. After all . . . I never told you *that*.
ANATOL. What!
MAX. Oh, never mind!
ANATOL. Never told me what? That you and he . . .
MIMI. And I never would have told it to you. Only a man could be so . . . unpleasant!

Two slight incidents—the arrival of the waiter with the ices and Mimi's making off with the cigars for her lover-—lower the tension of the climax slightly, and the answer to the problem of the play is made final by Max's speech to the speechless Anatol: "I said it'd go off all right."

CHARACTERIZATION IN DRAMA

In fiction there are a variety of methods available for the creation of character: the description of the character's appearance, habits, and manners or mannerisms; the exhibition or exposition of his feelings, emotions, and ideas; the indication of his personality traits through action or inaction; the relationship of the character to his immediate or remote environment, his judgments of other people, and other people's judgments of him; and the author's direct exposition of the character's major and minor traits. Which of these are particularly applicable to the drama?

Although the first-mentioned method—the description of the character's appearance, habits, and mannerisms—is available to the playwright, the form of the drama has a very definite effect on his use of it. He may sketch the general lines of the character's appearance, and give indications of the clothes he wears in each successive scene. He may also indicate the nature of the character's voice and any mannerisms that identify the type to which he belongs or that are a manifestation of his individuality. But this method of characterization in drama depends—even as every other method depends—on the actor's coöperation with the playwright. In other words, the playwright's descriptions of the character's appearance, habits, and mannerisms are directions which the actor, the director, the make-up man, and the costumer will attempt to carry out faithfully. The director, for instance, will attempt to select an actor whose physique resembles as closely as possible that indicated by the playwright; the make-up man and the costumer, each in his way, will aid in the process of accurate visualization.

But on the actor ultimately depends the fidelity and precision with which the playwright's notion of his character's appearance is visualized for the audience.

The playwright's use of description as a method of characterization may be conveniently illustrated from the plays in this book. Schnitzler, to be sure, contents himself with describing Mimi, the heroine of "A Farewell Supper" as "a lovely lady," who "doesn't seem to be in the best of tempers." Although Synge in his initial stage directions informs us merely that Maurya is "an old woman," he later uses stage directions to fill out the picture: "looking up at Cathleen and speaking querulously . . . sitting down on a stool by the fire . . . turning round to the fire and putting her shawl over her head . . . sways herself on her stool . . . standing up unsteadily . . . taking a stick Nora gives her . . . goes out slowly . . . comes in very slowly, without looking at the girls, and goes over to her stool at the other side of the fire. The cloth with the bread is still in her hand . . . starts, so that her shawl falls back from her head and shows her white tossed hair." But other playwrights are more generous with their descriptive details. Thus, Barrie, in addition to some novelistic comments on the hero and heroine of "The Will," offers the following details: "A young man and woman are shown in: very devoted to each other . . . it is the one thing obvious about them; more obvious than his cheap suit, which she presses carefully beneath the mattress every night, or than the strength of his boyish face. . . . He is scarcely the less nervous of the two, but he enters stoutly in front of her as if to receive the first charge." As we might expect from the realistic mode in which *Beyond the Horizon* is written, O'Neill makes elaborate use of this method of characterization, not only on the first appearance of his major characters but on each appearance after the passage of an interval of years. Thus, we get three shockingly different descriptions of the hero, Robert Mayo:

He is a tall, slender young man of twenty-three. There is a touch of the poet about him expressed in his high forehead and wide, dark eyes. His features are delicate and refined, leaning to weakness in the mouth and chin. He is dressed in gray corduroy trousers pushed into high laced boots, and a blue flannel shirt with

*a bright colored tie. He is reading a book by the fading sunset
light. He shuts this, keeping a finger in to mark the place, and turns
his head toward the horizon, gazing out over the fields and hills.
His lips move as if he were reciting something to himself.* (ACT I)

*He, too, has aged. His shoulders are stooped as if under too
great a burden. His eyes are dull and lifeless, his face burned by
the sun and unshaven for days. Streaks of sweat have smudged the
layer of dust on his cheeks. His lips drawn down at the corners,
give him a hopeless, resigned expression. The three years have ac-
centuated the weakness of his mouth and chin. He is dressed in
overalls, laced boots, and a flannel shirt open at the neck.* (ACT II)

*Robert appears in the doorway, leaning weakly against it for
support. His hair is long and unkempt, his face and body emaciated. There are bright patches of crimson over his cheek bones
and his eyes are burning with fever. He is dressed in corduroy
pants, a flannel shirt, and wears worn carpet slippers on his bare
feet.* (ACT III)

The playwright may also utilize other characters as means of visualiz-
ing a character's appearance, dress, and habits. Thus, in the first scene
of *Hamlet,* the king, Claudius, establishes immediately that Hamlet is
wearing mourning—a fact that Shakespeare might have given in a
stage direction—and later, Ophelia gives a very vivid description of
Hamlet's appearance when he appears to her in one of his real or apparent frenzies. The Queen's remark, "But Hamlet he is fat and scant
of breath," just before the duel that precipitates the denouement of the
play, furnishes us a rather surprising realistic detail.

The use of one character's description of another character to fill
out details of appearance may be illustrated from Yeats's "Cathleen ni
Houlihan." To his bare description of her in the Cast of Characters as
The Poor Old Woman, other characters add details: "I see an old
woman coming up the path . . . she has her cloak over her face."
. . . "Do you think she could be the widow Casey that was put out of
her holding at Kilglass awhile ago?" "She is not. I saw the widow Casey
one time at the market at Ballina, a stout fresh woman." . . . "Is she

right, do you think? Or is she a woman from beyond the world?" "She doesn't know well what she's talking about, with the want and trouble she has gone through." . . . "Did you see an old woman going down the path?" "I did not, but I saw a young girl, and she had the walk of a queen."

Much more important as a method of dramatic characterization than the character's appearance and mannerisms is the revelation of the character through speech and action, through what the character says and what he does or does not do. In view of the limited number of overt actions that can be represented on the stage, characterization by means of speech may be even more important than characterization through action. If a character kills another character on or off the stage, the act of killing may in itself be surprising or shocking, but the significance of the act resides in what the character says about the motives that led him to the deed and about his reaction to it.

The extent to which the character may reveal himself through what he says is almost infinite. His opinion of himself—whether exalted or humble, excessively subjective or objective, extravagant or accurate—is revealed by his speech. Dialogue discloses what he thinks of other characters and how he feels toward them; his opinions of other characters will throw light on his own intelligence, judgment, and ethical and cultural demands. And, finally, the character's speeches provide insight into his scale of values—selfish or altruistic, idealistic or cynical, moral or immoral, religious or irreligious—and reveal what values constitute his life-goal, and whether that life-goal is materialistic or idealistic, self-regarding or self-abnegating, superficial or profound.

Self-characterization through speech is the method illustrated by the following quotations from plays in this collection. When Anatol, in Schnitzler's "A Farewell Supper," remarks to his confidant Max, "To a man with my nice sense of honour . . . my nice sense of honour, Max. . . . If I go on like this much longer, I shall lose my self-respect," we realize that although he thinks he has a nice sense of honor, he really has a very low sense of honor, and, although he thinks his self-respect is threatened, he has really lost it long before the play began. On the other hand, the spinster Genevieve, in Wilder's "The Long Christmas Dinner," is probably describing herself accurately when she says, "Oh,

I'm going to live and die abroad! Yes, I'm going to be the American old maid living and dying in a pension in Munich or Florence." Since a full-length play like *Beyond the Horizon* offers a much larger canvas than does the one-act play for the depiction of characters, it is not surprising that most of the first scene is devoted to characterization, and that some of the dialogue consists of the characters' views of their own natures. When, for instance, the hero Robert says, "You don't realize how I've bucked up in the past few years. Why, I bet right now I'm just as healthy as you are—I mean just as sound in wind and limb; and if I was staying on at the farm, I'd prove it to you," the reader will not miss the note of excessive self-assertion.

A character's comments on other people frequently throw more light on himself than on them or more light than is thrown on himself by self-analysis. Anatol's description of his new love in "A Farewell Supper," for instance, probably gives us a more accurate impression of his own incurably romantic nature than it does of the girl: "She's a little girl that . . . well, she's an andante of a girl. . . . She's like a waltz . . . simple, alluring, dreamy. Yes, that's what she's like. . . . When I'm with her I find I grow simple, too. If I take her a bunch of violets . . . the tears come into her eyes." His idea of the way in which Mimi will take the news of his break with her confirms our impression of his inability to read the characters of the girls with whom he becomes involved: "When it comes to the point . . . somehow I can't tell her. She'll cry. I know she'll cry, and I can't bear that. Suppose she cries and I fall in love with her again . . . then it won't be fair to the other one." In the same way, Sir Philip's comments on his children, in "The Will," are more revelatory of his own character than of theirs: "He's a rotter. . . . But I've shipped him off. The law had to wink at it, or I couldn't have done it. Why don't you say I pampered him and it serves me right. It's what they are all saying behind my back. Why don't you ask me about my girl? That's another way to rub it in." One of the reasons Andrew, in *Beyond the Horizon*, offers for his brother Robert's going to sea turns out to be, not only a complete misreading of his brother but an expression of his own unconscious nature: "There's always a chance of a good thing coming your way in some of those foreign ports or other. I've heard there are great opportunities for a young fellow with his eyes open in some of those new countries that are just being opened up. . . . I'll bet that's what you've been turning over in your mind under all your quietness!"

Dramatic speech is also an effective medium for the expression of the character's scale of values and of the nature of his life-goal. When, for instance, Mother Bayard at the beginning of "The Long Christmas Dinner," says to her son Roderick, "I used to think that only the wicked owned two horses. A new horse and a new house and a new wife!" . . . "Tz-Tz-Tz! I don't know what your dear father would say!" we are given a glimpse not only of a less lavish scale of living but also of a greater ethical severity. Both Peter and Bridget, in "Cathleen ni Houlihan," are given ample opportunity to suggest the values that they regard as most reliable. Their sense of the importance of money is brought out by the following exchange of speeches: "You seem to be well pleased to be handling the money, Peter." "Indeed, I wish that I had had the luck to get a hundred pounds, or twenty pounds itself, with the wife I married." But that their life-goal is not entirely materialistic, their discussion of the future of their younger son Patrick makes clear: "I do be thinking sometimes, now things are going so well with us, and the Cahels such a good back to us in the district, and Delia's own uncle a priest, we might be put in the way of making Patrick a priest some day, and he so good at his books." Since the tragedy of *Beyond the Horizon* arises from the failure of the three major characters to reach their life-goals, O'Neill is at very considerable pains to establish these goals clearly, especially those of the hero Robert Mayo. Much of the exposition in the first scene is devoted to clarifying his life-goal. His brother suggests that he wants to go to sea to regain his health or to become a ship's officer or to make profits from foreign merchandise. Robert rejects all these attempts to define his life-goal, and tries to put into words the objectives that going to sea may help him realize: "Supposing I was to tell you that it's just Beauty that's calling me, the beauty of the far off and unknown, the mystery and spell of the East, which lures me in the books I've read, the need of the freedom of great wide spaces, the joy of wandering on and on—in quest of the secret which is hidden just over there, beyond the horizon? Supposing I told you that was the one and only reason for my going?"

In forms of the drama in which the soliloquy is an accepted convention, the playwright shares with the writer of fiction a means of presenting the thought processes of his character directly to the audience. The astute playwright may thus deepen his characterization, may thus come close to plucking out the heart of the character's mystery. Read *Hamlet* without the famous soliloquies, and the hero will appear vastly more simple and less interesting than in the blinding light of his eternal self-examination and self-reproach. The modern playwright may use the soliloquy—if he can persuade his audience to accept it as a reputable dramatic convention—for the expression not only of the character's rational mental processes but also of his apparently irrational subconscious mental processes. The banning of the soliloquy by the realistic drama enhanced the superficial lifelikeness of the drama but prevented the playwright's direct use of material that might plumb the depths of his characters.

The revelation of the character through action is basic, of course, to our conception of drama and its function, and yet the stage sets rather strict limits on the actions that can be represented satisfactorily. Actions may be distinguished as those of acceptance and those of rejection. Thus, a character may reveal himself by taking (or refusing to take) a cup of tea or a vial of poison, by accepting or rejecting a proffered office, by accepting or rejecting a proffered friendship or love, by accepting or rejecting a particular view of himself, of someone else, or of life, or of God. The acceptance or rejection may be peaceful or violent, restrained or unrestrained. Juliet's acceptance of Romeo in the balcony scene and in the nuptial scenes is romantically unrestrained. In the scene in which the Nurse tells her that Romeo has killed Tybalt, she manifests dramatically the conflict between her love of Romeo as a husband and her hatred of him as her cousin's murderer; here the conflict between acceptance and rejection is perfectly lucid, as it is later in her soliloquy before she takes the sleeping potion. A character's mode of rejecting another character may range from a quiet "no," through such elaborate verbalization as Portia's farewell to her unsuccessful suitors—the Prince of Morocco and the Prince of Arragon, in *The Merchant of Venice*—to such explicit aggressiveness as

Shylock's whetting his knife in preparation for taking the pound of Antonio's flesh, in the same play, or to the violent physical aggressiveness of Laertes in the duel scene that brings Hamlet to his death. This last-mentioned scene is rich in examples of implied or overt aggressiveness: in the King's preparation of the poisoned cup for Hamlet, an act that is apparently one of acceptance and is really one of rejection, and in Laertes' use of a poisoned foil instead of the normally harmless foil.

The use of action, of gestures of acceptance or rejection, to suggest and reveal character is fundamental to any play the plot of which is satisfactorily motivated. Character may be suggested by even so trivial an act as attacking one's food with gusto. Mimi, the heroine of "A Farewell Supper," accompanies her consumption of oysters by the remark, "I *do* like oysters. They're the only things one can go on eating and eating. . . ." When, later, she says, "Ring the bell, Max, I'm so hungry," Anatol's comment on her character becomes clear in his words, "Hungry at such a moment! Hungry!" Similarly, Emily's tearfulness, in "The Will," when she hears the words, "I leave everything of which I die possessed to my beloved wife," is an act that expresses her tender devotion to her husband. When he says, "Don't give way, Emily," she replies, "It was those words 'of which I die possessed.' Surely he doesn't need to say that—please, Mr. Devizes?" Her second upset when the lawyer uses the word, "widow," further emphasizes her tenderheartedness. In the tense scene before Bartley's departure, in "Riders to the Sea," the boy's persistence in going to sea despite his mother's objections emphasizes his stubborn and headstrong nature, of which there is an echo in her refusal to bless him before he goes. The daughter, Cathleen, says, "Why wouldn't you give him your blessing and he looking round in the door? Isn't it sorrow enough is on every one in the house without your sending him out with an unlucky word behind him, and a hard word in his ear?" In *Beyond the Horizon*, the use of action to bring out character is more easily illustrated in the case of the aggressive Andrew Mayo than in that of his more passive brother Robert. The former's determination to escape from the painful situation caused by his brother's announcement of his engagement is expressed with natural violence in the following speech:

I don't care. I've done my share of work here. I've earned my right to quit when I want to. I'm sick and tired of the whole damn business. I hate the farm and every inch of ground in it. I'm sick of digging in the dirt and sweating in the sun like a slave without getting a word of thanks for it. I'm through, through for good and all; and if Uncle Dick won't take me on his ship, I'll find another. I'll get away somewhere, somehow.

And his similar decision to leave the farm almost immediately after his return to it further marks a brusquely active nature: "Yes, I'll take the berth. The sooner I go the sooner I'll be back, that's a certainty; and I won't come back with empty hands next time. You bet I won't! . . . I'll go to the house and repack my bag right away."

One method of characterization already mentioned needs further comment, namely, comments made by the other characters about the major character. If the playwright realizes that in real life every individual makes a slightly different impression on every perceptive individual who comes in contact with him, he can enrich his characterization immeasurably by exhibiting the range of views the other characters take of the major character. Thus, what the major character thinks of other characters may be—and usually is—supplemented by what the other characters think of him. If Hamlet's soliloquies are the major characterizing method by which we are allowed to see into the depths of Hamlet's soul, and if the method second in importance is Hamlet's expression of his opinion of every character of any importance in the play, from Claudius to the First Grave Digger, the method third in importance is the revelation of what the other characters think of Hamlet, and here, too, almost everyone of any importance expresses his opinion, from the Queen to Rosencrantz and Guildenstern.

The character of Maurya, in "Riders to the Sea," is built up, not only from what she says and what she does but also from what her daughters say about her. Nora quotes the young priest as saying of Maurya, "She'll be getting her death with crying and lamenting. . . . Herself does be saying prayers half through the night, and the Almighty God won't leave her destitute, with no son living." Later, Cathleen remarks, "It's the life of a young man to be going on the sea, and who would listen to an old woman with one thing and she saying it over?" and, again, "She's that sorry, God help her, you wouldn't know the thing she'd do." O'Neill makes extensive use of this method of characterization to fill out our impressions of his hero. Thus, after Robert Mayo's attempt to run the farm has failed, his mother-in-law gives an altogether unsympathetic reading of his character, and his mother comes to his defense. The mother-in-law expresses her disapprobation of Robert in no uncertain terms: "It do make me mad, Kate Mayo, to see folks that God gave all the use of their limbs to potterin' round and wastin' time doin' every thing the wrong way. . . . And it ain't that I haven't pointed the right way to 'em. . . . He's had three years to learn, and he's gettin' worse 'stead of better. He hasn't got it in him, that's what. . . . He doesn't want to learn." His mother defends him: "Robert never had any experience in farming. You can't expect him to learn in a day." . . . "You can't say but Robbie works hard, Sarah." . . . "Robbie's had bad luck against him." Thus, we get two complementary ways of interpreting him and evaluating him, in addition to the revelation of his character through his own speeches and actions.

The playwright—unlike the writer of fiction or the poet—cannot express his opinion of his character directly but must content himself with implying his attitude. The responsibility of the reader of drama for the formal analysis of a character is, therefore, heavier than that of the reader of fiction. You will find no ready-made authoritative analysis of the character; instead, to arrive at a satisfactory grasp of the character, you must synthesize the result of the methods the playwright has used: what the character looks and acts like, what the character says and does, and what the other characters say of him. You must guard against accepting any one character's estimate of the main character, unless such a one is pretty obviously the playwright's spokesman, and even then it is within your rights to reject—on the basis of evidence that the playwright himself may have unconsciously given—the author's estimate placed in the mouth of a character speaking for him.

You have a right to expect the emergence, through the characterization and through your own analysis of the character, of a pattern of personality traits that is lucid and intelligible, a pattern made up of dominant and subordinate traits that interact to make an organized personality. The pattern may be simple or it may be complex, but, if it is complex, it should contain no element that cannot be related to the other elements in the pattern. The character may very well be divided, may very well be at war with himself, but—if this is the case—all the elements in the personality must be participants in the conflict.

SETTING IN DRAMA

The function of setting in drama is identical with that of setting in fiction, namely, the provision of an environment that will not only be appropriate to the action but also augment imaginatively the total effect of the action. Similarly, the importance of setting is—in both fiction and drama—a variable. If the setting is as remote and unfamiliar as a South American jungle or an Eskimo's igloo, the writer of either fiction or drama must take pains to make it suggestive and plausible. If the setting is reasonably familiar, either writer has the special responsibility of accurate observation and representation, since he does not want to run the risk of alienating you by his infidelities to fact.

Beyond these general resemblances, the problem of setting is a very different one for the writer of plays than for the writer of short stories or novels. The latter is primarily dependent upon his own skill in describing setting; he is dependent, secondarily, on your willingness and ability to respond sensitively to the imagery out of which the setting is built. The success of the playwright's settings, on the other hand, depends not merely on his own skill and the responsiveness of his audience, but also on the fidelity and imaginativeness with which the scene designer, the electrician, and the property man carry out his directions. In a sense, then, the playwright's role in relation to setting is that of the person of artistic tastes who has a general idea of the interior or exterior he wants constructed and who furnishes a rough sketch from which the technicians work. The scene designer, then, has the role of the draughtsman who makes blueprints that will, when followed, ob-

jectify the artist's initial ideas. Thereafter, the scene builders and painters, the property man, and the electricians act as the contractor and
workmen who carry out the directions set down for them by the
draughtsman. The same procedure accompanies the production of costumes; if they are successful embodiments of the playwright's ideas,
their success will depend upon the skill of the costume designer and
workers in executing the original notions of the playwright.

The authors of "Cathleen ni Houlihan" and "Riders to the Sea" furnish rough sketches of the same type of setting for the use of stage
technicians. Yeats contents himself with the briefest of descriptions: "Interior of a cottage close to Killala, in 1798. Bridget is standing at a
table undoing a parcel. Peter is sitting at one side of the fire, Patrick at
the other." Synge's sketch is somewhat more detailed: "Cottage kitchen,
with nets, oil-skins, spinning-wheel, some new boards standing by the
wall, etc. Cathleen, a girl of about eighteen, finishes kneading cake,
and puts it down in the pot-oven by the fire; then wipes her hands, and
begins to spin at the wheel. Nora, a young girl, puts her head in at the
door." Both these sketches call for fairly detailed information about
Irish cottage interiors and real skill in executing the designs made from
them.

Further details about the setting appear in the stage directions within
the play itself. In Yeats's play, for instance, we read of the dresser on
which Bridget deposits Michael's clothes and of a large box in the corner into which Peter puts the bag of money. Synge's even more detailed
stage directions heighten considerably the responsibility of the scene
designer and the other technicians. The cottage has a turf-loft and a
ladder by which Cathleen climbs up to it to hide the bundle of clothes
and, as her mother appears, to throw down some turf.

The extent to which the playwright assumes responsibility for the setting and participates in its production varies widely with the kind of
theater in which he is operating and the mode of drama that he is writing. In so far as one can gather from the dramatic texts and records
that have come down to us, playwrights in ancient Greece and Rome,
in Elizabethan England, and in seventeenth-century France, assumed no
responsibility for the creation and production of settings beyond that of
indicating very roughly the general nature of the setting required for a

particular play. The permanent set—the façade of a temple or palace —in the open-air Greek theater restricted very definitely the type of setting that the playwright might use, but it also laid the lightest possible burden upon him as a creator of setting.

In the main, setting in classical and romantic drama was treated symbolically; that is to say, certain objects were conventionally assumed to stand for objects other than themselves. A few artificial rocks might stand for a desert place or a seashore; a table and a few chairs might represent almost any kind of interior. With the advent and development of realism, setting in drama made increasing demands on everyone concerned, playwright, scene designer, stage carpenter, property man, electrician. For the realistic treatment of setting is not symbolic but representational; it requires as faithful as possible a visual representation of the scene in which the action takes place. Here, the playwright's responsibility in the matter of setting is or may be heavy; he may feel it incumbent upon himself to describe in great detail the size and shape of rooms, the specific nature of the decoration, the furniture and its location, and a very large number of stage properties, some of which are essential if the action is to be represented realistically but many of which may serve merely to make the setting as circumstantial as possible. The responsibilities of the playwright's practical collaborators is even heavier. If the setting is an interior, it is their responsibility to create one that shall be representationally accurate and convincing, one in which doors, windows, and lights are "practicable" and in which the costumes represent with fidelity the region and the period of action of the play.

O'Neill's *Beyond the Horizon* illustrates clearly the realistic treatment of setting. The descriptions of the successive states in which we see the Mayos' sitting room are extremely detailed and call for painstaking execution and stage management. O'Neill establishes the basic elements in this important set in the initial stage directions to Scene II of Act I:

On the left, two windows looking out on the fields. Against the wall between the windows, an old-fashioned walnut desk. In the left corner, rear, a sideboard with a mirror. In the rear wall to the right of the sideboard, a window looking out on the road. Next to the window a door leading out into the yard. Farther right, a black horse-hair sofa, and another door opening on a bedroom. In the corner, a straight-backed chair. In the right wall, near the middle, an open doorway leading to the kitchen. Farther forward a double-heater stove with coal scuttle, etc. In the center of the newly carpeted floor, an oak dining-room table with a red cover. In the center of the table, a large oil reading lamp. Four chairs, three rockers with crocheted tidies on their backs, and one straight-backed, are placed about the table. The walls are papered a dark red with a scrolly-figured pattern.

O'Neill's description of this same room three years later is a graphic symbol of the progress of the tragedy:

All the windows are open, but no breeze stirs the soiled white curtains. A patched screen door is in the rear. Through it the yard can be seen, its small stretch of lawn divided by the dirt path leading to the door from the gate in the white picket fence which borders the road.

The room has changed, not so much in its outward appearance as in its general atmosphere. Little significant details give evidence of carelessness, of inefficiency, of an industry gone to seed. The chairs appear shabby from lack of paint; the table cover is spotted and askew; holes show in the curtains; a child's doll, with one arm gone, lies under the table; a hoe stands in a corner; a man's coat is flung on the couch in the rear; the desk is cluttered up with odds and ends; a number of books are piled carelessly on the sideboard.

Our last glimpse of this interior five years later reveals in almost microscopic detail the final stage in its deterioration:

The room, seen by the light of the shadeless oil lamp with a smoky chimney which stands on the table, presents an appearance of decay, of dissolution. The curtains at the windows are torn and dirty and one of them is missing. The closed desk is gray with

accumulated dust as if it had not been used in years. Blotches of
dampness disfigure the wall paper. Threadbare trails, leading to
the kitchen and outer doors, show in the faded carpet. The top of
the coverless table is stained with the imprints of hot dishes and
spilt food. The rung of one rocker has been clumsily mended with
a piece of plain board. A brown coating of rust covers the un-
blacked stove. A pile of wood is stacked up carelessly against the
wall by the stove.

O'Neill in his insistence on a realistic representation of his setting has perhaps gone beyond the point where the details described will express what he wants to express, not in the study but in the theater.

The value of setting in the classical or romantic drama is or may be its beauty or its imaginative suggestiveness; the value of the representational setting lies in the pleasure of recognition and the pleasure of applauding the ingenuity with which the scene designer, stage carpenter, and property men have constructed a set that has persuasive actuality. The goal of realism in setting is fidelity to physical fact. Not a little of the great success of the wartime play, *The Voice of the Turtle*, was due to the audience's delight in the skill with which a cross section of an apartment, including a kitchenette with an astonishing number of practicable devices, had been constructed on the stage, and their pleasure in watching the various uses to which the playwright put this elaborate mechanism.

In addition to the use of stage directions to describe setting, the playwright may use dialogue. Such a use for dialogue is obviously more probable and pertinent in dramas in which the setting is not highly realistic, since, in such dramas, the playwright may depend heavily on descriptions of setting embedded in the dialogue to supplement the symbolic devices set up on the stage to suggest the setting. Numerous examples of descriptive dialogue will occur to anyone who has read Shakespeare's plays. King Duncan's description of Macbeth's castle as he enters it establishes imaginatively, if ironically, something of the appearance and a good deal of the atmosphere of the place where the unsuspecting King is to be murdered. In *Hamlet*, before the permanent set on the bare open sunlit Elizabethan stage, one can see Shakespeare attempting to create the atmosphere of a chilly midnight watch on the medieval battlements of the royal Danish castle of Elsinore:

HAMLET. The air bites shrewdly; it is very cold.
HORATIO. It is a nipping and an eager air.
HAMLET. What hour now?
HORATIO. I think it lacks of twelve.
MARCELLUS. No, it is struck.
HORATIO. Indeed? I heard it not: it draws near the season
    Wherein the spirit held his wont to walk.

Even in the modern plays in this collection, passages in the dialogue are used to indicate details of the setting or the atmosphere of a particular scene. Wilder, in "The Long Christmas Dinner," relies heavily on this means of creating setting and atmosphere since the actual setting he prescribes for the play is symbolic and not realistic. The following speeches help to describe the house in which the action takes place and the long slow history of its decline: "At all events, now that I'm better I'm going to start doing something about the house." "Roderick! You're not going to change the house?" "Only touch it up here and there. It looks a hundred years old." . . . "It really is pretty old, Charles. And so ugly, with all that ironwork filigree and that dreadful cupola!" "Charles! You aren't going to change the house!" "No, no, I won't give up the house, but great heavens! it's fifty years old. This Spring we'll remove the cupola and build a new wing toward the tennis courts." . . . "I can stand everything but this terrible soot everywhere. We should have moved long ago. We're surrounded by factories. We have to change the window curtains every week. . . . I can't stand it. I can't stand it any more. I'm going abroad."

The playwright's responsibility for the settings of his scenes varies, then, from a rough indication to a detailed and accurate description of them. Your responsibility as the reader of a play varies with the amount of detail with which the setting is described. If the playwright has merely indicated his setting by some such phrase as, "The seacoast of Bohemia" or "The Roman Forum," you may need to call heavily upon both your information and imagination to construct the setting that the action requires. If, on the other hand, the playwright has described the setting in great detail, you must take on the responsibilities of the scene designer, the stage carpenter, the property man, and the electrician, and must, single-handed, carry out in imagination the instructions the playwright has set down. Much more diligent coöperation is required of you, as a reader, in the construction of settings for plays than in settings for stories, since in the latter the writer is combining in his own person the duties of all those essential to the construction of stage settings. The audience in the theater is called upon to observe and to respond sensitively to the beauty and imaginative suggestiveness of classical or romantic settings—or of the playwright's description of them—or to observe carefully and appreciate amiably the fidelity with which realistic settings have been created.

The playwright may augment the effect of the setting by references in the dialogue to such stage properties involved in the action as the caskets in the wooing scenes or Shylock's knife in the trial scene of The Merchant of Venice, the ass's head in the scenes between Titania and the transformed Bottom in Midsummer Night's Dream, the dimming candle in the apparition scene before the battle of Phillippi in Julius Caesar, or the poisonous asp in the scene of Cleopatra's suicide in Antony and Cleopatra. Thus, Synge's "Riders to the Sea" requires, in addition to the setting and costumes, the following stage properties: a rope, two coats for Bartley, a stocking and a shirt sleeve in a bundle, bread wrapped in a cloth, the plank on which Bartley's body is brought in, the sail covering it, and a bottle of Holy Water. The supper that Anatol orders served for Mimi in Schnitzler's play includes oysters, filets aux truffes, ices, and champagne. On the other hand, Barrie and Wilder deliberately keep stage properties to a minimum, and the courses and wine of Wilder's long Christmas dinner are served and consumed in pantomime.

If, then, the play is one in which the settings are not described in detailed stage directions, you must watch the text carefully for descriptive passages, atmosphere-creating phrases, or the mention of the stage properties that are essential to the proper carrying out of the action on the stage.

Critically, you may very well raise the question of the adequacy and the proportion or lack of proportion with which setting is treated in drama. You may further raise the question of what the setting contributes to the effectiveness of any particular play. It is, of course, impossible to generalize with regard to the significance of setting in drama. In some types of play—such as the Greek tragedies or the neoclassical comedies of Molière—setting is a relatively inconsiderable element; in the romantic dramas of the Elizabethan period, it is a more weighty consideration; in the realistic drama, its contribution is likely to be impressive, and in plays that specialize in atmosphere, it may be one of the major concerns of both playwright and reader (or audience).

STYLE IN DRAMA

The problem of style in drama is more sharply focused than the problem of style in fiction, since style in drama is inevitably limited to the only two constituents of the printed text: the stage directions and the dialogue.

In the main, the style of most stage directions—even in more or less realistic modern plays—tends to be neutral, tends merely to furnish directions for producing the play. Indeed, some stage directions—specially those having to do with interiors—may consist merely of a round plan of the stage with indications for the location of entrances and the positions of the pieces of furniture. On the other hand, many realistic playwrights feel it desirable to furnish their technical collaborators—and their readers—with elaborate verbal descriptions of whatever sets they have chosen for their play, and the more adroit of them appreciate the opportunity this type of stage direction offers for giving both technicians and lay readers a vivid visual account of the sets and to establish the tone of the play. In the hands of a brilliant stylist such as Bernard Shaw, the stage directions became almost as significant a part of the text of the play as the dialogue itself. Both Shaw and Barrie—once the latter had been won over to the idea of publishing his plays for the consumption of readers—regularly use the stage directions for novelistic and not for dramatic purposes; in other words, they communicate via the stage directions information or observations that help the reader (and possibly the technician) to imagine the total environment and to understand the characters but that could not possibly be conveyed to the audience through either setting or stage business.

Barrie, for instance, uses stage directions for sly and humorous personal comments, comments that might be said to be novelistically but not dramatically relevant, since they are frequently not of a sort to modify the behavior of the actors who attempt to carry out the author's dramatic intentions. Barrie's printed plays—carefully aimed at readers and not listeners in an audience—approach a form that is halfway between the drama and the novel.

But the basic problem of style in drama is that of style in dialogue, and, whether the play is written in prose or verse, certain qualities differentiate effective dialogue in drama from effective dialogue in fiction. The first requisite of effective dialogue in drama is that it shall lend itself to being spoken and heard with ease. Whether the dialogue is in verse or in prose, the astute dramatist will never lose sight of the fact that his lines are designed to be spoken by living actors and to be heard and understood by an audience that must, as it actually hears the words, get at least the general drift of what is being said, since it cannot—as the reader can—turn back the page to reread something it has imperfectly understood or misunderstood. Everyone who has had any experience with speaking in public will have learned the very great difference between written discourse and oral discourse; the first is denser, more closely packed, less repetitious than the second. So, the playwright who writes dialogue that is more effective to read than to hear runs the very great risk of losing the attention of an audience and thus of destroying the effect of his acted play.

These considerations have the most profound effects on both the extent and the density of dialogue in drama. While there are a few famous speeches that run to exorbitant length in successful plays, most playwrights see the wisdom of breaking up a very extended speech by plausible interruptions that give the audience a momentary relief from their concentration on it. Such extended soliloquies as Hamlet's usually occur at some point of high tension in the action, and their effectiveness is certainly enhanced by the interest and absorption of the audience in the situation out of which the soliloquy flowers. If the situation is sufficiently tense to arouse the audience and if the speech itself is not too closely packed and is designed to be spoken, the speech may, with impunity, run to rather considerable length.

But the density of the dialogue is an even more important consideration than the length of individual speeches. The density of the dialogue depends directly on two features: the complexity of the subject matter and the complexity of the style. If the feelings, emotions, thoughts, or ideas are complicated but are expressed in such a way that they can be followed, the dialogue will be dramatically effective. If, on the other hand, the feelings or emotions, thoughts or ideas are essentially simple but are expressed in a complicated style, the dialogue will be dramatically ineffective, whatever nondramatic value it may have. Two distinguished writers of the nineteenth century—Robert Browning and Henry James—attempted to write plays; neither was really successful. Their failures, however, were due to different reasons; Browning expressed simple ideas in an involved and complicated style; James expressed subtle ideas in an appropriately subtle style. The dialogue of both these writers requires the repeated attentiveness that the printed play may get, but that the acted play simply will not permit.

A further distinction may be made between dialogue in drama and dialogue in fiction, although it is one that requires almost immediate qualification. The distinction is this: In the main, dialogue in drama needs to preserve its functional relationship to the plot, needs to advance the action with a steadiness that fiction does not always demand. In other words, the audience is likely to become restive if extended dialogue does not seem to be relevant to the action and to contribute to it. All dialogue in fiction or drama is, of course, highly selective; it resembles, but is by no means identical with, the casualness and the indirection of most actual conversations. It is the particular business of the playwright to secure and to hold the interest of his audience, and the most certain means of doing so is to keep the dialogue pointed clearly in the direction in which the action is developing.

This sharp focusing of the dialogue may, of course, be ignored or neglected by the skillful dramatist, provided he does not lose the audience's interest by this neglect. What is indispensable is the maintenance of interest; any means by which it may be maintained is pragmatically defensible. For a considerable period, the audience will listen with pleasure to dialogue that does not advance the plot but that is witty or humorous or intellectually stimulating in and by itself. Shakespeare, for instance, introduces conversations between Hamlet and some other character that do not advance the plot but illuminate Hamlet's character or that of the other person involved. Thus, the scenes in which Hamlet indulges in verbal play with Polonius, though really nondramatic, are amusing in themselves and also throw light on the characters of both Hamlet and Polonius. An extreme illustration of Shakespeare's audacity in introducing an utterly nondramatic speech is the Queen Mab speech in *Romeo and Juliet*. In and by itself, it is a charming fairy poem, but it has no dramatic utility and it does not come too appropriately from the lips of shrewd and witty Mercutio. Because it is a, passage of verbal bravura, we are willing to enjoy it though the action of the play is suspended.

Since most stage plays from the time of Henrik Ibsen have been written in prose, the problem of prose style is more pressing and persistent than that of verse style in modern drama. Dramatic dialogue in prose shows a stylistic range no less considerable than that of dialogue in prose fiction. It may, for instance, move consistently on an informal colloquial level, and many modern playwrights have prided themselves on the fidelity and accuracy with which they have represented the speech habits of their characters. Over the years they have administered to audiences a series of slight shocks as they have drilled their way to lower and lower levels of colloquial speech. They have, however, been even less free than writers of fiction to plumb the depths, because the acted drama is a public and not a private experience; and a cross-sectional audience tends to draw a line at indecorousness or obscenity that a writer of fiction may feel free to ignore.

Although all the plays in this collection are in prose and, therefore, aim at an effect of colloquialism, the range of the dialogue style is very wide indeed. Three of these plays—"Riders to the Sea," "Cathleen ni Houlihan," and *Beyond the Horizon*—concern rural types, but since the characters in the first two are Irish and in the third Yankee, no one would be likely to mistake the Irish way of speech:

I'll have no call now to be up crying and praying when the wind breaks from the south, and you can hear the surf is in the east, and the surf is in the west, making a great stir with the two noises, and they hitting one on the other. I'll have no call now to be going down and getting Holy Water in the dark nights after Samhain and I won't care what way the sea is when the other women will be keening.

for the Yankee way of speech:

It was a crazy mistake for them two to get married. I argyed against it at the time, but Ruth was so spelled with Robert's wild poetry notions she wouldn't listen to sense. Andy was the one would have been the match for her. I always thought so in those days, same as your James did; and I know she liked Andy. Then 'long came Robert with his book-learnin' and high-fangled talk —and off she goes and marries him.

Indeed, although there are many stylistic elements in common between Synge's dialogue and Yeats's, Synge's more emphatic rhythms and more richly poetic vocabulary could hardly be mistaken for Yeats's subtler rhythms and less decorated prose:

It is a hard service they take that help me. Many that are red-cheeked now will be pale-cheeked; many that have been free to walk the hills and the bogs and the rushes will be sent to walk hard streets in far countries; many that have gathered money will not stay to spend it; many a child will be born, and there will be no father at its christening to give it a name.

The other plays included here—"A Farewell Supper," "The Will," and "The Long Christmas Dinner"—depict urban types, Viennese, British, and American. The dialogue style of the first two might be distinguished with difficulty, since the talk of the Viennese characters is refracted by the British translation. But with neither of these would the vocabulary and rhythms of Wilder's characters' speech be confused. Since the play has a musical rather than a dramatic structure, Wilder uses repetitions and variations in dialogue to emphasize the motifs that compose the musical structure of his play. His handling of one of the minor motifs— the weather on Christmas Day—demonstrates what a good ear he has for American speech and how deftly he weaves a pattern out of the repetitions and variations of his dialogue: "What a wonderful day for our first Christmas dinner: a beautiful sunny morning, a splendid sermon." . . . "Every least twig is wrapped around with ice. You almost never see that." . . . "It's too bad it's such a cold dark day today. We almost need the lamps." . . . "Pity it's such an overcast day today. And no snow." . . . "a fine bright one, too." . . . "It's a great blowy morning, Mother." . . . "It's glorious. Every least twig is wrapped around with ice. You almost never see that." . . . "It's really a splendid Christmas day today. . . . Every least twig is encircled with ice. You never see that." . . . "It certainly is a keen, cold morning. I used to go skating with Father on mornings like this."

Prose dialogue in drama may also aim at and maintain stylization on a high or formal plane. In historical dramas or costume plays, the dramatist has the task of differentiating the speech habits of his characters from those of contemporary characters. He will aim at a way of speech that is a kind of compromise between the colloquial style of the period and the more relaxed colloquialism of modern times. But he will be chary of affronting his audience by an admixture of slang or of diction that would destroy—even for only a moment—the illusion of historical remoteness. The writer of dramatic prose dialogue may also heighten its effect by utilizing some of the devices that we normally associate with verse dialogue: marked rhythms, vivid sensory diction, and striking similes or metaphors. Such a style as that of Synge, in "Riders to the Sea," is prose on the verge of becoming poetry; we accept it, partly because it is spoken by a primitive peasantry of whose actual speech habits we have had no experience.

Although the greatest plays in the western European tradition have been written in verse, there has been a long slow decline in the production of dramas in verse, since the middle of the eighteenth century. Very few verse plays written since that time have succeeded in reaching a wide audience, despite innumerable attempts to revive the poetic drama. For this state of affairs, various historical explanations have been offered; whatever the explanation, the characteristics of successful verse dialogue are not too difficult to distinguish. Dramatic verse dialogue, if it is to be satisfactory and effective, must meet the demands of both poetry and drama. It must have the qualities that we expect really good poetry to have, and at the same time, a functional relationship to the main business of the drama, the exhibition of characters in action. This dual demand, poetic and dramatic, is obviously a heavy one; it is not surprising that, in a period in which poetry has tended to be lyrical or meditative, very few poets have had the power to write poetry that is dramatic or dramas that are poetic.

DIRECTIONS FOR THE
ANALYSIS OF A PLAY[1]

I. "Factual" Values

Summarize the play in two or three sentences.

What elements in the summary seem familiar to you? Are they familiar through your personal experience of the locale, the characters, or the action, through your reading of nonimaginative or imaginative literature, or through their presentation in some artistic medium other than literature?

What elements in the summary seem unfamiliar to you? Why do they seem unfamiliar?

In the handling of the familiar elements in the play, what details seem to you to be the most telling, the most vivid? Why?

In handling the unfamiliar elements in the play, has the author succeeded in giving you a lively imaginative experience of the locale, the characters, or the action? Why or why not?

Does the "factual" value of the play depend on its familiarity or unfamiliarity? Why?

II. Psychological Values

A. Affective and Emotional

Make a diagram representing the succession of feelings and emotions experienced by the major character in the play. Are

[1] For definitions and discussions of the technical terms used in these Directions, see Appendix B, The Values of Drama.

the feelings and emotions impressive for their variety or their intensity or both?

Make a diagram of the succession of feelings and emotions experienced by the second most important character in the play. Compare and contrast the two diagrams.

To what extent do you find yourself following almost exclusively the line of the major character's feelings and emotions? To what extent is your emotional response to the play affected by the feelings and emotions of other characters in the play?

What is the author's feeling about the characters he has created? How do you know? To what extent is your response to the play influenced by the author's attitude?

B. Empathetic

To what extent do you find yourself identifying yourself with one character in the play? If the process of identification is easy, what makes it easy? If the identification is incomplete, what stands in the way of an almost complete identification?

C. Analytical

Since the playwright has no opportunity to make a direct analysis of his major character, does he substitute for such an analysis an analysis by some of the other characters in the play? Is this analysis an important element? If there is no analysis of the major characters by other characters in the play, does the major character challenge you to make your own analysis of him? Why or why not? Would the play gain by a more explicit analysis of the major characters by the other characters in the play?

III. Technical Values

A. Structure and Plot

Make a visual analysis of the play in four parallel columns as follows: (1) divide the play into its parts and number them; (2) indicate the time, place, and content of each part, in noun phrases; (3) indicate in each case whether the part consists of narration, action that is past; narration, action that is to come; narration, action going on; description; exposition of a state of mind or feeling; argumentation for or against an action or an attitude; (4) enter opposite each part the one of the following terms that is appropriate: exposition; development; turning point; climax; development; denouement. (The terms "exposition" and "development" may be applied to more than one part of the structure.)

Write a discussion of the relationship between the structure and the plot, covering the following questions: What is the problem that the plot develops and more or less satisfactorily solves? Do the turning point and the climax appear at the same point in the pattern of the play? Do you consider the means by which the climax is brought about satisfactory? Why or why not? Is the denouement acceptable in view of all that has preceded it? Why or why not?

Are the structure and the plot well designed to bring out what you regard as the theme of the play? Why or why not?

B. Characterization

Make an analysis of the major character in the play.

What are his basic traits? Which of the following means of characterization are used by the author to bring out these basic traits: (Give illustrations of each method used.) description of the character's appearance (physique, clothes, manners or mannerisms); expression of the character through speech, through action, through the relationship between what the character says and what he does; the relationship between the character and his physical and social environment (its influence upon him, his influence upon it, his estimation of the persons with whom he is associated, the estimation of him entertained by other persons); the character's ideas and attitudes toward himself, toward other people, toward life and the world; the analysis of the character by other characters.

To what extent is the character a type? an individual?

Evaluate the characterization in terms of the character's individuality; intelligibility; credibility; vitality; consistency, as between his personality and his actions, and as among his basic personality traits.

C. Style

What are the characteristics of the style of the dialogue? Is the style appropriate to the characters and to the tone of the play? Why or why not? Does the style of the dialogue constitute one of the major technical values of the play? Why or why not?

IV. Symbolical Values

What are the major symbols in the play? persons? objects? actions? terms?

What sort of pattern results from the relationship built up among the symbols?

What point or theme does the pattern of symbols emphasize?

Do you think the author is successful in making clear to you the significance the symbols have for him? Why or why not?

V. Ideational Values

State, in the form of a phrase, the theme toward which the pattern of symbols points. Is the theme made explicit by the author or has it been left implicit? If it is left implicit, how do you know what it is? How sure are you of what the theme is? Why?

Does the entire play seem relevant to the theme? If there are passages in the play that do not seem relevant to the theme, can their presence in the play be justified? Why or why not?

What is the author's attitude toward the theme? By what means is the attitude communicated? What is the dominant tone of the play? What are the subordinate tones? Is the combination of tones harmonious, effectively inharmonious, or ineffectively inharmonious? Why?

What ethical values are suggested by the play? What philosophical values are suggested by the play, that is, does the author suggest or express his view of human nature? of the world? of life? of the universe?

How important are the ethical and philosophical values in your final evaluation of the play? Why?

Do you consider that the play was deserving of the exhaustive analysis that you have given it? Why or why not?

Plays

Commentaries

and Questions

A Farewell Supper [1]

ARTHUR SCHNITZLER

In a private room at Sacher's restaurant one evening, about supper-time, we find ANATOL *and* MAX. MAX *is comfortable upon a sofa with a cigarette.* ANATOL *stands by the door discussing the menu with the waiter.*

MAX. Haven't you done?

ANATOL. Just. Don't forget now.
  This to the waiter, who disappears. ANATOL *begins to pace the room, nervously.*

MAX. Suppose she don't turn up after all.   5

ANATOL. It's only ten. She couldn't be here yet.

MAX. The ballet must be over long ago.

ANATOL. Give her time to take her paint off and dress. Shall I go over and wait for her?

MAX. Don't spoil the girl.   10

ANATOL (*mirthlessly laughing*). Spoil her . . . spoil her!

MAX. I know . . . you behave like a brute to her. Well . . . that's one way of spoiling a woman.

ANATOL. No doubt. (*Then, suddenly stopping before his friend*) But, my dear Max . . . when I tell you . . . oh, Lord!   15

MAX. Well?

[1] From *Anatol* by Arthur Schnitzler. Translated by H. Granville-Barker. Reprinted by permission of Field Roscoe & Co.

ANATOL. . . . What a critical evening this is!

MAX. Critical! Have you asked her to marry you?

ANATOL. Worse than that.

MAX (*sitting up very straight*). You've married her? Well!

5 ANATOL. What a Philistine you are. When will you learn that
there are spiritual crises besides which such commonplace matters as. . . .

MAX (*subsiding again*). We know! If you've only got one of
those on I wouldn't worry her with it.

10 ANATOL (*grimly*). Wouldn't you? What makes this evening critical, my friend, is that it's to be the last.

MAX (*sitting up again*). What?

ANATOL. Yes . . . our farewell supper.

MAX. What am I doing at it?

15 ANATOL. You are to be the undertaker . . . to our dead love.

MAX. Thank you! I shall have a pleasant evening.

ANATOL. All the week I've been putting it off.

MAX. You should be hungry enough for it by this time.

ANATOL. Oh, we've had supper every night. But I've never
20 known how to begin . . . the right words to use. I tell you
. . . it's nervous work.

MAX. If you expect me to prompt you . . .

ANATOL. I expect you to stand by me. Smooth things down . . .
keep her quiet . . . explain.

25 MAX. Then suppose you explain first.

ANATOL *considers for half a second. Then* . . .

ANATOL. She bores me.

MAX. I see! And there's another she . . . who doesn't?

ANATOL. Yes.

30 MAX (*with fullest comprehension*). Ah!

ANATOL (*quite rapturously*). And what another!

MAX. Please describe her.

ANATOL. She makes me feel as I've never felt before. She . . . I
can't describe her.

35 MAX. No . . . one never can till it's all over.

ANATOL.   She's a little girl that . . . well, she's an andante of a
girl.

MAX.   Not out of the ballet again?

ANATOL.   No, no! She's like a waltz . . . simple, alluring, dreamy.
Yes, that's what she's like. Don't you know . . . ? No, of course   5
you don't! And how can I explain? When I'm with her I find I
grow simple too. If I take her a bunch of violets . . . the tears
come into her eyes.

MAX.   Try her with some diamonds.

ANATOL.   I knew you wouldn't understand in the least. I should   10
no more think of bringing her to a place like this . . . ! Those
little eighteenpenny places suit her. You know . . . Soup or
Fish: Entrée: Sweets or Cheese. We've been to one every night
this week.

MAX.   You said you'd had supper with Mimi.   15

ANATOL.   So I have. Two suppers every night this week! One
with the girl I want to win, and the other with the girl I want to
lose. And I haven't done either yet.

MAX.   Suppose you take Mimi to the Soup or Fish and bring
the little Andante girl here. That might do it.   20

ANATOL.   That shows you don't understand. Such a child! If
you'd seen her face when I ordered a one and tenpenny bottle
of wine.

MAX.   Tears in her eyes?

ANATOL.   She wouldn't let me.   25

MAX.   What have you been drinking?

ANATOL.   Shilling claret before ten. After ten, champagne. Such
is life.

MAX.   Your life!

ANATOL.   But I've had enough of it. To a man with my nice sense   30
of honour . . . my nice sense of honour, Max.

MAX.   I heard.

ANATOL.   If I go on like this much longer I shall lose my self-
respect.

MAX.   So shall I if I have much more to do with you.   35

ANATOL.   How can I play-act at love if I don't feel it?

MAX.   No doubt it's better acting when you do.

ANATOL.   I remember telling Mimi in so many words . . . when
we first met . . . when we swore that nothing should part us
. . . My dear, I said, whichever first discovers that the thing is
wearing thin must tell the other one straight out.

MAX.   Besides swearing that nothing should part you. Good!

ANATOL.   If I've said that once I've said it fifty times. We are perfectly free, and when the time comes we'll go each our own
way without any fuss. Only remember, I said, what I can't stand
is deceit.

MAX.   Then I'm sure supper ought to go off very well.

ANATOL.   Yes . . . but when it comes to the point . . . somehow
I can't tell her. She'll cry. I know she'll cry, and I can't bear
that. Suppose she cries and I fall in love with her again . . .
then it won't be fair to the other one.

MAX.   And the one thing you can't stand is deceit.

ANATOL.   It'll be easier with you here. There's an honest, un-
romantic air about you that would dry any tears.

MAX.   Happy to oblige. And how shall I start? Tell her she's better off without you. How can I?

ANATOL.   Something of that sort. Tell her she won't be losing so
much.

MAX.   Yes. . . .

ANATOL.   There are hundreds of better-looking men . . . men
better off.

MAX.   Handsomer, richer . . . and cleverer.

ANATOL (*half humorously*).   I shouldn't exaggerate.
  At this point the waiter shows in the MIMI *in question. A
  lovely lady.*

WAITER.   This way, Madame.
  She doesn't seem to be in the best of tempers.

MIMI.   Oh . . . so here you are!

ANATOL (*cheerfully*).   Here we are. (*He takes off her wrap with
much tenderness.*) Let me.

MIMI. You're a nice one, aren't you? I looked up and down. . . .

ANATOL. A good thing you hadn't far to come.

MIMI. If you say you'll be there for me you ought. Hullo, Max.
Come on . . . let's feed.

There's a knock at the door.   5

MIMI. Come in! What's he knocking for?

It is the WAITER *again, expectant of his orders, which* ANATOL
gives him. . . .

ANATOL. Bring supper.

MIMI *sits at the table and, cat-like, fusses her appearance.*   10

MIMI. You weren't in front.

ANATOL (*with careful candour*). No . . . I had to. . . .

MIMI. You didn't miss much. It was precious dull.

MAX. What was on before the ballet?

MIMI. I don't know. I go straight to the dressing-room and then   15
I go on the stage. I don't bother about anything else. Anatol
. . . I've a bit of news for you.

ANATOL (*his brow wrinkling a little*). Have you, my dear? Important?

MIMI. Myes: . . may surprise you a bit . . . praps.   20

The supper arrives . . . oysters first.

ANATOL. Well . . . I've some for you, too.

MIMI. Wait a second. It's no concern of his.

*This with a cock of the head towards the well-mannered, un-
conscious waiter.*   25

ANATOL. You needn't wait . . . we'll ring.

The WAITER *departs. Supper has begun.*

ANATOL. Well?

MIMI (*between her oysters*). I think praps it will surprise you,
Anatol . . . though I don't see why it should. Praps it won't   30
. . . and it oughtn't to.

MAX. They've raised your salary!

ANATOL (*watching her*). Tsch.

MIMI (*ignoring this levity*). No . . . why should it? I say . . .
are these Ostend or Whitstable?   35

ANATOL. Ostend . . . Ostend.

MIMI. I do like oysters. They're the only things you can go on eating and eating. . . .

MAX (*who is doing his full share*). And eating and eating and
5   eating.

MIMI. That's what I always say.

ANATOL. Well . . . what's this news?

MIMI. D'you remember something you once said?

ANATOL. Which of the hundreds?

10   MIMI. Mimi . . . oh, I remember your saying it. . . . The one thing I can't bear is deceit!

ANATOL, *not to mention* MAX, *is really taken aback.*

ANATOL. What!

MIMI. Always tell me the whole truth before it's too late.

15   ANATOL. Yes, I meant. . . .

MIMI (*roguish for a moment*). I say . . . suppose it was!

ANATOL. What d'you mean?

MIMI. Oh, it's all right . . . it isn't. Though it might be to-morrow.

20   ANATOL (*hot and cold*). Will you please explain what you mean?

MAX (*unheeded*). What's this?

MIMI (*meeting a fierce eye*). You eat your oysters, Anatol, or I won't.

ANATOL. Damn the oysters!

25   MIMI. You go on with them.

ANATOL. You go on with what you were saying. I don't like these jokes.

MIMI. Now didn't we agree that when it came to the point we weren't to make any fuss but . . . ! Well . . . it has come.

30   ANATOL (*bereft of breath*). D'you mean . . . ?

MIMI. Yes, I do. This is the last time we have supper together.

ANATOL. Oh! Why . . . would you mind telling me?

MIMI. All is over between us.

ANATOL. Is it!

35   MAX (*unable to be silent longer*). Admirable!

MIMI (*a little haughty*). Nothing admirable about it. It's true.

ANATOL (*with trembling calm*). My dear Mimi . . . please let
me understand. Some one has asked you to marry him?

MIMI. Oh . . . I wouldn't throw you over for that.

ANATOL. Throw me over!

MIMI (*with her last oyster*). It's no use, Anatol. I'm in love . . .   5
head over ears.

> MAX *goes into such a fit of laughter that choking follows, and
> he has to be patted on the back.* ANATOL *does the friendly of-
> fice, somewhat distractedly.*

MIMI (*very haughty indeed*). There's nothing to laugh at, Max.   10

MAX. Oh . . . oh . . . oh!

ANATOL. Never mind him. Now . . . will you please tell
me . . . ?

MIMI. I am telling you. I'm in love with somebody else and I'm
telling you straight out like you told me.   15

ANATOL. Yes, but damn it . . . who?

MIMI. Now my dear . . . don't lose your temper.

ANATOL. I want to know.

MIMI. Ring the bell, Max, I'm so hungry.

> MAX, *recovering, does so.*   20

ANATOL. Hungry . . . at such a moment! Hungry!

MAX (*passing back to his chair, says in* ANATOL's *ear*). Ah . . .
but it'll be the first supper she's had to-night.

> *The waiter arrives,* ANATOL *rends him savagely.*

ANATOL. And what do you want?   25

WAITER (*perfectly polite*). You rang, sir?

MAX. Bring the next thing.

> *While the plates are cleared* ANATOL *fumes, but* MIMI *makes
> casual conversation.*

MIMI. Berthe Hoflich is going to Russia . . . it's settled.   30

MAX. Letting her go without any fuss?

MIMI. Oh . . . not more than a bit.

ANATOL. Where's the wine? Are you asleep to-night?

WAITER. Beg pardon, sir . . . the wine. (*He points it out under*
ANATOL's *nose.*)   35

ANATOL. No, no . . . the champagne.

The WAITER *goes out for that and for the next course. As the door shuts on him.* . . .

ANATOL. Now then . . . will you please explain?

MIMI. Never take a man at his word! How many times have you
5   told me . . . when we feel it's coming to an end, say so and end
it calmly and quietly?

ANATOL (*with less and less pretence of self-control*). For the last
time. . . .

MIMI. He calls this quietly!

10 ANATOL. My dear girl . . . doesn't it occur to you that I have
some right to know who . . . ?

    MIMI *hasn't let her appetite be disturbed; and at this moment
she is relishing the wine, her eyes closed.*

MIMI. Ah!

15 ANATOL. Oh, drink it up . . . drink it up!

MIMI. Where's the hurry?

ANATOL (*really rather rudely*). You generally get it down quick
enough.

MIMI (*still sipping*). Ah . . . but it's good-bye to claret, too,
20 Anatol. It may be for years, it may be for ever.

ANATOL (*puzzled*). Oh . . . why?

MIMI (*with fine resignation*). No more claret for me . . . no
more oysters . . . no more champagne! (*At this moment the
WAITER begins to hand the next course.*) And no more filets aux
25 truffes! All done with now.

MAX. Oh . . . what a sentimental tummy! Have some?

MIMI (*with gusto*). I will.

MAX. You've no appetite, Anatol.

    The WAITER *having served them disappears once more, and
30 once more* ANATOL *plunges into trouble.*

ANATOL. Well, now . . . who's the lucky fellow?

MIMI (*serene and enjoying her filet aux truffes*). If I told you
you wouldn't be any the wiser.

ANATOL. But what sort of a chap? How did you come across
35 him? What does he look like?

MIMI (*seraphic*). He's a perfect picture of a man.

ANATOL. Oh, that's enough, of course.

MIMI. It's got to be. (*She re-starts her chant of self-sacrifice.*) No more oysters . . . !

ANATOL. Yes . . . you said that.

MIMI. No more champagne! 5

ANATOL. Damn it . . . is that his only excuse for existence . . . not being able to stand you oysters and champagne?

MAX. He couldn't live by that.

MIMI. What's the odds as long as I love him! I'm going to try throwing myself away for once. . . . I've never felt like this 10 about any one before.

MAX (*with a twinkle*). Anatol could have given you an eighteen-penny supper, you know.

ANATOL. Is he a clerk? Is he a chimney-sweep? Is he a candle-stick-maker? 15

MIMI. Don't you insult him.

MAX. Tell us.

MIMI. He's an Artist.

ANATOL. Music-hall artist?

MIMI (*with dignity*). He's a fellow-artist of mine. 20

ANATOL. Oh . . . an old friend? You've been seeing a lot of him? Now then . . . how long have you been deceiving me?

MIMI. Should I be telling you if I had? I'm taking you at your word and speaking out before it's too late.

ANATOL. How long have you been in love with him? You've been 25 t h i n k i n g things . . . haven't you?

MIMI. Well . . . I couldn't help that.

ANATOL (*his temper rising fast*). Oh!

MAX. Anatol!

ANATOL. Do I know the fellow? 30

MIMI. I don't suppose you've ever noticed him. He's in the cho-rus. He'll come to the front.

ANATOL. When did this affair start?

MIMI. To-night.

ANATOL. That's not true. 35

MIMI. It is. To-night I knew it was my fate.

ANATOL. Your fate! Max . . . her fate!

MIMI. Yes . . . my fate. Why not?

ANATOL. Now . . . I want the whole story. I've a right to it.
You still belong to me, remember. How long has this been going
5   on . . . how did it begin? When had he the impudence . . . ?

MAX. Yes . . . I think you ought to tell us that.

MIMI (*impatient for the first time*). Oh . . . this is all the thanks
I get for doing the straight thing. Suppose I'd gone like Florrie
with von Glehn. He hasn't found out yet about her and Hubert.

10 ANATOL. He will.

MIMI. Well, he may. And then again he mayn't. But you
wouldn't have. I know a thing or two more than you do.

   For proper emphasis she pours out another glass of wine.

ANATOL. Haven't you had enough?

15 MIMI. What . . . when it's the last I shall get?

MAX (*with a nod*). For a week or so.

MIMI (*with a wink*). Don't you think it. I'm going to stick to
Carl. I love him for himself alone. He won't badger and bully
me, the dear!

20 ANATOL. You and he have been carrying on under my nose for
. . . how long? To-night indeed!

MIMI. Don't believe it if you don't want to.

MAX. Mimi . . . tell the truth. You two won't part friends unless
you do.

25 ANATOL (*recovering some complacency*). And then I've a bit of
news for you.

MIMI. Well . . . it began like this. . . .

   Once more the WAITER, *with the champagne this time.* MIMI
   stops very discreetly.

30 ANATOL. Oh, never mind him.

   *So she gets ahead, but in whispers, till the intruder shall have
   departed, which he does very soon.*

MIMI. A fortnight ago he gave me a rose. Oh, so shy he was! I
laughed . . . I couldn't help it.

35 ANATOL. Why didn't you tell me?

MIMI.   Start telling you those sort of things! I should never have done.

ANATOL.   Well?

MIMI.   And he hung round at rehearsals. It made me cross at first . . . and then it didn't.

ANATOL (*viciously*).   No, I'm sure it didn't.

MIMI.   Then we began to have little chats. And then I began to take such a fancy to him.

ANATOL.   What did you chat about?

   MIMI *tries the champagne now.*

MIMI.   Oh . . . things. He got expelled from school. Then he went into business, and that wasn't any good. Then he thought perhaps he could act.

ANATOL.   And never a word to me!

MIMI.   And then we found out we used to live close to each other as children. Just fancy!

ANATOL.   Most touching!

MIMI (*simply*).   Wasn't it?

ANATOL.   Well?

   The champagne (one fears it is) has an instant effect. She be-comes a little vague and distant.

MIMI.   That's all. It's my fate. You can't struggle against your fate, can you? Can't . . . struggle . . . against. . . .

   She stops suddenly. ANATOL *waits for a minute, then. . . .*

ANATOL.   But I've not been told what happened to-night.

MIMI.   What happened. . . .

   Her eyes close.

MAX (*with fine effect*).   Hush . . . she sleeps.

ANATOL   Well, wake her up. Take that wine away from her. I want to know what happened to-night. Mimi . . . Mimi!

   She wakes up, refreshed apparently.

MIMI.   To-night? He told me he loved me.

ANATOL.   What did you say?

MIMI.   I said I was awfully glad. And I mustn't play the silly fool with him, must I? So it's good-bye to you.

ANATOL. It's him you're considering, not me.

MIMI (*with friendly candour*). I don't think I ever really liked you, Anatol.

ANATOL. Thank you. I'm happy to say that leaves me cold.

5 MIMI. Don't be nasty.

ANATOL. Would you be surprised to hear that I hope to get on very well without you for the future?

MIMI. Really?

ANATOL *throws his belated bomb.*

10 ANATOL. I am in love, too.

And it is received by MIMI *with the indifference of scepticism.*

MIMI. Think of that!

ANATOL. And have been for some time. Ask Max. I was telling

15 him when you came in.

She smiles at this in the most irritating way.

MIMI. Yes . . . I'm sure you were.

ANATOL (*piling it up*). She's younger and rather prettier than you.

20 MIMI. I'm sure she is.

ANATOL. And I'd throw six hundred and seventy of your sort into the sea for her. (*But* MIMI, *not in the least impressed or distressed, laughs loud.*) You needn't laugh. Ask Max.

MIMI. If I were you I should have invented all that a little earlier.

25 ANATOL (*aghast*). But it's true. I haven't cared that much about you since . . . ! You've been boring me till I could only stay in the room with you by sitting and thinking of her. I've had to shut my eyes tight and think it was her I was kissing.

MIMI (*as comfortable as ever*). Ditto to that, my dear.

30 ANATOL *takes a nasty turn.*

ANATOL. Well . . . that's not all. Say ditto to this if you can.

She notices the change in his tone, puts down her wine-glass, and looks squarely at him.

MIMI. To what?

35 ANATOL. I could have told you all you've been telling me months ago. And weeks ago I could have told you a good deal more.

MIMI.   D'you mean . . . ?

ANATOL.   Yes, I do. I have behaved very badly to you . . . dear
Mimi.

MIMI *gets up outraged.*

MIMI.   Oh . . . you cad!

ANATOL (*grateful for the abuse*).   And only just in time, too . . .
it seems! You wanted to get there first, did you? Well . . .
thank God, I have no illusions!

But MIMI *has gone to collect her things: her hat, her cloak.
And she puts them on too, not waiting a moment.*

MIMI.   Oh . . . it only shows!

ANATOL.   Doesn't it! Shows what?

MIMI.   What a brute a man can be!

ANATOL.   A brute . . . am I?

MIMI.   Yes, a brute . . . a tactless brute. (*For a moment she
gives him undivided attention.*) After all . . . I never told you
that.

Abysses open!

ANATOL.   What!

MAX.   Oh, never mind!

ANATOL.   Never told me what? That you and he. . . .

MIMI (*with most righteous indignation*).   And I never would
have told it you. Only a man could be so . . . unpleasant!

Heaven knows what might happen, ANATOL *so twitches with
rage and amazement. But the timely calm* WAITER *saves the
situation with yet another course.*

WAITER.   I beg pardon.

ANATOL.   Oh, go to . . . ! (*He swallows the word, and recovers
a little.*)

MIMI.   Ices!

*And, pleased as a child, she goes back to her chair to begin on
hers.* ANATOL, *in his turn, is deeply shocked.*

ANATOL.   Can you eat ices at a moment like this?

MAX (*starting on his too*).   Yes, of course she can. It's good-bye
to them for ever.

MIMI (*between the spoonfuls*).   No more ices . . . no more

claret . . . no more champagne . . . no more oysters! (*Then,
as she gets up to go*) And, thank goodness . . . no more Anatol.
(*But on her way to the door she notices on the sideboard the
cigars. She helps herself to a handful. Then turns with the sweet-
est of smiles.*) Not for me. They're for him!
    She departs.
MAX.   I said it'd go off all right.
    ANATOL *is speechless.*

This little play is one of a series entitled *Anatol*, which exhibits the
amatory adventures of a young Viennese man about town. The stage
directions of the first play in the series characterize him as follows:
"That he has taste, besides means to indulge it, may be seen by his
rooms, the furniture he buys, the pictures he hangs on his walls. And if
such things indicate character, one would judge, first by the material
comfort of the place and then by the impatience for new ideas which
his sense of what is beautiful to live with seems to show, that though a
hedonist, he is sceptical of even that easy faith."

This play has been chosen as the first example for dramatic analysis
because it illustrates in small compass all the technical elements essential to drama and also, like any work of art, embodies the various values which make literature worth while. We have a series of consecutive
incidents carefully arranged to build a plot; even on this small scale,
we can distinguish the structural elements of exposition, development,
turning point, climax, and denouement. Furthermore, the plot involves
easily distinguishable though not especially complicated characters.
Anatol could never be mistaken for Max, nor Max for Anatol, and
Mimi, although a type like the others, has a few delightful individualiz-
ing traits. Probably not all ballet dancers show quite Mimi's gusto in attacking the fine food and liquor with which Anatol has been plying her.
Although the setting may seem relatively unimportant, it would not be
easy to stage this play as elegantly as it deserves. Serving what looks
like an elaborate supper on the stage involves not only a considerable
number of stage properties but an arrangement of them so carefully

planned that the very busy waiter will find everything at hand the moment it is needed. Schnitzler, unlike Wilder in "The Long Christmas Dinner," does not leave the creation of the illusion of food to the actors' pantomime and the audience's imagination! Finally, the dialogue has a distinct and winning style. To decide how much of it is due to Schnitzler and how much to Granville-Barker would involve us in a detailed linguistic inquiry with which we cannot concern ourselves. But it is worth noting that Barker called his version of the play a paraphrase, because he felt that "in a faithful translation the peculiar charm of these dialogues" would disappear. Whatever its source, however, the dialogue has a deftness, lightness, and plausibility that constitute one of the attractions of this play.

"A Farewell Supper" will serve to illustrate not only the technical elements and values of the drama but also the other values of literature. "Factually," the substance of this play may be inconsequential, but its concern, however light-handed, with the eternal problem of man's relation to woman gives it universality of appeal. In the second place, the play obviously offers the reader a lively psychological experience. Schnitzler makes delectable comedy out of the pattern of Anatol's emotions, the venerable but still effective device of "the tables turned." The lightness, if not the triviality, of the play prevents its having, to any marked degree, the values we have called symbolical and ideational. But, in the first respect, neither Anatol nor Mimi would be intelligible to us if they were not characters some of whose elements we recognize in ourselves or in our friends. And, in the second respect, although it may seem to do violence to the play to stress its ethical values, the alert reader will see in it an expression of a view of life and of ethical standards of which he may not approve but which it may do him no harm to enjoy, on the stage!

Analyze the structure of the play by answering the following questions: How much of the play is devoted to exposition? What is the problem of the play? Where is it most clearly stated? At what point does the complicating development begin? What is the turning point in the action of the play? By what means does Schnitzler maintain and deepen interest after the turning point? At what point in the play does the climax come? By what means does Schnitzler maintain the interest between the climax and the denouement? Is the denouement effective? Why or why not?

Since Schnitzler has established the characters of Anatol and Max in the four playlets that precede this one, it is perhaps not fair to expect him to pay much attention to characterizing them here. But what major characteristics of Anatol and Max are brought out in this play?

Since Mimi appears in only this playlet in Schnitzler's series, he characterizes her sufficiently to differentiate her from the other girls with whom Anatol becomes involved. What are her major traits? Which of these traits are brought out by what she says? By what she does? Which of her traits are brought out by what Anatol and Max say of her? By what they say to her?

Essential to the comic effect of this play are the turns and twists in the pattern made by the feelings and emotions that Anatol experiences. Make a diagram showing what these feelings and emotions are and the order in which they occur.

In the German original, Mimi, as she leaves, picks up a handful of cigarettes. Was Barker well advised to change them to cigars? Why or why not?

What view of life does Schnitzler suggest in this play? Check your inferences by reading the other plays that make up *Anatol.*

The Will[1]

JAMES M. BARRIE

The scene is any lawyer's office.

*It may be, and no doubt will be, the minute reproduction of some
actual office, with all the characteristic appurtenances thereof,
every blot of ink in its proper place; but for the purpose in hand
any bare room would do just as well. The only thing essential
to the room, save the two men sitting in it, is a framed engraving
on the wall of Queen Victoria, which dates sufficiently the
opening scene, and will be changed presently to King Edward;
afterwards to King George, to indicate the passing of time. No
other alteration is called for. Doubtless different furniture came
in, and the tiling of the fire-place was renewed, and at last some
one discovered that the flowers in the window-box were dead,
but all that is as immaterial to the action as the new blue-bottles;
the succession of monarchs will convey allegorically the one
thing necessary, that time is passing, but that the office of
Devizes, Devizes, and Devizes goes on.*

The two men are DEVIZES SENIOR *and* JUNIOR. SENIOR, *who is middle-aged, succeeded to a good thing years ago, and as the curtain rises we see him bent over his table making it a better thing.
It is pleasant to think that before he speaks he adds another thir-
teen and fourpence, say, to the fortune of the firm.*

[1] Reprinted from *Half-Hours* by James M. Barrie. Copyright, 1914, by Charles Scrib-
ner's Sons, 1943, by Cynthis Asquith. Used by permission of the publishers.

JUNIOR *is quite a gay dog, twenty-three, and we catch him skil-
fully balancing an office ruler on his nose. He is recently from
Oxford—*

> If you show him in Hyde Park, lawk, how they will stare,
> Tho' a very smart figure in Bloomsbury Square.

Perhaps JUNIOR *is a smarter figure in the office (among the clerks)
than he was at Oxford, but this is one of the few things about
him that his shrewd father does not know.*

*There moves to them by the only door into the room a middle-
aged clerk called* SURTEES, *who is perhaps worth looking at,
though his manner is that of one who has long ceased to think of
himself as of any importance to either God or man. Look at him
again, however (which few would do), and you may guess that
he. has lately had a shock—touched a living wire—and is a little
dazed by it. He brings a card to* MR. DEVIZES, SENIOR, *who looks
at it and shakes his head.*

MR. DEVIZES.   'Mr. Philip Ross.' Don't know him.
SURTEES (*who has an expressionless voice*).   He says he wrote
you two days ago, sir, explaining his business.
MR. DEVIZES.   I have had no letter from a Philip Ross.
5   ROBERT.   Nor I.
> *He is more interested in his feat with the ruler than in a pos-
> sible client, but* SURTEES *looks at him oddly.*
MR. DEVIZES.   Surtees looks as if he thought you had.
> ROBERT *obliges by reflecting in the light of* SURTEES's *counte-*
10   *nance.*
ROBERT.   Ah, you think it may have been that one, Surty?
MR. DEVIZES (*sharply*).   What one?
ROBERT.   It was the day before yesterday. You were out, father,
and Surtees brought me in some letters. His mouth was wide
15   open. (*Thoughtfully*) I suppose that was why I did it.
MR. DEVIZES.   What did you do?
ROBERT.   I must have suddenly recalled a game we used to play at
Oxford. You try to fling cards one by one into a hat. It requires
great skill. So I cast one of the letters at Surtees's open mouth,

and it missed him and went into the fire. It may have been Philip Ross's letter.

MR. DEVIZES (*wrinkling his brows*). Too bad, Robert.

ROBERT (*blandly*). Yes, you see I am out of practice.

SURTEES. He seemed a very nervous person, sir, and quite young. Not a gentleman of much consequence.

ROBERT (*airily*). Why not tell him to write again?

MR. DEVIZES. Not fair.

SURTEES. But she——

ROBERT. She? Who?

SURTEES. There is a young lady with him, sir. She is crying.

ROBERT. Pretty?

SURTEES. I should say she is pretty, sir, in a quite inoffensive way.

ROBERT (*for his own gratification*). Ha!

MR. DEVIZES. Well, when I ring show them in.

ROBERT (*with roguish finger*). And let this be a lesson to you, Surty, not to go about your business with your mouth open. (SURTEES *tries to smile as requested, but with poor success.*) Nothing the matter, Surty? You seem to have lost your sense of humour.

SURTEES (*humbly enough*). I'm afraid I have, sir. I never had very much, Mr. Robert.

He goes quietly. There has been a suppressed emotion about him that makes the incident poignant.

ROBERT. Anything wrong with Surtees, father?

MR. DEVIZES. Never mind him. I am very angry with you, Robert.

ROBERT (*like one conceding a point in a debating society*). And justly.

MR. DEVIZES (*frowning*). All we can do is to tell this Mr. Ross that we have not read his letter.

ROBERT (*bringing his knowledge of the world to bear*). Is that necessary?

MR. DEVIZES. We must admit that we don't know what he has come about.

ROBERT (*tolerant of his father's limitations*). But don't we?

MR. DEVIZES.   Do you?

ROBERT.   I rather think I can put two and two together.

MR. DEVIZES.   Clever boy! Well, I shall leave them to you.

ROBERT.   Right.

5   MR. DEVIZES.   Your first case, Robert.

ROBERT (*undismayed*).   It will be as good as a play to you to sit
there and watch me discovering before they have been two minutes in the room what is the naughty thing that brings them
here.

10   MR. DEVIZES (*drily*).   I am always ready to take a lesson from the
new generation. But of course we old fogies could do that also.

ROBERT.   How?

MR. DEVIZES.   By asking them.

ROBERT.   Pooh. What did I go to Oxford for?

15   MR. DEVIZES.   God knows. Are you ready?

ROBERT.   Quite.

MR. DEVIZES *rings.*

MR. DEVIZES.   By the way, we don't know the lady's name.

ROBERT.   Observe me finding it out.

20   MR. DEVIZES.   Is she married or single?

ROBERT.   I'll know at a glance. And mark me, if she is married it
is our nervous gentleman who has come between her and her
husband; but if she is single it is little Wet Face who has come
between him and his wife.

25   MR. DEVIZES.   A Daniel!

A young man and woman are shown in: very devoted to each
other, though ROBERT *does not know it. Yet it is the one thing*
obvious about them; more obvious than his cheap suit, which
she presses so carefully beneath the mattress every night, or
30   *than the strength of his boyish face. Thinking of him as he*
then was by the light of subsequent events one wonders
whether if he had come alone something disquieting could
have been read in that face which was not there while she was
by. Probably not; it was certainly already there, but had not
yet reached the surface. With her, too, though she is to be
35   *what is called changed before we see them again, all seems se-*

rene; no warning signals; nothing in the way of their happiness in each other but this alarming visit to a lawyer's office. The stage direction might be 'Enter two lovers.' He is scarcely the less nervous of the two, but he enters stoutly in front of her as if to receive the first charge. She has probably nodded valiantly to him outside the door, where she let go his hand.

ROBERT (*master of the situation*).   Come in, Mr. Ross (*and he bows reassuringly to the lady*). My partner—indeed my father.
    MR. DEVIZES *bows but remains in the background.*

PHILIP (*with a gulp*).   You got my letter?

ROBERT.   Yes—yes.

PHILIP.   I gave you the details in it.

ROBERT.   Yes, I have them all in my head. (*Cleverly*) You will sit down, Miss— I don't think I caught the name.
    As much as to say, 'You see, father, I spotted that she was single at once.'

MR. DEVIZES (*who has also formed his opinion*).   You didn't ask for it, Robert.

ROBERT (*airily*).   Miss—?

PHILIP.   This is Mrs. Ross, my wife.
    ROBERT *is a little taken aback, and has a conviction that his father is smiling.*

ROBERT.   Ah yes, of course; sit down, please, Mrs. Ross.
    She sits as if this made matters rather worse.

PHILIP (*standing guard by her side*).   My wife is a little agitated.

ROBERT.   Naturally. (*He tries a 'feeler.'*) These affairs—very painful at the time—but one gradually forgets.

EMILY (*with large eyes*).   That is what Mr. Ross says, but somehow I can't help—(*the eyes fill*). You see, we have been married only four months.

ROBERT.   Ah—that does make it—yes, certainly. (*He becomes the wife's champion, and frowns on* PHILIP.)

PHILIP.   I suppose the sum seems very small to you?

ROBERT (*serenely*).   I confess that is the impression it makes on me.

PHILIP. I wish it was more.

ROBERT (*at a venture*). You are sure you can't make it more?

PHILIP. How can I?

ROBERT. Ha!

5 EMILY (*with sudden spirit*). I think it's a great deal.

PHILIP. Mrs. Ross is so nice about it.

ROBERT (*taking a strong line*). I think so. But she must not be taken advantage of. And of course we shall have something to say as to the amount.

10 PHILIP (*blankly*). In what way? There it is.

ROBERT (*guardedly*). Hum. Yes, in a sense.

EMILY (*breaking down*). Oh dear!

ROBERT (*more determined than ever to do his best for this wronged woman*). I am very sorry, Mrs. Ross. (*Sternly*) I

15 hope, sir, you realise that the mere publicity to a sensitive woman——

PHILIP. Publicity?

ROBERT (*feeling that he has got him on the run*). Of course for her sake we shall try to arrange things so that the names do not

20 appear. Still——

PHILIP. The names?

By this time EMILY *is in tears.*

EMILY. I can't help it. I love him so.

ROBERT (*still benighted*). Enough to forgive him? (*Seeing him-*

25 *self suddenly as a mediator*) Mrs. Ross, is it too late to patch things up?

PHILIP (*now in flame*). What do you mean, sir?

MR. DEVIZES (*who has been quietly enjoying himself*). Yes, Robert, what do you mean precisely?

30 ROBERT. Really I—(*he tries brow-beating*) I must tell you at once, Mr. Ross, that unless a client gives us his fullest confidence we cannot undertake a case of this kind.

PHILIP. A case of what kind, sir? If you are implying anything against my good name——

35 ROBERT. On your honour, sir, is there nothing against it?

PHILIP. I know of nothing, sir.

EMILY. Anything against my husband, Mr. Devizes! He is an angel.

ROBERT (*suddenly seeing that little Wet Face must be the culprit*). Then it is you.

EMILY. Oh, sir, what is me? 5

PHILIP. Answer that, sir.

ROBERT. Yes, Mr. Ross, I will. (*But he finds he cannot.*) On second thoughts I decline. I cannot believe it has been all this lady's fault, and I decline to have anything to do with such a painful case. 10

MR. DEVIZES (*promptly*). Then I will take it up.

PHILIP (*not to be placated*). I think your son has insulted me.

EMILY. Philip, come away.

MR. DEVIZES. One moment, please. As *I* did not see your letter, may I ask Mr. Ross what is your business with us? 15

PHILIP. I called to ask whether you would be so good as to draw up my will.

ROBERT (*blankly*). Your will! Is that all?

PHILIP. Certainly.

MR. DEVIZES. Now we know, Robert. 20

ROBERT. But Mrs. Ross's agitation?

PHILIP (*taking her hand*). She feels that to make my will brings my death nearer.

ROBERT. So that's it.

PHILIP. It was all in the letter. 25

MR. DEVIZES (*coyly*). Anything to say, Robert?

ROBERT. Most—ah—extremely— (*He has an inspiration.*) But even now I'm puzzled. You are Edgar Charles Ross?

PHILIP. No, Philip Ross.

ROBERT (*brazenly*). Philip Ross? We have made an odd mistake, 30 father. (*There is a twinkle in* MR. DEVIZES's *eye. He watches interestedly to see how his son is to emerge from the mess.*) The fact is, Mrs. Ross, we are expecting to-day a Mr. Edgar Charles Ross on a matter—well—of a kind— Ah me. (*With fitting gravity*) His wife, in short. 35

EMILY (*who has not read the newspapers in vain*). How awful. How sad.

ROBERT. Sad indeed. You will quite understand that professional etiquette prevents my saying one word more.

5 PHILIP. Yes, of course—we have no desire— But I did write.

ROBERT. Assuredly. But about a will. That is my father's department. No doubt you recall the letter now, father?

MR. DEVIZES (*who if he won't hinder won't help*). I can't say I do.

10 ROBERT (*unabashed*). Odd. You must have overlooked it.

MR. DEVIZES. Ha. At all events, Mr. Ross, I am quite at your service now.

PHILIP. Thank you.

ROBERT (*still ready to sacrifice himself on the call of duty*). You
15 don't need me any more, father?

MR. DEVIZES. No, Robert; many thanks. You run off to your club now and have a bit of lunch. You must be tired. Send Surtees in to me. (*To his clients*) My son had his first case to-day.

PHILIP (*politely*). I hope successfully.

20 MR. DEVIZES. Not so bad. He rather bungled it at first, but he got out of a hole rather cleverly. I think you'll make a lawyer yet, Robert.

ROBERT. Thank you, father. (*He goes jauntily, with a flower in his button-hole.*)

25 MR. DEVIZES. Now, Mr. Ross.

The young wife's hand goes out for comfort and finds PHILIP's *waiting for it.*

PHILIP. What I want myself is that the will should all go into one sentence, 'I leave everything of which I die possessed to my
30 beloved wife.'

MR. DEVIZES (*thawing to the romance of this young couple*). Well, there have been many worse wills than that, sir.

EMILY *is emotional.*

PHILIP. Don't give way, Emily.

35 EMILY. It was those words, 'of which I die possessed.' (*Imploringly*) Surely he doesn't need to say that—please, Mr. Devizes?

MR. DEVIZES.   Certainly not. I am confident I can draw up the
will without mentioning death at all.

EMILY (*huskily*).   Oh, thank you.

MR. DEVIZES.   At the same time, of course, in a legal document in
which the widow is the sole——

EMILY *again needs attention.*

PHILIP (*reproachfully*).   What was the need of saying 'widow'?

MR. DEVIZES.   I beg your pardon, Mrs. Ross. I unreservedly with-
draw the word 'widow.' Forgive a stupid old solicitor. (*She
smiles gratefully through her tears.* SURTEES *comes in.*) Surtees,
just take a few notes, please. (SURTEES *sits in the background
and takes notes.*) The facts of the case, as I understand, Mrs.
Ross, are these: Your husband (*Quickly*)—who is in the prime
of health—but knows life to be uncertain——

EMILY.   Oh!

MR. DEVIZES.   —though usually, as we learn from holy script itself, it lasts seven times ten years—and believing that he will in
all probability live the allotted span, nevertheless, because of his
love of you thinks it judicious to go through the form—it is a
mere form—of making a will.

EMILY (*fervently*).   Oh, thank you.

MR. DEVIZES.   Any details, Mr. Ross?

PHILIP.   I am an orphan. I live at Belvedere, 14 Tulphin Road,
Hammersmith.

EMILY (*to whom the address has a seductive sound*).   We live
there.

PHILIP.   And I am a clerk in the employ of Curar and Gow, the
foreign coaling agents.

MR. DEVIZES.   Yes, yes. Any private income?

They cannot help sniggering a little at the quaint question.

PHILIP.   Oh no!

MR. DEVIZES.   I see it will be quite a brief will.

PHILIP (*to whom the remark sounds scarcely worthy of a great
occasion*).   My income is a biggish one.

MR. DEVIZES.   Yes?

EMILY (*important*).   He has £170 a year.

MR. DEVIZES.   Ah.

PHILIP.   I began at £60. But it is going up, Mr. Devizes, by leaps
and bounds. Another £15 this year.

MR. DEVIZES.   Good.

5 PHILIP (*darkly*).   I have a certain ambition.

EMILY (*eagerly*).   Tell him, Philip.

PHILIP (*with a big breath*).   We have made up our minds to
come to £365 a year before I—retire.

EMILY.   That is a pound a day.

10 MR. DEVIZES (*smiling sympathetically on them*).   So it is. My
best wishes.

PHILIP.   Thank you. Of course the furnishing took a good deal.

MR. DEVIZES.   It would.

EMILY.   He insisted on my having the very best. (*She ceases. She
15 is probably thinking of her superb spare bedroom.*)

PHILIP.   But we are not a penny in debt; and I have £200 saved.

MR. DEVIZES.   I think you have made a brave beginning.

EMILY.   They have the highest opinion of him in the office.

PHILIP.   Then I am insured for £500.

20 MR. DEVIZES.   I am glad to hear that.

PHILIP.   Of course I would like to leave her a house in Kensing-
ton and a carriage and pair.

MR. DEVIZES.   Who knows, perhaps you will.

EMILY.   Oh!

25 MR. DEVIZES.   Forgive me.

EMILY.   What would houses and horses be to me without him!

MR. DEVIZES (*soothingly*).   Quite so. What I take Mr. Ross to
mean is that when he dies—if he ever should die—everything is
to go to his—his spouse.

30 PHILIP (*dogged.*)   Yes.

EMILY (*dogged*).   No.

PHILIP (*sighing*).   This is the only difference we have ever had.
Mrs. Ross insists on certain bequests. You see, I have two cousins, ladies, not well off, whom I have been in the way of helping
35 a little. But in my will, how can I?

MR. DEVIZES.   You must think first of your wife.

PHILIP.   But she insists on my leaving £50 to each of them. (*He looks appealingly to his wife.*)

EMILY (*grandly*).   £100.

PHILIP.   £50.

EMILY.   Dear, £100.

MR. DEVIZES.   Let us say £75.

PHILIP (*reluctantly*).   Very well.

EMILY.   No, £100.

PHILIP.   She'll have to get her way. Here are their names and addresses.

MR. DEVIZES.   Anything else?

PHILIP (*hurriedly*).   No.

EMILY.   The convalescent home, dear. He was in it a year ago, and they were so kind.

PHILIP.   Yes, but——

EMILY.   £10. (*He has to yield, with a reproachful, admiring look.*)

MR. DEVIZES.   Then if that is all, I won't detain you. If you look in to-morrow, Mr. Ross, about this time, we shall have everything ready for you.

   Their faces fall.

EMILY.   Oh, Mr. Devizes, if only it could all be drawn up now, and done with.

PHILIP.   You see, sir, we are screwed up to it to-day.

   'Our fate is in your hands,' they might be saying, and the lawyer smiles to find himself such a power.

MR. DEVIZES (*looking at his watch*).   Well, it certainly need not take long. You go out and have lunch somewhere, and then come back.

EMILY.   Oh, don't ask me to eat.

PHILIP.   We are too excited.

EMILY.   Please may we just walk about the street?

MR. DEVIZES (*smiling*).   Of course you may, you ridiculous young wife.

EMILY.   I know it's ridiculous of me, but I am so fond of him.

MR. DEVIZES.   Yes, it is ridiculous. But don't change; especially if you get on in the world, Mr. Ross.

PHILIP.   No fear!

5 EMILY (*backing from the will, which may now be said to be in existence*).   And please don't give us a copy of it to keep. I would rather not have it in the house.

MR. DEVIZES (*nodding reassuringly*).   In an hour's time. (*They go, and the lawyer has his lunch, which is simpler than ROB-*

10 *ERT'S: a sandwich and a glass of wine. He speaks as he eats.*) You will get that ready, Surtees. Here are the names and addresses he left. (*Cheerily*) A nice couple.

SURTEES (*who is hearing another voice*).   Yes, sir.

MR. DEVIZES (*unbending*).   Little romance of its kind. Makes one

15 feel quite gay.

SURTEES.   Yes, sir.

MR. DEVIZES (*struck perhaps by the deadness of his voice*).   You don't look very gay, Surtees.

SURTEES.   I'm sorry, sir. We can't all be gay. (*He is going out

20 without looking at his employer.*) I'll see to this, sir.

MR. DEVIZES.   Stop a minute. Is there anything wrong? (SURTEES *has difficulty in answering, and* MR. DEVIZES *goes to him kindly.*) Not worrying over that matter we spoke about? (SUR-TEES *inclines his head.*) Is the pain worse?

25 SURTEES.   It's no great pain, sir.

MR. DEVIZES (*uncomfortably*).   I'm sure it's not—what you fear. Any specialist would tell you so.

SURTEES (*without looking up*).   I have been to one, sir—yester-day.

30 MR. DEVIZES.   Well?

SURTEES.   It's—that, sir.

MR. DEVIZES.   He couldn't be sure.

SURTEES.   Yes, sir.

MR. DEVIZES.   An operation——

35 SURTEES.   Too late, he said, for that. If I had been operated on long ago there might have been a chance.

MR. DEVIZES.   But you didn't have it long ago.

SURTEES.   Not to my knowledge, sir; but he says it was there all
the same, always in me, a black spot, not so big as a pin's head,
but waiting to spread and destroy me in the fulness of time. All
the rest of me as sound as a bell. (*That is the voice that* SURTEES   5
has been hearing.)

MR. DEVIZES (*helpless*).   It seems damnably unfair.

SURTEES (*humbly*).   I don't know, sir. He says there's a spot of
that kind in pretty nigh all of us, and if we don't look out it
does for us in the end.   10

MR. DEVIZES (*hurriedly*).   No, no, no.

SURTEES.   He called it the accursed thing. I think he meant we
should know of it and be on the watch. (*He pulls himself together.*) I'll see to this at once, sir.

> *He goes out.* MR. DEVIZES *continues his lunch.*   15

> *The curtain falls here for a moment only, to indicate the pass-
> ing of a number of years. When it rises we see that the en-
> graving of Queen Victoria has given way to one of King Ed-
> ward.*

> ROBERT *is discovered, immersed in affairs. He is now a mid-*   20
> *dle-aged man who has long forgotten how to fling cards into*
> *a hat. To him comes* SENNET, *a brisk clerk.*

SENNET.   Mrs. Philip Ross to see you, sir.

ROBERT.   Mr. Ross, don't you mean, Sennet?

SENNET.   No, sir.   25

ROBERT.   Ha. It was Mr. Ross I was expecting. Show her in.
(*Frowning*) And, Sennet, less row in the office, if you please.

SENNET (*glibly*).   It was these young clerks, sir——

ROBERT.   They mustn't be young here, or they go. Tell them that.

SENNET (*glad to be gone*).   Yes, sir.   30

> *He shows in* MRS. ROSS. *We have not seen her for twenty
> years and would certainly not recognise her in the street. So
> shrinking her first entrance into this room, but she sails in now
> like a galleon. She is not so much dressed as richly upholstered.*

She is very sure of herself. Yet she is not a different woman from the EMILY *we remember; the pity of it is that somehow this is the same woman.*

ROBERT (*who makes much of his important visitor and is also won-* ⁵ *dering why she has come*).   This is a delightful surprise, Mrs. Ross. Allow me. (*He removes her fine cloak with proper solici- tude, and* EMILY *walks out of it in the manner that makes it worth possessing.*) This chair, alas, is the best I can offer you.

EMILY (*who is still a good-natured woman if you attempt no non-* ¹⁰ *sense with her*).   It will do quite well.

ROBERT (*gallantly*).   Honoured to see you in it.

EMILY (*smartly*).   Not you. You were saying to yourself, 'Now, what brings the woman here?'

ROBERT.   Honestly, I——

¹⁵ EMILY.   And I'll tell you. You are expecting Mr. Ross, I think?

ROBERT (*cautiously*).   Well—ah——

EMILY.   Pooh. The cunning of you lawyers. I know he has an appointment with you, and that is why I've come.

ROBERT.   He arranged with you to meet him here?

²⁰ EMILY (*preening herself*).   I wouldn't say that. I don't know that he will be specially pleased to find me here when he comes.

ROBERT. (*guardedly*).   Oh?

EMILY (*who is now a woman that goes straight to her goal*).   I know what he is coming about. To make a new will.

²⁵ ROBERT (*admitting it*).   After all, not the first he has made with us, Mrs. Ross.

EMILY (*promptly*).   No, the fourth.

ROBERT (*warming his hands at the thought*).   Such a wonderful career. He goes from success to success.

³⁰ EMILY (*complacently*).   Yes, we're big folk.

ROBERT.   You are indeed.

EMILY (*sharply*).   But the last will covered everything.

ROBERT (*on guard again*).   Of course it is a matter I cannot well discuss even with you. And I know nothing of his intentions.

³⁵ EMILY.   Well, I suspect some of them.

ROBERT.   Ah.

EMILY. And that's why I'm here. Just to see that he does nothing
foolish.
She settles herself more comfortably as MR. Ross *is an-*
nounced. A city magnate walks in. You know he is that be-
fore you see that he is PHILIP ROSS.   5
PHILIP (*speaking as he enters*). How do, Devizes, how do. Well,
let us get at this thing at once. Time is money, you know, time
is money. (*Then he sees his wife.*) Hello, Emily.
EMILY (*unperturbed*). You didn't ask me to come, Philip, but I
thought I might as well.   10
PHILIP. That's all right.
His brow had lowered at first sight of her, but now he gives
her cleverness a grin of respect.
EMILY. It is the first will you have made without taking me into
your confidence.   15
PHILIP. No important changes. I just thought to save you the—
unpleasantness of the thing.
EMILY. How do you mean?
PHILIP (*fidgeting*). Well, one can't draw up a will without feel-
ing for the moment that he is bringing his end nearer. Is that not   20
so, Devizes?
ROBERT (*who will quite possibly die intestate*). Some do have
that feeling.
EMILY. But what nonsense. How can it have any effect of that
kind one way or the other?   25
ROBERT. Quite so.
EMILY (*reprovingly*). Just silly sentiment, Philip. I would have
thought it would be a pleasure to you handling such a big sum.
PHILIP (*wincing*). Not handling it, giving it up.
EMILY. To those you love.   30
PHILIP (*rather shortly*). I'm not giving it up yet. You talk as if
I was on my last legs.
EMILY (*imperturbably*). Not at all. It's you that are doing that.
ROBERT (*to the rescue*). Here is my copy of the last will. I
don't know if you would like me to read it out?   35
PHILIP. It's hardly necessary.

EMILY.   We have our own copy at home and we know it well.

PHILIP (*sitting back in his chair*).   What do you think I'm worth to-day, Devizes?

    Every one smiles. It is as if the sun had peeped in at the window.

ROBERT.   I daren't guess.

PHILIP.   An easy seventy thou.

EMILY.   And that's not counting the house and the country cottage. We call it a cottage. You should see it!

ROBERT.   I have heard of it.

EMILY (*more sharply, though the sun still shines*).   Well, go on, Philip. I suppose you are not thinking of cutting me out of anything.

PHILIP (*heartily*).   Of course not. There will be more to you than ever.

EMILY (*coolly*).   There's more to leave.

PHILIP (*hesitating*).   At the same time——

EMILY.   Well? It's to be mine absolutely of course. Not just a life interest.

PHILIP (*doggedly*).   That is a change I was thinking of.

EMILY.   Just what I have suspected for days. Will you please to say why?

ROBERT (*whose client after all is the man*).   Of course it is quite common.

EMILY.   I didn't think my husband was quite common.

ROBERT.   I only mean that as there are children——

PHILIP.   That's what I mean too.

EMILY.   And I can't be trusted to leave my money to my own children! In what way have I ever failed them before?

PHILIP (*believing it too*).   Never, Emily, never. A more devoted mother— If you have one failing it is that you spoil them.

EMILY.   Then what's your reason?

PHILIP (*less sincerely*).   Just to save you worry when I'm gone.

EMILY.   It's no worry to me to look after my money.

PHILIP (*bridling*).   After all, it's my money.

EMILY.   I knew that was what was at the back of your mind.

PHILIP (*reverently*). It's such a great sum.

EMILY. One would think you were afraid I would marry again.

PHILIP (*snapping*). One would think you looked to my dying next week.

EMILY. Tuts.   5

PHILIP *is unable to sit still.*

PHILIP. My money. If you were to invest it badly and lose it. I tell you, Devizes, I couldn't lie quiet in my grave if I thought my money was lost by injudicious investments.

EMILY (*coldly*). You are thinking of yourself, Philip, rather   10
than of the children.

PHILIP. Not at all.

ROBERT (*hastily*). How are the two children?

EMILY. Though I say it myself, there never were better. Harry is at Eton, you know, the most fashionable school in the coun-   15
try.

ROBERT. Doing well, I hope.

PHILIP (*chuckling*). We have the most gratifying letters from him. Last Saturday he was caught smoking cigarettes with a lord. (*With pardonable pride*) They were sick together.   20

ROBERT. And Miss Gwendolen? She must be almost grown up now.

The parents exchange important glances.

EMILY. Should we tell him?

PHILIP. Under the rose, you know, Devizes.   25

ROBERT. Am I to congratulate her?

EMILY. No names, Philip.

PHILIP. No, no names—but she won't be a plain Mrs., no, sir.

ROBERT. Well done, Miss Gwendolen. (*With fitting jocularity*)
Now I see why you want a new will.   30

PHILIP. Yes, that's my main reason, Emily.

EMILY. But none of your life interests for me, Philip.

PHILIP (*shying*). We'll talk that over presently.

ROBERT. Will you keep the legacies as they are?

PHILIP. Well, there's that £500 for the hospitals.   35

EMILY. Yes, with so many claims on us, is that necessary?

PHILIP (*becoming stouter*). I'm going to make it £1000.

EMILY. Philip!

PHILIP. My mind is made up. I want to make a splash with the hospitals.

5 ROBERT (*hurrying to the next item.*) There is £50 a year each to two cousins, ladies.

PHILIP. I suppose we'll keep that as it is, Emily?

EMILY. It was just gifts to them of £100 each at first.

PHILIP. I was poor at that time myself.

10 EMILY. Do you think it's wise to load them with so much money? They'll not know what to do with it.

PHILIP. They're old.

EMILY. But they're wiry. £75 a year between them would surely be enough.

15 PHILIP. It would be if they lived together, but you see they don't. They hate each other like cat and dog.

EMILY. That's not nice between relatives. You could leave it to them on condition that they do live together. That would be a Christian action.

20 PHILIP. There's something in that.

ROBERT. Then the chief matter is whether Mrs. Ross——.

EMILY. Oh, I thought that was settled.

PHILIP (*with a sigh*). I'll have to give in to her, sir.

ROBERT. Very well. I suppose my father will want to draw up

25 the will. I'm sorry he had to be in the country to-day.

EMILY (*affable now that she has gained her point*). I hope he is wearing well?

ROBERT. Wonderfully. He is away playing golf.

PHILIP (*grinning*). Golf. I have no time for games. (*Consid-*

30 *erately*) But he must get the drawing up of my will. I couldn't deprive the old man of that.

ROBERT. He will be proud to do it again.

PHILIP (*well satisfied*). Ah! There's many a one would like to look over your father's shoulder when he's drawing up my

35 will. I wonder what I'll cut up for in the end. But I must be going.

EMILY. Can I drop you anywhere? I have the greys out.

PHILIP. Yes, at the club.

Now MRS. Ross *walks into her cloak.*

Good-day, Devizes. I won't have time to look in again, so tell
the old man to come to me.   5

ROBERT (*deferentially*). Whatever suits you best. (*Ringing.*)
He will be delighted. I remember his saying to me on the day
you made your first will——

PHILIP (*chuckling*). A poor little affair that.

ROBERT. He said to me you were a couple whose life looked like   10
being a romance.

PHILIP. And he was right—eh, Emily?—though he little thought
what a romance.

EMILY. No, he little thought what a romance.

They make a happy departure, and ROBERT *is left reflecting.*   15

*The curtain again falls, and rises immediately, as the engrav-
ing shows, on the same office in the reign of King George. It
is a foggy morning and a fire burns briskly.* MR. DEVIZES,
SENIOR, *arrives for the day's work just as he came daily for
over half a century. But he has no right to be here now. A
year or two ago they got him to retire, as he was grown
feeble; and there is an understanding that he does not go out
of his house alone. He has, as it were, escaped to-day, and his
feet have carried him to the old office that is the home of his
mind. He was almost portly when we saw him first, but he
has become little again and as light as the schoolboy whose
deeds are nearer to him than many of the events of later years.
He arrives at the office, thinking it is old times, and a clerk
surveys him uncomfortably from the door.*

CREED (*not quite knowing what to do*). Mr. Devizes has not
come in yet, sir.

MR. DEVIZES (*considering*). Yes, I have. Do you mean Mr.
Robert?

CREED. Yes, sir.

MR. DEVIZES (*querulously*). Always late. Can't get that boy to   20 settle down. (*Leniently*) Well, well, boys will be boys—eh, Surtees?

CREED (*wishing* MR. ROBERT *would come*). My name is Creed, sir.

5 MR. DEVIZES (*sharply*). Creed? Don't know you. Where is Surtees?

CREED. There is no one of that name in the office, sir.

MR. DEVIZES (*growing timid*). No? I remember now. Poor Surtees! (*But his mind cannot grapple with troubles.*) Tell him
10 I want him when he comes in.

He is changing, after his old custom, into an office coat.

CREED. That is Mr. Dev—Mr. Robert's coat, sir.

MR. DEVIZES. He has no business to hang it there. That is my nail.

15 CREED. He has hung it there for years, sir.

MR. DEVIZES. Not at all. I must have it. Why does Surtees let him do it? Help me into my office coat, boy.

CREED helps him into the coat he has taken off, and the old man is content.

20 CREED (*seeing him lift up the correspondence*). I don't think Mr. Devizes would like you to open the office letters, sir.

MR. DEVIZES (*pettishly*). What's that? Go away, boy. Send Surtees.

To the relief of CREED, ROBERT *arrives, and, taking in the*
25 *situation, signs to the clerk to go. He has a more youthful manner than when last we saw him, has* ROBERT, *but his hair is iron grey. He is kindly to his father.*

ROBERT. You here, father?

MR. DEVIZES (*after staring at him*). Yes, you are Robert. (*A*
30 *little frightened*) You are an old man, Robert.

ROBERT (*without wincing*). Getting on, father. But why did they let you come? You haven't been here for years.

MR. DEVIZES (*puzzled*). Years? I think I just came in the old way, Robert, without thinking.

35 ROBERT. Yes, yes. I'll get some one to go home with you.

MR. DEVIZES (*rather abject*). Let me stay, Robert. I like being here. I won't disturb you. I like the smell of the office, Robert.

ROBERT.   Of course you may stay. Come over to the fire. (*He settles his father by the fire in the one arm-chair.*) There; you can have a doze by the fire.

MR. DEVIZES.   A doze by the fire. That is all I'm good for now.   5
Once—but my son hangs his coat there now. (*Presently he looks up fearfully.*) Robert, tell me something in a whisper: Is Surtees dead?

ROBERT (*who has forgotten the name*).   Surtees?

MR. DEVIZES.   My clerk, you know.   10

ROBERT.   Oh. Why, he has been dead this thirty years, father.

MR. DEVIZES.   So long! Seems like yesterday.

ROBERT.   It is just far back times that seem clear to you now.

MR. DEVIZES (*meekly*).   Is it?

    ROBERT *opens his letters, and his father falls asleep.* CREED   15
    comes.)

CREED.   Sir Philip Ross.

    The great SIR PHILIP *enters, nearly sixty now, strong of frame still, but a lost man. He is in mourning, and carries the broken pieces of his life with an air of braggadocio. It should*   20
    be understood that he is not a 'sympathetic' part, and any actor who plays him as such will be rolling the play in the gutter.

ROBERT (*on his feet at once to greet such a client*).   You, Sir Philip.   25

PHILIP (*head erect.*)   Here I am.

ROBERT (*because it will out*).   How are you?

PHILIP (*as if challenged*).   I'm all right—great. (*With defiant jocularity*) Called on the old business.

ROBERT.   To make another will?   30

PHILIP.   You've guessed it—the very first time. (*He sees the figure by the fire.*)

ROBERT.   Yes, it's my father. He's dozing. Shouldn't be here at all. He forgets things. It's just age.

PHILIP (*grimly*).   Forgets things. That must be fine.   35

ROBERT (*conventionally*).   I should like, Sir Philip, to offer you

my sincere condolences. In the midst of life we are— How
true that is. I attended the funeral.

PHILIP.   I saw you.

ROBERT.   A much esteemed lady. I had a great respect for her.

5 PHILIP (*almost with relish*).   Do you mind, when we used to
come here about the will, somehow she—we—always took for
granted I should be the first to go.

ROBERT (*devoutly*).   These things are hid from mortal eyes.

PHILIP (*with conviction*).   There's a lot hid. We needn't have
10 worried so much about the will if—well, let us get at it.
(*Fiercely*) I haven't given in, you know.

ROBERT.   We must bow our heads——

PHILIP.   Must we? Am I bowing mine?

ROBERT (*uncomfortably*).   Such courage in the great hour—yes
15 —and I am sure Lady Ross——

PHILIP (*with the ugly humour that has come to him*).   She
wasn't that.

ROBERT.   The honour came so soon afterwards—I feel she would
like to be thought of as Lady Ross. I shall always remember her
20 as a fine lady richly dressed who used——

PHILIP (*harshly*).   Stop it. That's not how I think of her. There
was a time before that—she wasn't richly dressed—(*he stamps
upon his memories*). Things went wrong, I don't know how.
It's a beast of a world. I didn't come here to talk about that. Let
25 us get to work.

ROBERT (*turning with relief from the cemetery*).   Yes, yes, and
after all life has its compensations. You have your son who——

PHILIP (*snapping*).   No, I haven't. (*This startles the lawyer.*)
I'm done with him.

30 ROBERT.   If he has been foolish——

PHILIP.   Foolish! (*Some dignity comes into the man.*) Sir, I have
come to a pass when foolish as applied to my own son would
seem to me a very pretty word.

ROBERT.   Is it as bad as that?

35 PHILIP.   He's a rotter.

ROBERT.   It is very painful to me to hear you say that.

PHILIP.   More painful, think you, than for me to say it? (*Clench-ing his fists*) But I've shipped him off. The law had to wink at it, or I couldn't have done it. Why don't you say I pampered him and it serves me right? It's what they are all saying behind my back. Why don't you ask me about my girl? That's another   5
way to rub it in.

ROBERT.   Don't, Sir Philip. I knew her. My sympathy——

PHILIP.   A chauffeur, that is what he was. The man who drove her own car.

ROBERT.   I was deeply concerned——   10

PHILIP.   I want nobody's pity. I've done with both of them, and if you think I'm a broken man you're much mistaken. I'll show them. Have you your papers there? Then take down my last will. I have everything in my head. I'll show them.

ROBERT.   Would it not be better to wait till a calmer——   15

PHILIP.   Will you do it now, or am I to go across the street?

ROBERT.   If I must.

PHILIP.   Then down with it. (*He wets his lips.*) I, Philip Ross, of 77 Bath Street, W., do hereby revoke all former wills and testa-ments, and I leave everything of which I die possessed——   20

ROBERT.   Yes?

PHILIP.   Everything of which I die possessed——

ROBERT.   Yes?

PHILIP.   I leave it—I leave it— (*The game is up.*) My God, Devizes, I don't know what to do with it.   25

ROBERT.   I—I—really—come——

PHILIP (*cynically*).   Can't you make any suggestions?

ROBERT.   Those cousins are dead, I think?

PHILIP.   Years ago.

ROBERT (*troubled*).   In the case of such a large sum——   30

PHILIP (*letting all his hoarded gold run through his fingers*). The money I've won with my blood. God in heaven! (*Showing his teeth*) Would that old man like it to play with? If I bring it to you in sacks, will you fling it out of the window for me?

ROBERT.   Sir Philip!   35

PHILIP (*taking a paper from his pocket*).   Here, take this. It has the names and addresses of the half-dozen men I've fought with most for gold; and I've beaten them. Draw up a will leaving all my money to be divided between them, with my respectful curses, and bring it to my house and I'll sign it.

5 ROBERT (*properly shocked*).   But really I can't possibly——

PHILIP.   Either you or another; is it to be you?

ROBERT.   Very well.

PHILIP.   Then that's settled. (*He rises with a laugh. He regards* MR. DEVIZES *quizzically.*) So you weren't in at the last will

10 after all, old Sleep by the Fire.

To their surprise the old man stirs.

MR. DEVIZES.   What's that about a will?

ROBERT.   You are awake, father?

MR. DEVIZES (*whose eyes have opened on* PHILIP's *face*). I

15 don't know you, sir.

ROBERT.   Yes, yes, father, you remember Mr. Ross. He is Sir Philip now.

MR. DEVIZES (*courteously*).   Sir Philip? I wish you joy, sir, but I don't know you.

20 ROBERT (*encouragingly*).   Ross, father.

MR. DEVIZES.   I knew a Mr. Ross long ago.

ROBERT.   This is the same.

MR. DEVIZES (*annoyed*).   No, no. A bright young fellow he was, with such a dear, pretty wife. They came to make a will.

25 (*He chuckles.*) And bless me, they had only twopence halfpenny. I took a fancy to them; such a happy pair.

ROBERT (*apologetically*).   The past is clearer to him than the present nowadays. That will do, father.

PHILIP (*brusquely*).   Let him go on.

30 MR. DEVIZES.   Poor souls, it all ended unhappily, you know.

PHILIP (*who is not brusque to him*).   Yes, I know. Why did things go wrong, sir? I sit and wonder, and I can't find the beginning.

MR. DEVIZES.   That's the sad part of it. There was never a be-

35 ginning. It was always there. He told me all about it.

ROBERT.   He is thinking of something else; I don't know what.

PHILIP. Quiet. What was it that was always there?

MR. DEVIZES. It was always in them—a spot no bigger than a pin's head, but waiting to spread and destroy them in the fulness of time.

ROBERT. I don't know what he has got hold of. 5

PHILIP. He knows. Could they have done anything to prevent it, sir?

MR. DEVIZES. If they had been on the watch. But they didn't know, so they weren't on the watch. Poor souls.

PHILIP. Poor souls. 10

MR. DEVIZES. It's called the accursed thing. It gets nearly everybody in the end, if they don't look out.

He sinks back into his chair and forgets them.

ROBERT. He is just wandering.

PHILIP. The old man knows. 15

He slowly tears up the paper he had given ROBERT.

ROBERT (*relieved*). I am glad to see you do that.

PHILIP. A spot no bigger than a pin's head. (*A wish wells up in him, too late perhaps.*) I wish I could help some young things before that spot has time to spread and destroy them as it has 20 destroyed me and mine.

ROBERT (*brightly*). With such a large fortune——

PHILIP (*summing up his life*). It can't be done with money, sir.

He goes away; God knows where.

———————

As the opening stage directions suggest, Barrie was temperamentally opposed to the realistic movement that reached its climax in the drama during his lifetime. In consequence, almost every one of Barrie's plays gives some evidence of his hostility to either the spirit or the form of the realistic drama. *Peter Pan* is the most fantastically imaginative of his plays, but in even such highly successful dramas as *What Every Woman Knows* and *Dear Brutus* there are anti-realistic elements.

Although there is no element of fantasy in "The Will," the boldness with which it compresses the life history of two characters into a one-act play is symptomatic of Barrie's belief that the drama should not be a merely photographic representation of life. The life histories of Philip and Emily Ross contain material enough for a full-length play or possibly a novel. The most dramatic events in their lives were the criminality of the son, the elopement of the daughter, the death of the wife, and the knighting of Philip.

But Barrie will have none of these obviously dramatic events. Instead, he suggests the life history and the character developments of this pair in brief cross sections of their lives at three moments when the characters reveal themselves clearly. From their long life lines, he selects three points, strikingly alike and yet unlike, and, from what happens at these points, we are expected to construct the pattern of their whole lives. The similarities in the points selected give the play a unity and coherence that it would not have if the points were any three of the climactic scenes mentioned. The distances between the points he has selected, moreover, give him an opportunity to bring out the effects on character of the dramatic occurrences off stage.

The substance of the play does not involve much action on the stage; what we get instead is the results of unseen action upon character. To compensate for the lack of action on the stage, Barrie introduces some degree of tension into each of his three scenes. In each scene, the tension develops between the two major characters of the play; this tension is present in even the last scene, despite the fact that one of the major characters has recently died. But it is Philip's relationship, not only to his children but to his late wife, that lies at the root of the emotional state from which he is suffering in the final scene.

Barrie's high-handed attitude toward realism in the drama is also suggested by the lightning changes that he forces upon his actors in their passage from youth to old age. A playwright more interested than Barrie in the minutiae of realism would have provided more time for the changes in make-up and costume needed to visualize the advancing ages of the characters. Barrie allows time for only such changes as will suggest symbolically the stage at which his characters have arrived.

Barrie's impatience with the restrictions of the dramatic form is evident in the way in which he prepared his plays for the reading public. His reluctance to print his plays may have been due in part to the economic motive, the idea that, if people had a chance to read his plays, they might not go to the theater to see them. More certainly, as the printed plays make clear, he felt that the bare theatrical script of a play made too heavy demands on the reader, demands which setting, costume, lighting, and excellent acting would supply in the theater. Barrie, therefore, introduced, in the form of stage directions and parenthetical comments, observations that are essentially not dramatic but novelistic. It is almost as though Barrie felt that the theatrical script must, to a degree, be novelized before its values could get across to the person who reads it but does not see it acted.

———

In the stage directions with which the play opens, what portions are stage directions in the conventional sense and what portions are comments such as a novelist might make on either setting or characters? Would the novelistic comments be of any use to anyone connected with the production of the play? Why or why not?

Of what expository value is the fact of the destruction of Philip's letter? Is its destruction satisfactorily motivated? Why or why not?

Which of Barrie's comments on Philip and Emily Ross, as they enter, are dramatic, and which are novelistic? Is Robert Devizes' misunderstanding of the relationship of the Rosses satisfactorily motivated? Why or why not?

Why does Barrie include the scene in which Surtees reveals the fact that he is suffering from cancer? Is its inclusion made to seem natural? Why or why not?

By what means, other than the change of the pictures, does Barrie establish the lapse of time between the first and the second scene of the play? Between the second and third scene?

What changes have taken place in the characters of Philip and Emily between the first and the second scenes? By what methods does Barrie bring out these changes?

What does Barrie gain by introducing the elder Devizes in the third scene? Is his recollection of Surtees' ailment made to seem plausible? Why or why not? Is his final effect on Philip made to seem plausible? Why or why not?

What is the theme of the play? Where is it stated most explicitly?

Riders to the Sea [1]

A Play in One Act

JOHN MILLINGTON SYNGE

PERSONS

MAURYA, *an old woman*
BARTLEY, *her son*
CATHLEEN, *her daughter*
NORA, *a younger daughter*
MEN AND WOMEN

SCENE. *An Island off the west of Ireland.*
Cottage kitchen, with nets, oil-skins, spinning-wheel, some new boards standing by the wall, etc. CATHLEEN, *a girl of about twenty, finishes kneading cake, and puts it down in the pot-oven by the fire; then wipes her hands, and begins to spin at the wheel.* NORA, *a young girl, puts her head in at the door.*

NORA (*in a low voice*). Where is she?
CATHLEEN. She's lying down, God help her, and maybe sleeping, if she's able.
    NORA *comes in softly, and takes a bundle from under her shawl.*

5

[1] Reprinted by permission of Random House, Inc., and George Allen & Unwin Ltd.

91

CATHLEEN (*spinning the wheel rapidly*).   What is it you have?

NORA.   The young priest is after bringing them. It's a shirt and a plain stocking were got off a drowned man in Donegal.

5   CATHLEEN *stops her wheel with a sudden movement, and leans out to listen.*

NORA.   We're to find out if it's Michael's they are, some time herself will be down looking by the sea.

CATHLEEN.   How would they be Michael's, Nora? How would he go the length of that way to the far north?

10   NORA.   The young priest says he's known the like of it. "If it's Michael's they are," says he, "you can tell herself he's got a clean burial by the grace of God, and if they're not his, let no one say a word about them, for she'll be getting her death," says he, "with crying and lamenting."

15   *The door which* NORA *half closed is blown open by a gust of wind.*

CATHLEEN (*looking out anxiously*).   Did you ask him would he stop Bartley going this day with the horses to the Galway fair?

NORA.   "I won't stop him," says he, "but let you not be afraid.

20   Herself does be saying prayers half through the night, and the Almighty God won't leave her destitute," says he, "with no son living."

CATHLEEN.   Is the sea bad by the white rocks, Nora?

NORA.   Middling bad, God help us. There's a great roaring in

25   the west, and it's worse it'll be getting when the tide's turned to the wind. (*She goes over to the table with the bundle.*) Shall I open it now?

CATHLEEN.   Maybe she'd wake up on us, and come in before we'd done. (*Coming to the table*) It's a long time we'll be, and

30   the two of us crying.

NORA.   (*Goes to the inner door and listens.*)   She's moving about on the bed. She'll be coming in a minute.

CATHLEEN.   Give me the ladder, and I'll put them up in the turf-loft, the way she won't know of them at all, and maybe when

35   the tide turns she'll be going down to see would he be floating from the east.

They put the ladder against the gable of the chimney; CATH-
LEEN *goes up a few steps and hides the bundle in the turf-
loft.* MAURYA *comes from the inner room.*

MAURYA (*looking up at* CATHLEEN *and speaking querulously*).
Isn't it turf enough you have for this day and evening?

CATHLEEN. There's a cake baking at the fire for a short space
(*throwing down the turf*) and Bartley will want it when the
tide turns if he goes to Connemara.

NORA *picks up the turf and puts it round the pot-oven.*

MAURYA (*sitting down on a stool at the fire*). He won't go this
day with the wind rising from the south and west. He won't go
this day, for the young priest will stop him surely.

NORA. He'll not stop him, mother, and I heard Eamon Simon
and Stephen Pheety and Colum Shawn saying he would go.

MAURYA. Where is he itself?

NORA. He went down to see would there be another boat sailing
in the week, and I'm thinking it won't be long till he's here
now, for the tide's turning at the green head, and the hooker's
tacking from the east.

CATHLEEN. I hear some one passing the big stones.

NORA (*looking out*). He's coming now, and he in a hurry.

BARTLEY. (*Comes in and looks round the room; speaking sadly
and quietly.*) Where is the bit of new rope, Cathleen, was
bought in Connemara?

CATHLEEN (*coming down*). Give it to him, Nora; it's on a nail
by the white boards. I hung it up this morning, for the pig
with the black feet was eating it.

NORA (*giving him a rope*). Is that it, Bartley?

MAURYA. You'd do right to leave that rope, Bartley, hanging by
the boards. (BARTLEY *takes the rope.*) It will be wanting in
this place, I'm telling you, if Michael is washed up to-morrow
morning, or the next morning, or any morning in the week, for
it's a deep grave we'll make him by the grace of God.

BARTLEY (*beginning to work with the rope*). I've no halter the
way I can ride down on the mare, and I must go now quickly.
This is the one boat going for two weeks or beyond it, and the

fair will be a good fair for horses I heard them saying below.

MAURYA.   It's a hard thing they'll be saying below if the body is
washed up and there's no man in it to make the coffin, and I
after giving a big price for the finest white boards you'd find in
5   Connemara.

She looks round at the boards.

BARTLEY.   How would it be washed up, and we after looking
each day for nine days, and a strong wind blowing a while back
from the west and south?

10 MAURYA.   If it wasn't found itself, that wind is raising the sea,
and there was a star up against the moon, and it rising in the
night. If it was a hundred horses, or a thousand horses you had
itself, what is the price of a thousand horses against a son where
there is one son only?

15 BARTLEY (*working at the halter, to* CATHLEEN).   Let you go
down each day, and see the sheep aren't jumping in on the rye,
and if the jobber comes you can sell the pig with the black
feet if there is a good price going.

MAURYA.   How would the like of her get a good price for a pig?

20 BARTLEY (*to* CATHLEEN).   If the west wind holds with the last
bit of the moon let you and Nora get up weed enough for another cock for the kelp. It's hard set we'll be from this day with
no one in it but one man to work.

MAURYA.   It's hard set we'll be surely the day you're drownd'd
25   with the rest. What way will I live and the girls with me, and I
an old woman looking for the grave?

BARTLEY *lays down the halter, takes off his old coat, and puts
on a newer one of the same flannel.*

BARTLEY (*to* NORA).   Is she coming to the pier?

30 NORA (*looking out*).   She's passing the green head and letting
fall her sails.

BARTLEY (*getting his purse and tobacco*).   I'll have half an hour
to go down, and you'll see me coming again in two days, or in
three days, or maybe in four days if the wind is bad.

35 MAURYA (*turning round to the fire, and putting her shawl over*

her head). Isn't it a hard and cruel man won't hear a word
from an old woman, and she holding him from the sea?

CATHLEEN. It's the life of a young man to be going on the sea,
and who would listen to an old woman with one thing and she
saying it over?

BARTLEY (*taking the halter*). I must go now quickly. I'll ride
down on the red mare, and the gray pony'll run behind me.
. . . The blessing of God on you.

He goes out.

MAURYA (*crying out as he is in the door*). He's gone now, God
spare us, and we'll not see him again. He's gone now, and when
the black night is falling I'll have no son left me in the world.

CATHLEEN. Why wouldn't you give him your blessing and he
looking round in the door? Isn't it sorrow enough is on every
one in this house without your sending him out with an unlucky word behind him, and a hard word in his ear?

*MAURYA takes up the tongs and begins raking the fire aim-
lessly without looking round.*

NORA (*turning toward her*). You're taking away the turf from
the cake.

CATHLEEN (*crying out*). The Son of God forgive us, Nora,
we're after forgetting his bit of bread.

She comes over to the fire.

NORA. And it's destroyed he'll be going till dark night, and he
after eating nothing since the sun went up.

CATHLEEN (*turning the cake out of the oven*). It's destroyed
he'll be, surely. There's no sense left on any person in a house
where an old woman will be talking forever.

MAURYA sways herself on her stool.

CATHLEEN (*cutting off some of the bread and rolling it in a cloth;
to MAURYA*). Let you go down now to the spring well and
give him this and he passing. You'll see him then and the dark
word will be broken, and you can say "God speed you," the
way he'll be easy in his mind.

MAURYA (*taking the bread*). Will I be in it as soon as himself?

CATHLEEN.   If you go now quickly.

MAURYA (*standing up unsteadily*).   It's hard set I am to walk.

CATHLEEN (*looking at her anxiously*).   Give her the stick, Nora, or maybe she'll slip on the big stones.

5 NORA.   What stick?

CATHLEEN.   The stick Michael brought from Connemara.

MAURYA (*taking a stick* NORA *gives her*).   In the big world the old people do be leaving things after them for their sons and children, but in this place it is the young men do be leaving
10 things behind for them that do be old.

> *She goes out slowly.* NORA *goes over to the ladder.*

CATHLEEN.   Wait, Nora, maybe she'd turn back quickly. She's that sorry, God help her, you wouldn't know the thing she'd do.

15 NORA.   Is she gone round by the bush?

CATHLEEN (*looking out*).   She's gone now. Throw it down quickly, for the Lord knows when she'll be out of it again.

NORA (*getting the bundle from the loft*).   The young priest said he'd be passing tomorrow, and we might go down and speak
20 to him below if it's Michael's they are surely.

CATHLEEN (*taking the bundle*).   Did he say what way they were found?

NORA (*coming down*).   "There were two men," says he, "and they rowing round with poteen before the cocks crowed, and
25 the oar of one of them caught the body, and they passing the black cliffs of the north."

CATHLEEN (*trying to open the bundle*).   Give me a knife, Nora, the string's perished with the salt water, and there's a black knot on it you wouldn't loosen in a week.

30 NORA (*giving her a knife*).   I've heard tell it was a long way to Donegal.

CATHLEEN (*cutting the string*).   It is surely. There was a man in here a while ago—the man sold us that knife—and he said if you set off walking from the rocks beyond, it would be seven
35 days you'd be in Donegal.

NORA.   And what time would a man take, and he floating?

> CATHLEEN *opens the bundle and takes out a bit of a stocking.*
> *They look at them eagerly.*

CATHLEEN (*in a low voice*). The Lord spare us, Nora! isn't it a queer hard thing to say if it's his they are surely?

NORA. I'll get his shirt off the hook the way we can put the one flannel on the other. (*She looks through some clothes hanging in the corner.*) It's not with them, Cathleen, and where will it be?

CATHLEEN. I'm thinking Bartley put it on him in the morning, for his own shirt was heavy with the salt in it (*pointing to the corner.*) There's a bit of a sleeve was of the same stuff. Give me that and it will do.

> NORA *brings it to her and they compare the flannel.*

CATHLEEN. It's the same stuff, Nora; but if it is itself aren't there great rolls of it in the shops of Galway, and isn't it many another man may have a shirt of it as well as Michael himself?

NORA (*who has taken up the stocking and counted the stitches, crying out*). It's Michael, Cathleen, it's Michael; God spare his soul, and what will herself say when she hears this story, and Bartley on the sea?

CATHLEEN (*taking the stocking*). It's a plain stocking.

NORA. It's the second one of the third pair I knitted, and I put up threescore stitches, and I dropped four of them.

CATHLEEN. (*Counts the stitches.*) It's that number is in it (*crying out*). Ah, Nora, isn't it a bitter thing to think of him floating that way to the far north, and no one to keen him but the black hags that do be flying on the sea?

NORA (*swinging herself round, and throwing out her arms on the clothes*). And isn't it a pitiful thing when there is nothing left of a man who was a great rower and fisher, but a bit of an old shirt and a plain stocking?

CATHLEEN (*after an instant*). Tell me is herself coming, Nora? I hear a little sound on the path.

NORA (*looking out*). She is, Cathleen. She's coming up to the door.

CATHLEEN. Put these things away before she'll come in. Maybe

it's easier she'll be after giving her blessing to Bartley, and we
won't let on we've heard anything the time he's on the sea.

NORA (*helping* CATHLEEN *to close the bundle*).   We'll put them
here in the corner.

5   *They put them into a hole in the chimney corner.* CATHLEEN
goes back to the spinning-wheel.

NORA.   Will she see it was crying I was?

CATHLEEN.   Keep your back to the door the way the light'll not
be on you.

10   NORA *sits down at the chimney corner, with her back to the
door.* MAURYA *comes in very slowly, without looking at the
girls, and goes over to her stool at the other side of the fire.
The cloth with the bread is still in her hand. The girls look at
each other, and* NORA *points to the bundle of bread.*

15   CATHLEEN (*after spinning for a moment*).   You didn't give him
his bit of bread?

MAURYA *begins to keen softly, without turning round.*

CATHLEEN.   Did you see him riding down?

MAURYA *goes on keening.*

20   CATHLEEN (*a little impatiently*).   God forgive you; isn't it a better thing to raise your voice and tell what you seen, than to be
making lamentation for a thing that's done? Did you see Bartley, I'm saying to you.

MAURYA (*with a weak voice*).   My heart's broken from this day.

25   CATHLEEN (*as before*).   Did you see Bartley?

MAURYA.   I seen the fearfulest thing.

CATHLEEN. (*Leaves her wheel and looks out.*)   God forgive you;
he's riding the mare now over the green head, and the gray
pony behind him.

30   MAURYA. (*Starts, so that her shawl falls back from her head and
shows her white tossed hair. With a frightened voice.*)   The
gray pony behind him.

CATHLEEN (*coming to the fire*).   What is it ails you, at all?

MAURYA (*speaking very slowly*).   I've seen the fearfulest thing
35   any person has seen, since the day Bride Dara seen the dead
man with a child in his arms.

CATHLEEN AND NORA. Uah.

They crouch down in front of the old woman at the fire.

NORA. Tell us what it is you seen.

MAURYA. I went down to the spring well, and I stood there saying a prayer to myself. Then Bartley came along, and he riding 5
on the red mare with the gray pony behind him. (*She puts up
her hands, as if to hide something from her eyes.*) The Son of
God spare us, Nora!

CATHLEEN. What is it you seen?

MAURYA. I seen Michael himself. 10

CATHLEEN (*speaking softly*). You did not, mother; it wasn't
Michael you seen, for his body is after being found in the Far
North, and he's got a clean burial by the grace of God.

MAURYA (*a little defiantly*). I'm after seeing him this day, and
he riding and galloping. Bartley came first on the red mare; and 15
I tried to say, "God speed you," but something choked the
words in my throat. He went by quickly; and "the blessing of
God on you," says he, and I could say nothing. I looked up
then, and I crying, at the gray pony, and there was Michael
upon it—with fine clothes on him, and new shoes on his feet. 20

CATHLEEN. (*Begins to keen.*) It's destroyed we are from this
day. It's destroyed, surely.

NORA. Didn't the young priest say the Almighty God wouldn't
leave her destitute with no son living?

MAURYA (*in a low voice, but clearly*). It's little the like of him 25
knows of the sea. . . . Bartley will be lost now, and let you
call in Eamon and make me a good coffin out of the white
boards, for I won't live after them. I've had a husband, and a
husband's father, and six sons in this house—six fine men,
though it was a hard birth I had with every one of them and 30
they coming to the world—and some of them were found and
some of them were not found, but they're gone now the lot of
them. . . . There were Stephen, and Shawn, were lost in the
great wind, and found after in the Bay of Gregory of the
Golden Mouth, and carried up the two of them on the one 35
plank, and in by that door.

She pauses for a moment, the girls start as if they heard something through the door that is half open behind them.

NORA (*in a whisper*). Did you hear that, Cathleen? Did you hear a noise in the northeast?

5 CATHLEEN (*in a whisper*). There's some one after crying out by the seashore.

MAURYA. (*Continues without hearing anything*). There was Sheamus and his father, and his own father again, were lost in a dark night, and not a stick or sign was seen of them when the
10 sun went up. There was Patch after was drowned out of a curagh that turned over. I was sitting here with Bartley, and he a baby, lying on my two knees, and I seen two women, and three women, and four women coming in, and they crossing themselves, and not saying a word. I looked out then, and there
15 were men coming after them, and they holding a thing in the half of a red sail, and water dripping out of it—it was a dry day, Nora—and leaving a track to the door.

She pauses again with her hand stretched out toward the door. It opens softly and old women begin to come in, cross-
20 *ing themselves on the threshold, and kneeling down in front of the stage with red petticoats over their heads.*

MAURYA (*half in a dream, to* CATHLEEN). Is it Patch, or Michael, or what is it at all?

CATHLEEN. Michael is after being found in the Far North, and
25 when he is found there how could he be here in this place?

MAURYA. There does be a power of young men floating round in the sea, and what way would they know it if it was Michael they had, or another man like him, for when a man is nine days in the sea, and the wind blowing, it's hard set his own mother
30 would be to say what man was it.

CATHLEEN. It's Michael, God spare him, for they're after sending us a bit of his clothes from the Far North.

She reaches out and hands MAURYA *the clothes that belonged to* MICHAEL. MAURYA *stands up slowly, and takes them in*
35 *her hands.* NORA *looks out.*

NORA. They're carrying a thing among them and there's water dripping out of it and leaving a track by the big stones.

CATHLEEN (*in a whisper to the women who have come in*). Is it Bartley it is?

ONE OF THE WOMEN.   It is surely, God rest his soul.

Two younger women come in and pull out the table. Then men carry in the body of BARTLEY, laid on a plank, with a bit of a sail over it, and lay it on the table.   5

CATHLEEN (*to the women, as they are doing so*).   What way was he drowned?

ONE OF THE WOMEN.   The gray pony knocked him into the sea, and he was washed out where there is a great surf on the white   10
rocks.

MAURYA has gone over and knelt down at the head of the table. The women are keening softly and swaying themselves with a slow movement. CATHLEEN and NORA kneel at the other end of the table. The men kneel near the door.   15

MAURYA (*raising her head and speaking as if she did not see the people around her*).   They're all gone now, and there isn't anything more the sea can do to me. . . . I'll have no call now to be up crying and praying when the wind breaks from the south, and you can hear the surf is in the east, and the surf is in   20
the west, making a great stir with the two noises, and they hitting one on the other. I'll have no call now to be going down and getting Holy Water in the dark nights after Samhain, and I won't care what way the sea is when the other women will be keening. (*To* NORA) Give me the Holy Water, Nora, there's   25
a small sup still on the dresser.

NORA gives it to her.

MAURYA. (*Drops MICHAEL's clothes across BARTLEY's feet, and sprinkles the Holy Water over him.*)   It isn't that I haven't prayed for you, Bartley, to the Almighty God. It isn't that I   30
haven't said prayers in the dark night till you wouldn't know what I'd be saying; but it's a great rest I'll have now, and it's time surely. It's a great rest I'll have now, and great sleeping in the long nights after Samhain, if it's only a bit of wet flour we do have to eat, and maybe a fish that would be stinking.   35

She kneels down again, crossing herself, and saying prayers under her breath.

CATHLEEN (*to an old man*).   Maybe yourself and Eamon would
make a coffin when the sun rises. We have fine white boards
`herself bought, God help her, thinking Michael would be
found, and I have a new cake you can eat while you'll be work-
5   ing.

THE OLD MAN (*looking at the boards*).   Are there nails with
them?

CATHLEEN.   There are not, Colum; we didn't think of the nails.

ANOTHER MAN.   It's a great wonder she wouldn't think of the
10   nails, and all the coffins she's seen made already.

CATHLEEN.   It's getting old she is, and broken.

> MAURYA *stands up again very slowly and spreads out the*
> *pieces of* MICHAEL'S *clothes beside the body, sprinkling them*
> *with the last of the Holy Water.*

15   NORA (*in a whisper to* CATHLEEN).   She's quiet now and easy;
but the day Michael was drowned you could hear her crying
out from this to the spring well. It's fonder she was of Michael,
and would any one have thought that?

CATHLEEN (*slowly and clearly*).   An old woman will be soon
20   tired with anything she will do, and isn't it nine days herself is
after crying and keening, and making great sorrow in the
house?

MAURYA. (*Puts the empty cup mouth downwards on the table,*
and lays her hands together on BARTLEY'S *feet.*)   They're all
25   together this time, and the end is come. May the Almighty
God have mercy on Bartley's soul, and on Michael's soul, and
on the souls of Sheamus and Patch, and Stephen and Shawn
(*bending her head*); and may He have mercy on my soul,
Nora, and on the soul of every one is left living in the world.

30   > *She pauses, and the keen rises a little more loudly from the*
> *women, then sinks away.*

MAURYA (*continuing*).   Michael has a clean burial in the Far
North, by the grace of the Almighty God. Bartley will have a
fine coffin out of the white boards, and a deep grave surely.
35   What more can we want than that? No man at all can be living
forever, and we must be satisfied.

> *She kneels down again and the curtain falls slowly.*

Synge's play is one of the indubitable masterpieces of the modern theater and compares favorably with the finest tragedies ever written. Most writers of tragedy have worked with a canvas more than five times the size of Synge's, and yet by a miracle of concentration he has managed to arouse those emotions of pity and fear which, since Aristotle, have been an integral part of our conception of tragedy.

Synge uses various devices to compress the life story of Maurya into a half-hour's playing time: beginning of the play very close to the final catastrophe, various means—the rope, the clothes, the coffin-boards—to involve the death of Michael in the action of the play, and Maurya's retrospective narrative that moves us because she herself is so deeply moved by it. Perhaps the most audacious instance of concentration is the very brief interval between the exit of Bartley and the bringing in of his dead body. Despite the distinction between real time and stage time, the playwright must persuade us that, on the scale of stage time, the events he depicts could have happened.

Unlike the central figure in most tragedies written before the twentieth century, Maurya is a passive rather than an active character. She does not act; she is acted upon. The significance of death to Bartley himself is hardly suggested; on the other hand, his death is the turning point in the course of Maurya's feelings and attitudes. If the reader is interested in theoretical speculations, he may very well consider whether this play would have had a more powerful effect if Maurya had been more active, whether there are implications in Maurya's passivity as to modern man's view of himself and his place in the universe, or whether the play suggests the desirability of modifying Aristotle's conception (quoted below) of the ideal tragic hero. But, whatever theoretical conclusions one arrives at, and whether or not the play is a tragedy in the noblest sense, it continues to give its audience, in the theater and in the study, a deeply moving aesthetic experience.

Not the least of the sources of the play's power is the immense skill with which Synge has utilized Anglo-Irish speech. In both diction and rhythm, the dialogue is as beautiful as any ever written in English. Its full effect, to be sure, can be felt only when it is spoken by a gifted Irish actor, but even a reader who is merely responding to the rhythms suggested by the printed page can catch something of its melody, and can appreciate the aesthetic economy of such phrases as "they holding a thing in the half of a red sail, and water dripping out of it and leaving a track to the door."

What does Synge gain by delaying the identification of Michael's clothes? What does he gain by placing Bartley's departure at so early a point in the play? Does he succeed in not only maintaining but in deepening the interest and suspense between Bartley's departure and the news of his death? Why or why not?

To what extent is Synge successful in persuading the reader to accept the fact of the death by drowning of Maurya's husband and her six sons? Why? To accept death of Bartley in the brief period after he leaves the stage? Why?

Translate one of Maurya's long speeches from Anglo-Irish into normal literary English. What does it lose by such translation?

Maurya is a devoutly religious person. Is the state of mind in which we see her at the end of the play consistent with her religious faith? Why or why not?

Aristotle characterized the ideal tragic hero as "a man who is not eminently good or just yet whose misfortune is brought about not by vice or depravity but by some error or frailty" or, as another translation has it, as a man who "is not extraordinary in virtue or righteousness but because of some error of some kind found in men of high reputation and good fortune" is brought to disaster. Discuss the extent to which Maurya does and does not conform to this definition.

Does the play arouse any other major emotions than pity and fear? Aristotle said that tragedy purges the observer of these particular emotions after they have been aroused. If you feel that there is some alleviation of the emotions aroused by this play, by what means is the alleviation secured?

Cathleen ni Houlihan [1]

WILLIAM BUTLER YEATS

PERSONS IN THE PLAY

PETER GILLANE
MICHAEL GILLANE, *his Son, going to be married*
PATRICK GILLANE, *a lad of twelve,* MICHAEL's *Brother*
BRIDGET GILLANE, PETER's *Wife*
DELIA CAHEL, *engaged to* MICHAEL
THE POOR OLD WOMAN
NEIGHBOURS

SCENE. *Interior of a cottage close to Killala, in 1798.* BRIDGET *is standing at a table undoing a parcel.* PETER *is sitting at one side of the fire,* PATRICK *at the other.*

PETER. What is that sound I hear?
PATRICK. I don't hear anything. (*He listens.*) I hear it now. It's like cheering. (*He goes to the window and looks out.*) I wonder what they are cheering about. I don't see anybody.
PETER. It might be a hurling.
PATRICK. There's no hurling to-day. It must be down in the town the cheering is.

5

[1] From William Butler Yeats, *The Hour Glass.* Copyright, 1904, by The Macmillan Company. Reprinted by permission of The Macmillan Company, Mrs. Yeats, and Macmillan & Co., Ltd.

BRIDGET.   I suppose the boys must be having some sport of their own. Come over here, Peter, and look at Michael's wedding clothes.

PETER (*shifts his chair to table*).   Those are grand clothes, indeed.

BRIDGET.   You hadn't clothes like that when you married me, and no coat to put on of a Sunday more than any other day.

PETER.   That is true, indeed. We never thought a son of our own would be wearing a suit of that sort for his wedding, or have so good a place to bring a wife to.

PATRICK (*who is still at the window*).   There's an old woman coming down the road. I don't know is it here she is coming?

BRIDGET.   It will be a neighbour coming to hear about Michael's wedding. Can you see who it is?

PATRICK.   I think it is a stranger, but she's not coming to the house. She's turned into the gap that goes down where Murteen and his sons are shearing sheep. (*He turns towards* BRIDGET.) Do you remember what Winny of the Cross Roads was saying the other night about the strange woman that goes through the country whatever time there's war or trouble coming?

BRIDGET.   Don't be bothering us about Winny's talk, but go and open the door for your brother. I hear him coming up the path.

PETER.   I hope he has brought Delia's fortune with him safe, for fear the people might go back on the bargain and I after making it. Trouble enough I had making it.

PATRICK *opens the door and* MICHAEL *comes in.*

BRIDGET.   What kept you, Michael? We were looking out for you this long time.

MICHAEL.   I went round by the priest's house to bid him be ready to marry us to-morrow.

BRIDGET.   Did he say anything?

MICHAEL.   He said it was a very nice match, and that he was never better pleased to marry any two in his parish than myself and Delia Cahel.

PETER.   Have you got the fortune, Michael?

MICHAEL.   Here it is.

MICHAEL *puts bag on table and goes over and leans against chimney-jamb*. BRIDGET, *who has been all this time examining the clothes, pulling the seams and trying the lining of the pockets, etc., puts the clothes on the dresser.*

PETER (*getting up and taking the bag in his hand and turning out the money*).   Yes, I made the bargain well for you, Michael. Old John Cahel would sooner have kept a share of this a while longer. 'Let me keep the half of it until the first boy is born,' says he. 'You will not,' says I. 'Whether there is or is not a boy, the whole hundred pounds must be in Michael's hands before he brings your daughter to the house.' The wife spoke to him then, and he gave in at the end.

BRIDGET.   You seem well pleased to be handling the money, Peter.

PETER.   Indeed, I wish I had had the luck to get a hundred pounds, or twenty pounds itself, with the wife I married.

BRIDGET.   Well, if I didn't bring much I didn't get much. What had you the day I married you but a flock of hens and you feeding them, and a few lambs and you driving them to the market at Ballina. (*She is vexed and bangs a jug on the dresser.*) If I brought no fortune I worked it out in my bones, laying down the baby, Michael that is standing there now, on a stook of straw, while I dug the potatoes, and never asking big dresses or anything but to be working.

PETER.   That is true, indeed.

He pats her arm.

BRIDGET.   Leave me alone now till I ready the house for the woman that is to come into it.

PETER.   You are the best woman in Ireland, but money is good, too. (*He begins handling the money again and sits down.*) I never thought to see so much money within my four walls. We can do great things now we have it. We can take the ten acres of land we have the chance of since Jamsie Dempsey died, and stock it. We will go to the fair at Ballina to buy the stock. Did Delia ask any of the money for her own use, Michael?

MICHAEL.   She did not, indeed. She did not seem to take much notice of it, or to look at it at all.

BRIDGET. That's no wonder. Why would she look at it when she had yourself to look at, a fine, strong young man? It is proud she must be to get you; a good steady boy that will make use of the money, and not be running through it or spending it on
5   drink like another.

PETER. It's likely Michael himself was not thinking much of the fortune either, but of what sort the girl was to look at.

MICHAEL (*coming over towards the table*). Well, you would like a nice comely girl to be beside you, and to go walking with
10 you. The fortune only lasts for a while, but the woman will be there always.

PATRICK (*turning round from the window*). They are cheering again down in the town. Maybe they are landing horses from Enniscrone. They do be cheering when the horses take the
15 water well.

MICHAEL. There are no horses in it. Where would they be going and no fair at hand? Go down to the town, Patrick, and see what is going on.

PATRICK (*opens the door to go out, but stops for a moment on the*
20 *threshold*). Will Delia remember, do you think, to bring the greyhound pup she promised me when she would be coming to the house?

MICHAEL. She will surely.

    PATRICK *goes out, leaving the door open.*

25 PETER. It will be Patrick's turn next to be looking for a fortune, but he won't find it so easy to get it and he with no place of his own.

BRIDGET. I do be thinking sometimes, now things are going so well with us, and the Cahels such a good back to us in the dis-
30 trict, and Delia's own uncle a priest, we might be put in the way of making Patrick a priest some day, and he so good at his books.

PETER. Time enough, time enough, you have always your head full of plans, Bridget.

35 BRIDGET. We will be well able to give him learning, and not to

send him tramping the country like a poor scholar that lives on charity.

MICHAEL. They're not done cheering yet.

He goes over to the door and stands there for a moment, putting up his hand to shade his eyes.

BRIDGET. Do you see anything?

MICHAEL. I see an old woman coming up the path.

BRIDGET. Who is it, I wonder? It must be the strange woman Patrick saw a while ago.

MICHAEL. I don't think it's one of the neighbours anyway, but she has her cloak over her face.

BRIDGET. It might be some poor woman heard we were making ready for the wedding and came to look for her share.

PETER. I may as well put the money out of sight. There is no use leaving it out for every stranger to look at.

He goes over to a large box in the corner, opens it and puts the bag in and fumbles at the lock.

MICHAEL. There she is, father! (*An* OLD WOMAN *passes the window slowly, she looks at* MICHAEL *as she passes.*) I'd sooner a stranger not to come to the house the night before my wedding.

BRIDGET. Open the door, Michael; don't keep the poor woman waiting.

The OLD WOMAN *comes in.* MICHAEL *stands aside to make way for her.*

OLD WOMAN. God save all here!

PETER. God save you kindly!

OLD WOMAN. You have good shelter here.

PETER. You are welcome to whatever shelter we have.

BRIDGET. Sit down there by the fire and welcome.

OLD WOMAN (*warming her hands*). There is a hard wind outside.

MICHAEL watches her curiously from the door. PETER *comes over to the table.*

PETER. Have you travelled far to-day?

OLD WOMAN.   I have travelled far, very far; there are few have
travelled so far as myself, and there's many a one that doesn't
make me welcome. There was one that had strong sons I
thought were friends of mine, but they were shearing their
5   sheep, and they wouldn't listen to me.

PETER.   It's a pity indeed for any person to have no place of their
own.

OLD WOMAN.   That's true for you indeed, and it's long I'm on the
roads since I first went wandering.

10   BRIDGET.   It is a wonder you are not worn out with so much
wandering.

OLD WOMAN.   Sometimes my feet are tired and my hands are
quiet, but there is no quiet in my heart. When the people see
me quiet, they think old age has come on me and that all the stir
15   has gone out of me. But when the trouble is on me I must be
talking to my friends.

BRIDGET.   What was it put you wandering?

OLD WOMAN.   Too many strangers in the house.

BRIDGET.   Indeed you look as if you'd had your share of trouble.

20   OLD WOMAN.   I have had trouble indeed.

BRIDGET.   What was it put the trouble on you?

OLD WOMAN.   My land that was taken from me.

PETER.   Was it much land they took from you?

OLD WOMAN.   My four beautiful green fields.

25   PETER (*aside to* BRIDGET).   Do you think could she be the widow
Casey that was put out of her holding at Kilglass a while ago?

BRIDGET.   She is not. I saw the widow Casey one time at the
market in Ballina, a stout fresh woman.

PETER (*to* OLD WOMAN).   Did you hear a noise of cheering, and
30   you coming up the hill?

OLD WOMAN.   I thought I heard the noise I used to hear when
my friends came to visit me. (*She begins singing half to herself.*)

> I will go cry with the woman,
> For yellow-haired Donough is dead,
35   > With a hempen rope for a neckcloth,
> And a white cloth on his head,——

MICHAEL (*coming from the door*).   What is it that you are singing, ma'am?

OLD WOMAN.   Singing I am about a man I knew one time, yel-
low-haired Donough that was hanged in Galway. (*She goes on
singing, much louder.*)   5

> I am come to cry with you, woman,
> My hair is unwound and unbound;
> I remember him ploughing his field,
> Turning up the red side of the ground,
> And building his barn on the hill   10
> With the good mortared stone;
> Oh! we'd have pulled down the gallows
> Had it happened in Enniscrone!

MICHAEL.   What was it brought him to his death?

OLD WOMAN.   He died for love of me: many a man has died for   15
love of me.

PETER (*aside to* BRIDGET).   Her trouble has put her wits astray.

MICHAEL.   Is it long since that song was made? Is it long since he
got his death?

OLD WOMAN.   Not long, not long. But there were others that   20
died for love of me a long time ago.

MICHAEL.   Were they neighbours of your own, ma'am?

OLD WOMAN.   Come here beside me and I'll tell you about them.
(MICHAEL *sits down beside her at the hearth.*) There was a red
man of the O'Donells from the north, and a man of the O'Sul-   25
livans from the south, and there was one Brian that lost his life
at Clontarf by the sea, and there were a great many in the
west, some that died hundreds of years ago, and there are some
that will die to-morrow.

MICHAEL.   Is it in the west that men will die to-morrow?   30

OLD WOMAN.   Come nearer, nearer to me.

BRIDGET.   Is she right, do you think? Or is she a woman from
beyond the world?

PETER.   She doesn't know well what she's talking about, with the
want and the trouble she has gone through.   35

BRIDGET.   The poor thing, we should treat her well.

PETER.   Give her a drink of milk and a bit of the oaten cake.

BRIDGET.   Maybe we should give her something along with that,
to bring her on her way. A few pence or a shilling itself, and
5   we with so much money in the house.

PETER.   Indeed I'd not begrudge it to her if we had it to spare,
but if we go running through what we have, we'll soon have
to break the hundred pounds, and that would be a pity.

BRIDGET.   Shame on you, Peter. Give her the shilling and your
10   blessing with it, or our own luck will go from us.

    PETER *goes to the box and takes out a shilling.*

BRIDGET (*to the* OLD WOMAN).   Will you have a drink of milk,
ma'am?

OLD WOMAN.   It is not food or drink that I want.

15 PETER (*offering the shilling*).   Here is something for you.

OLD WOMAN.   This is not what I want. It is not silver I want.

PETER.   What is it you would be asking for?

OLD WOMAN.   If any one would give me help he must give me
himself, he must give me all.

20   PETER *goes over to the table staring at the shilling in his hand
        in a bewildered way, and stands whispering to* BRIDGET.

MICHAEL.   Have you no one to care you in your age, ma'am?

OLD WOMAN.   I have not. With all the lovers that brought me
their love I never set out the bed for any.

25 MICHAEL.   Are you lonely going the roads, ma'am?

OLD WOMAN.   I have my thoughts and I have my hopes.

MICHAEL.   What hopes have you to hold to?

OLD WOMAN.   The hope of getting my beautiful fields back
again; the hope of putting the strangers out of my house.

30 MICHAEL.   What way will you do that, ma'am?

OLD WOMAN.   I have good friends that will help me. They are
gathering to help me now. I am not afraid. If they are put down
to-day they will get the upper hand to-morrow. (*She gets up.*)
I must be going to meet my friends. They are coming to help
35   me and I must be there to welcome them. I must call the neighbours together to welcome them.

MICHAEL.   I will go with you.

BRIDGET.   It is not her friends you have to go and welcome,
Michael; it is the girl coming into the house you have to welcome. You have plenty to do, it is food and drink you have to
bring to the house. The woman that is coming home is not   5
coming with empty hands; you would not have an empty house
before her. (*To the* OLD WOMAN) Maybe you don't know,
ma'am, that my son is going to be married to-morrow.

OLD WOMAN.   It is not a man going to his marriage that I look to
for help.   10

PETER (*to* BRIDGET).   Who is she, do you think, at all?

BRIDGET.   You did not tell us your name yet, ma'am.

OLD WOMAN.   Some call me the Poor Old Woman, and there are
some that call me Cathleen, the daughter of Houlihan.

PETER.   I think I knew some one of that name, once. Who was it, 15
I wonder? It must have been some one I knew when I was a
boy. No, no; I remember, I heard it in a song.

OLD WOMAN (*who is standing in the doorway*).   They are wondering that there were songs made for me; there have been
many songs made for me. I heard one on the wind this morning. 20
(*Sings*)

> Do not make a great keening
> When the graves have been dug to-morrow.
> Do not call the white-scarfed riders
> To the burying that shall be to-morrow.   25
> Do not spread food to call strangers
> To the wakes that shall be to-morrow;
> Do not give money for prayers
> For the dead that shall die to-morrow. . . .

they will have no need of prayers, they will have no need of   30
prayers.

MICHAEL.   I do not know what that song means, but tell me
something I can do for you.

PETER.   Come over to me, Michael.

MICHAEL.   Hush, father, listen to her.   35

OLD WOMAN.   It is a hard service they take that help me. Many
that are red-cheeked now will be pale-cheeked; many that have
been free to walk the hills and the bogs and the rushes, will be
sent to walk hard streets in far countries; many a good plan will
5   be broken; many that have gathered money will not stay to
spend it; many a child will be born and there will be no father
at its christening to give it a name. They that have red cheeks
will have pale cheeks for my sake, and for all that, they will
think they are well paid.

10   *She goes out; her voice is heard outside singing.*

> They shall be remembered for ever,
> They shall be alive for ever,
> They shall be speaking for ever,
> The people shall hear them for ever.

15 BRIDGET (*to* PETER).   Look at him, Peter; he has the look of a
man that has got the touch. (*Raising her voice*) Look here,
Michael, at the wedding clothes. Such grand clothes as these
are! You have a right to fit them on now, it would be a pity
to-morrow if they did not fit The boys would be laughing at
20   you. Take them, Michael, and go into the room and fit them
on.

    She puts them on his arm.

MICHAEL.   What wedding are you talking of? What clothes will
I be wearing to-morrow?

25 BRIDGET.   These are the clothes you are going to wear when you
marry Delia Cahel to-morrow.

MICHAEL.   I had forgotten that.

    *He looks at the clothes and turns towards the inner room, but
stops at the sound of cheering outside.*

30 PETER.   There is the shouting come to our own door. What is
it has happened?

    NEIGHBOURS *come crowding in,* PATRICK *and* DELIA *with
them.*

PATRICK.   There are ships in the Bay; the French are landing at
35   Killala!

PETER *takes his pipe from his mouth and his hat off, and stands up. The clothes slip from* MICHAEL'S *arm.*

DELIA. Michael! (*He takes no notice.*) Michael! (*He turns towards her.*) Why do you look at me like a stranger?
She drops his arm. BRIDGET *goes over towards her.* 5

PATRICK. The boys are all hurrying down the hillside to join the French.

DELIA. Michael won't be going to join the French.

BRIDGET (*to* PETER). Tell him not to go, Peter.

PETER. It's no use. He doesn't hear a word we're saying. 10

BRIDGET. Try and coax him over to the fire.

DELIA. Michael, Michael! You won't leave me! You won't join the French, and we going to be married!
She puts her arms about him, he turns towards her as if about to yield. 15

OLD WOMAN'S *voice outside.*

They shall be speaking for ever,
The people shall hear them for ever.

MICHAEL *breaks away from* DELIA, *stands for a second at the door, then rushes out, following the* OLD WOMAN'S *voice.* 20
BRIDGET *takes* DELIA, *who is crying silently, into her arms.*

PETER (*to* PATRICK, *laying a hand on his arm*). Did you see an old woman going down the path?

PATRICK. I did not, but I saw a young girl, and she had the walk of a queen. 25

Every work of art by embodying a pattern of symbols achieves a profounder significance than that of its merely literal meaning. In most works of art, however, the literal meaning and the symbolic significance parallel each other, and readers not given to analysis may fail to discover the two planes of meaning, even though they can hardly be completely unaware of some of the symbolic overtones. Yeats's "Cathleen ni Houlihan" is symbolic in a different sense from that we have just suggested, because it is a play that is almost meaningless unless it is read symbolically. The luring away of a young man on the eve of his marriage by a strange old woman who refuses food and money, sings mystifying songs, and demands the sacrifice of the lives and happiness of her followers is, in literal terms, unintelligible. It is only as one sees that the old woman is not a woman but a symbol and realizes what it is she symbolizes that the play becomes meaningful. In other words, one of the characters in this play is only a symbol and not a character that has *both* literal and symbolic significance. Such a play as this makes a demand on the reader that realistic plays do not make: it asks the reader to accept a symbol as a character. It is incumbent on the playwright to use such means as will induce the audience to accept this violation of the realistic drama code. The means Yeats uses to achieve this end should be investigated carefully.

The casual reader may miss the significance of the fact that this play is set in a definite period in the history of Ireland. The stage directions indicate that the place of the action is Killala, and the time 1798, and later one of the characters says, "There are ships in the Bay; the French are landing in Killala. . . . The boys are all hurrying down the hillside to join the French." The incidents referred to were the aftermath of the Irish Rebellion of 1798, which was put down by the British after shocking brutalities had been committed by both sides. The French, with whom England was at war, sent two small military expeditions to aid the Irish, but they did not arrive until after the Rebellion had been suppressed. One of the forces, however, captured and held Killala, but, after a brief period, was overcome and captured. These historical details may serve to suggest the atmosphere with which the year 1798 is invested for an Irish audience and the significance of this incident in the long and painful story of England's relations to Ireland. Thus, the play becomes a document in the history of the Irish struggle for economic and political liberty, and it has its maximum effect only in such a context. On the other hand, it has a wider meaning as a dramatic illustration of the unending struggle of man to secure or to preserve his liberties and of the perpetual conflict between private and public obligations and responsibilities.

This play dramatizes a conflict between opposed values, and Yeats has given every character in the play an opportunity to state or to suggest the values he holds highest. What are the things the young boy Patrick values? Are they appropriate to him? Why or why not? To what extent are the values of Peter and Bridget identical? To what extent are they different?

Is the situation in which Michael finds himself well calculated to emphasize the values to which Yeats is giving priority in this play? Why or why not?

By what means does Yeats gradually make clear the significance of the Poor Old Woman? To whom does she refer in the lines, "There was one that had strong sons I thought were friends of mine, but they were shearing their sheep, and they wouldn't listen to me"? Is it important or unimportant that the audience should be able to identify the men who have sacrificed themselves for her? What effect does the final speech of the play have on the reader's feelings toward the Old Woman?

Michael is the only character in the play who suffers from the claims of conflicting sets of values. Does Yeats emphasize this conflict? Why or why not? Would he have been well advised to give Michael's conflict greater emphasis? Why or why not?

Translate into normal literary English the Old Woman's speech beginning, "It is a hard service they take that help me." What does it lose in translation?

Do you think it fair to compare this play with "Riders to the Sea"? Why or why not? In the light of your study of these two plays, which do you consider the better play? Give the reasons that support your judgment.

The Long Christmas Dinner[1]

THORNTON WILDER

*The dining-room of the Bayard home. Close to the footlights a
long dining table is handsomely spread for Christmas dinner.
The carver's place with a great turkey before it is at the spec-
tator's right.*

A door, left back, leads into the hall.

*At the extreme left, by the proscenium pillar, is a strange portal
trimmed with garlands of fruits and flowers. Directly opposite
is another edged and hung with black velvet. The portals de-
note birth and death.*

*Ninety years are to be traversed in this play which represents in
accelerated motion ninety Christmas dinners in the Bayard
household. The actors are dressed in inconspicuous clothes and
must indicate their gradual increase in years through their acting. Most of them carry wigs of white hair which they adjust
upon their heads at the indicated moment, simply and without*

[1] Reprinted from *The Long Christmas Dinner & Other Plays in One Act* by Thornton
Wilder. Copyright, 1931, by Yale University Press and Coward-McCann, Inc. All in-
quiries about any performance whatsoever should be addressed to Samuel French, Inc.,
25 West 45 Street, New York 19, N. Y.

comment. The ladies may have shawls concealed beneath the table that they gradually draw up about their shoulders as they grow older.

Throughout the play the characters continue eating imaginary food with imaginary knives and forks.

There is no curtain. The audience arriving at the theatre sees the stage set and the table laid, though still in partial darkness. Gradually the lights in the auditorium become dim and the stage brightens until sparkling winter sunlight streams through the dining room windows.

Enter LUCIA. *She inspects the table, touching here a knife and there a fork. She talks to a servant girl who is invisible to us.*

LUCIA.   I reckon we're ready now, Gertrude. We won't ring the chimes today. I'll just call them myself.
    She goes into the hall and calls:
Roderick. Mother Bayard. We're all ready. Come to dinner.
    Enter RODERICK *pushing* MOTHER BAYARD *in a wheel chair.*   5

MOTHER BAYARD.   . . . and a new horse too, Roderick. I used to think that only the wicked owned two horses. A new horse and a new house and a new wife!

RODERICK.   Well, Mother, how do you like it? Our first Christmas dinner in the new house, hey?   10

MOTHER BAYARD.   Tz-Tz-Tz! I don't know what your dear father would say!

LUCIA.   Here, Mother Bayard, you sit between us.
    RODERICK *says grace.*

MOTHER BAYARD.   My dear Lucia, I can remember when there   15 were still Indians on this very ground, and I wasn't a young girl either. I can remember when we had to cross the Mississippi on a new-made raft. I can remember when St. Louis and Kansas City were full of Indians.

LUCIA (*tying a napkin around* MOTHER BAYARD'S *neck*). Imagine   20 that! There!—What a wonderful day for our first Christmas dinner: a beautiful sunny morning, snow, a splendid sermon.

Dr. McCarthy preaches a splendid sermon. I cried and cried.

RODERICK (*extending an imaginary carvingfork*). Come now, what'll you have, Mother? A little sliver of white?

LUCIA.   Every least twig is wrapped around with ice. You almost never see that. Can I cut it up for you, dear? (*over her shoulder*) Gertrude, I forgot the jelly. You know,—on the top shelf. —Mother Bayard, I found your mother's gravy-boat while we were moving. What was her name, dear? What were all your names? You were . . . a . . . Genevieve Wainright. Now your mother——

MOTHER BAYARD.   Yes, you must write it down somewhere. I was Genevieve Wainright. My mother was Faith Morrison. She was the daughter of a farmer in New Hampshire who was something of a blacksmith too. And she married young John Wainright——

LUCIA (*memorizing on her fingers*).   Genevieve Wainright. Faith Morrison.

RODERICK.   It's all down in a book somewhere upstairs. We have it all. All that kind of thing is very interesting. Come, Lucia, just a little wine. Mother, a little red wine for Christmas day. Full of iron. "Take a little wine for thy stomach's sake."

LUCIA.   Really, I can't get used to wine! What would my father say? But I suppose it's all right.

Enter COUSIN BRANDON *from the hall. He takes his place by* LUCIA.

COUSIN BRANDON (*rubbing his hands*).   Well, well, I smell turkey. My dear cousins, I can't tell you how pleasant it is to be having Christmas dinner with you all. I've lived out there in Alaska so long without relatives. Let me see, how long have you had this new house, Roderick?

RODERICK.   Why, it must be . . . .

MOTHER BAYARD.   Five years. It's five years, children. You should keep a diary. This is your sixth Christmas dinner here.

LUCIA.   Think of that, Roderick. We feel as though we had lived here twenty years.

COUSIN BRANDON.   At all events it still looks as good as new.

RODERICK (*over his carving*).   What'll you have, Brandon, light or dark?—Frieda, fill up Cousin Brandon's glass.

LUCIA.   Oh, dear, I can't get used to these wines. I don't know what my father'd say, I'm sure. What'll you have, Mother 5 Bayard?

During the following speeches MOTHER BAYARD'S *chair, without any visible propulsion, starts to draw away from the table, turns toward the right, and slowly goes toward the dark portal.* 10

MOTHER BAYARD.   Yes, I can remember when there were Indians on this very land.

LUCIA (*softly*).   Mother Bayard hasn't been very well lately, Roderick.

MOTHER BAYARD.   My mother was a Faith Morrison. And in 15 New Hampshire she married a young John Wainright, who was a Congregational minister. He saw her in his congregation one day. . . .

LUCIA.   Mother Bayard, hadn't you better lie down, dear?

MOTHER BAYARD.   . . . and right in the middle of his sermon he 20 said to himself: "I'll marry that girl." And he did, and I'm their daughter.

LUCIA (*half rising and looking after her with anxiety*).   Just a little nap, dear?

MOTHER BAYARD.   I'm all right. Just go on with your dinner. I 25 was ten, and I said to my brother——

She goes out. A very slight pause.

COUSIN BRANDON.   It's too bad it's such a cold dark day today. We almost need the lamps. I spoke to Major Lewis for a moment after church. His sciatica troubles him, but he does pretty 30 well.

LUCIA (*dabbing her eyes*).   I know Mother Bayard wouldn't want us to grieve for her on Christmas day, but I can't forget her sitting in her wheel chair right beside us, only a year ago. And she would be so glad to know our good news. 35

RODERICK (*patting her hand*).   Now, now. It's Christmas. (*Formally*) Cousin Brandon, a glass of wine with you, sir.

COUSIN BRANDON (*half rising, lifting his glass gallantly*).   A glass of wine with you, sir.

5   LUCIA.   Does the Major's sciatica cause him much pain?

COUSIN BRANDON.   Some, perhaps. But you know his way. He says it'll be all the same in a hundred years.

LUCIA.   Yes, he's a great philosopher.

RODERICK.   His wife sends you a thousand thanks for her Christ-
10   mas present.

LUCIA.   I forget what I gave her.—Oh, yes, the workbasket!

Through the entrance of birth comes a nurse wheeling a perambulator trimmed with blue ribbons. LUCIA *rushes toward it, the men following.*

15   O my wonderful new baby, my darling baby! Who ever saw such a child! Quick, nurse, a boy or a girl? A boy! Roderick, what shall we call him? Really, nurse, you've never seen such a child!

RODERICK.   We'll call him Charles after your father and grand-
20   father.

LUCIA.   But there are no Charleses in the Bible, Roderick.

RODERICK.   Of course, there are. Surely there are.

LUCIA.   Roderick!— Very well, but he will always be Samuel to me.—What miraculous hands he has! Really, they are the most
25   beautiful hands in the world. All right, nurse. Have a good nap, my darling child.

RODERICK.   Don't drop him, nurse. Brandon and I need him in our firm.

Exit nurse and perambulator into the hall. The others return
30   *to their chairs,* LUCIA *taking the place left vacant by* MOTHER
BAYARD *and* COUSIN BRANDON *moving up beside her.* COUSIN
BRANDON *puts on his white hair.*

Lucia, a little white meat? Some stuffing? Cranberry sauce, anybody?

35   LUCIA (*over her shoulder*).   Margaret, the stuffing is very good today.—Just a little, thank you.

RODERICK. Now something to wash it down. (*Half rising*) Cousin Brandon, a glass of wine with you, sir. To the ladies, God bless them.

LUCIA. Thank you, kind sirs.

COUSIN BRANDON. Pity it's such an overcast day today. And no snow.   5

LUCIA. But the sermon was lovely. I cried and cried. Dr. Spaulding does preach such a splendid sermon.

RODERICK. I saw Major Lewis for a moment after church. He says his rheumatism comes and goes. His wife says she has something for Charles and will bring it over this afternoon.   10

Enter nurse again with perambulator. Pink ribbons. Same rush toward the left.

LUCIA. O my lovely new baby! Really, it never occurred to me that it might be a girl. Why, nurse, she's perfect.   15

RODERICK. Now call her what you choose. It's your turn.

LUCIA. Loolooloolo. Aië. Aië. Yes, this time I shall have my way. She shall be called Genevieve after your mother. Have a good nap, my treasure.

She looks after it as the nurse wheels the perambulator into   20
the hall.

Imagine! Sometime she'll be grown up and say "Good morning, Mother. Good morning, Father."—Really, Cousin Brandon, you don't find a baby like that every day.

COUSIN BRANDON. *And* the new factory.   25

LUCIA. A new factory? Really? Roderick, I shall be very uncomfortable if we're going to turn out to be rich. I've been afraid of that for years.—However, we mustn't talk about such things on Christmas day. I'll just take a little piece of white meat, thank you. Roderick, Charles is destined for the ministry. 30
I'm sure of it.

RODERICK. Woman, he's only twelve. Let him have a free mind. *We* want him in the firm, I don't mind saying. Anyway, no time passes as slowly as this when you're waiting for your urchins to grow up and settle down to business.   35

LUCIA. I don't want time to go any faster, thank you. I love the

children just as they are.—Really, Roderick, you know what
the doctor said: One glass a meal. (*Putting her hand over his
glass*) No, Margaret, that will be all.

5   RODERICK *rises, glass in hand. With a look of dismay on his
    face he takes a few steps toward the dark portal.*

RODERICK.   Now I wonder what's the matter with me.

LUCIA.   Roderick, do be reasonable.

RODERICK (*tottering, but with gallant irony*).   But, my dear, statistics show that we steady, moderate drinkers. . . .

10 LUCIA (*rises, gazing at him in anguish*).   Roderick! My dear!
    What . . . ?

RODERICK (*returns to his seat with a frightened look of relief*).
Well, it's fine to be back at table with you again. How many
good Christmas dinners have I had to miss upstairs? And to be

15 back at a fine bright one, too.

LUCIA.   O my dear, you gave us a very alarming time! Here's
your glass of milk.—Josephine, bring Mr. Bayard his medicine
from the cupboard in the library.

RODERICK.   At all events, now that I'm better I'm going to start

20 doing something about the house.

LUCIA.   Roderick! You're not going to change the house?

RODERICK.   Only touch it up here and there. It looks a hundred
years old.

25 CHARLES *enters casually from the hall. He kisses his mother's
    hair and sits down.*

LUCIA.   Charles, you carve the turkey, dear. Your father's not
well.—You always said you hated carving, though you *are* so
clever at it.

Father and son exchange places.

30 CHARLES.   It's a great blowy morning, mother. The wind comes
over the hill like a lot of cannon.

LUCIA.   And such a good sermon. I cried and cried. Mother Bayard loved a good sermon so. And she used to sing the Christmas
hymns all around the year. Oh, dear, oh, dear, I've been think-

35 ing of her all morning!

RODERICK.   Sh, Mother. It's Christmas day. You mustn't think of
such things.—You mustn't be depressed.

LUCIA. But sad things aren't the same as depressing things. I must be getting old: I like them.

CHARLES. Uncle Brandon, you haven't anything to eat. Pass his plate, Hilda . . . and some cranberry sauce. . . .

Enter GENEVIEVE. *She kisses her father's temple and sits* 5 *down.*

GENEVIEVE. It's glorious. Every least twig is wrapped around with ice. You almost never see that.

LUCIA. Did you have time to deliver those presents after church, Genevieve? 10

GENEVIEVE. Yes, Mama. Old Mrs. Lewis sends you a thousand thanks for hers. It was just what she wanted, she said. Give me lots, Charles, lots.

RODERICK (*rising and starting toward the dark portal*). Statistics, ladies and gentlemen, show that we steady, moderate. . . . 15

CHARLES. How about a little skating this afternoon, Father?

RODERICK. I'll live till I'm ninety.

LUCIA. I really don't think he ought to go skating.

RODERICK (*at the very portal, suddenly astonished*). Yes, but . . . but . . . not yet! 20

He goes out.

LUCIA (*dabbing her eyes*). He was so young and so clever, Cousin Brandon. (*Raising her voice for* COUSIN BRANDON's *deafness*) I say he was so young and so clever.—Never forget your father, children. He was a good man.—Well, he wouldn't 25 want us to grieve for him today.

CHARLES. White or dark, Genevieve? Just another sliver, Mother?

LUCIA (*putting on her white hair*). I can remember our first Christmas dinner in this house, Genevieve. Twenty-five years 30 ago today. Mother Bayard was sitting here in her wheel chair. She could remember when Indians lived on this very spot and when she had to cross the river on a new-made raft.

CHARLES AND GENEVIEVE. She couldn't have, Mother. That can't be true. 35

LUCIA. It certainly was true—even I can remember when there was only one paved street. We were very happy to walk on

boards. (*Louder, to* Cousin Brandon) We can remember when
there were no sidewalks, can't we, Cousin Brandon?

Cousin Brandon (*delighted*). Oh, yes! And those were the
days.

5 Charles and Genevieve (*sotto voce*). (*This is a family refrain.*)
Those were the days.

Lucia. . . . and the ball last night, Genevieve? Did you have
a nice time? I hope you didn't *waltz*, dear. I think a girl in our
position ought to set an example. Did Charles keep an eye on
10 you?

Genevieve. He had none left. They were all on Leonora Banning. He can't conceal it any longer, Mother. I think he's engaged to marry Leonora Banning.

Charles. I'm not engaged to marry anyone.

15 Lucia. Well, she's very pretty.

Genevieve. I shall never marry, Mother—I shall sit in this house
beside you forever, as though life were one long, happy Christmas dinner.

Lucia. O my child, you mustn't say such things!

20 Genevieve (*playfully*). You don't want me? You don't want
me?

Lucia *bursts into tears.*

Why, Mother, how silly you are! There's nothing sad about
that—what could possibly be sad about that.

25 Lucia (*drying her eyes*). Forgive me. I'm just unpredictable,
that's all.

Charles *goes to the door and leads in* Leonora Banning.

Leonora (*kissing* Lucia's *temple*). Good morning, Mother
Bayard. Good morning, everybody. It's really a splendid
30 Christmas day today.

Charles. Little white meat? Genevieve, Mother, Leonora?

Leonora. Every least twig is encircled with ice.—You never see
that.

Charles (*shouting*). Uncle Brandon, another?—Rogers, fill my
35 uncle's glass.

Lucia (*to* Charles). Do what your father used to do. It would please Cousin Brandon so. You know—(*pretending to raise a glass*)—"Uncle Brandon, a glass of wine——"

CHARLES (*rising*).   Uncle Brandon, a glass of wine with you, sir.

BRANDON.   A glass of wine with you, sir. To the ladies, God bless them every one.

THE LADIES.   Thank you, kind sirs.

GENEVIEVE.   And if I go to Germany for my music I promise to be back for Christmas. I wouldn't miss that.

LUCIA.   I hate to think of you over there all alone in those strange pensions.

GENEVIEVE.   But, darling, the time will pass so fast that you'll hardly know I'm gone. I'll be back in the twinkling of an eye.

Enter Left, the nurse and preambulator. Green ribbons.

LEONORA.   Oh, what an angel! The darlingest baby in the world. Do let me hold it, nurse.

But the nurse resolutely wheels the perambulator across the stage and out the dark door.

Oh, I did love it so!

LUCIA goes to her, puts her arm around LEONORA's shoulders, and they encircle the room whispering—LUCIA then hands her over to CHARLES who conducts her on the same circuit.

GENEVIEVE (*as her mother sits down,—softly*).   Isn't there anything I can do?

LUCIA (*raises her eyebrows, ruefully*).   No, dear. Only time, only the passing of time can help in these things.

CHARLES and LEONORA return to the table.

Don't you think we could ask Cousin Ermengarde to come and live with us here? There's plenty for everyone and there's no reason why she should go on teaching the First Grade for ever and ever. She wouldn't be in the way, would she, Charles?

CHARLES.   No, I think it would be fine.—A little more potato and gravy, anybody? A little more turkey, Mother?

BRANDON rises and starts slowly toward the dark portal.

LUCIA rises and stands for a moment with her face in her hands.

COUSIN BRANDON (*muttering*). It was great to be in Alaska in
those days. . . .

GENEVIEVE (*half rising, and gazing at her mother in fear*).
Mother, what is . . . ?

5 LUCIA (*hurriedly*). Hush, my dear. It will pass.—Hold fast to
your music, you know. (*As* GENEVIEVE *starts toward her*) No,
no. I want to be alone for a few minutes.

> *She turns and starts after* COUSIN BRANDON *toward the Right.*

CHARLES. If the Republicans collected all their votes instead of
10 going off into cliques among themselves, they might prevent
his getting a second term.

GENEVIEVE. Charles, Mother doesn't tell us, but she hasn't been
very well these days.

CHARLES. Come, Mother, we'll go to Florida for a few weeks.

15   *Exit* BRANDON.

LUCIA (*smiling at* GENEVIEVE *and waving her hand*). Don't be
foolish. Don't grieve.

> *She clasps her hands under her chin; her lips move, whisper-*
> *ing; she walks serenely into the portal.*

20 GENEVIEVE *stares after her, frozen.*
> *At the same moment the nurse and perambulator enter from*
> *the Left. Pale yellow ribbons.* LEONORA *rushes to it.*

LEONORA. O my darlings . . . twins . . . Charles, aren't they
glorious! Look at them. Look at them.

25 GENEVIEVE (*sinks down on the table her face buried in her arms*).
But what will I do? What's left for me to do?

CHARLES (*bending over the basket*). Which is which?

LEONORA. I feel as though I were the first mother who ever had
twins.—Look at them now!—But why wasn't Mother Bayard
30 allowed to stay and see them!

GENEVIEVE (*rising suddenly distraught, loudly*). I don't want to
go on. I can't bear it.

CHARLES (*goes to her quickly*). (*They sit down. He whispers to*
her earnestly, taking both her hands.) But Genevieve, Gene-
35 vieve! How frightfully Mother would feel to think that . . .
Genevieve!

GENEVIEVE (*shaking her head wildly*). I never told her how wonderful she was. We all treated her as though she were just a friend in the house. I thought she'd be here forever.

LEONORA (*timidly*). Genevieve darling, do come one minute and hold my babies' hands. We shall call the girl Lucia after her grandmother,—will that please you? Do just see what adorable little hands they have.

GENEVIEVE *collects herself and goes over to the perambulator. She smiles brokenly into the basket.*

GENEVIEVE. They are wonderful, Leonora.

LEONORA. Give him your finger, darling. Just let him hold it.

CHARLES. And we'll call the boy Samuel.—Well, now everybody come and finish your dinners. Don't drop them, nurse; at least don't drop the boy. We need him in the firm.

LEONORA (*stands looking after them as the nurse wheels them into the hall*). Someday they'll be big. Imagine! They'll come in and say "Hello, Mother!" (*She makes clucking noises of rapturous consternation.*)

CHARLES. Come, a little wine, Leonora, Genevieve? Full of iron. Eduardo, fill the ladies' glasses. It certainly is a keen, cold morning. I used to go skating with Father on mornings like this and Mother would come back from church saying—

GENEVIEVE (*dreamily*). I know: saying "Such a splendid sermon. I cried and cried."

LEONORA. Why did she cry, dear?

GENEVIEVE. That generation all cried at sermons. It was their way.

LEONORA. Really, Genevieve?

GENEVIEVE. They had had to go since they were children and I suppose sermons reminded them of their fathers and mothers, just as Christmas dinners do us. Especially in an old house like this.

LEONORA. It really is pretty old, Charles. And so ugly, with all that ironwork filigree and that dreadful cupola.

GENEVIEVE. Charles! You aren't going to change the house!

CHARLES. No, no. I won't give up the house, but great heavens!

it's fifty years old. This Spring we'll remove the cupola and build a new wing toward the tennis courts.

From now on GENEVIEVE *is seen to change. She sits up more straightly. The corners of her mouth become fixed. She becomes a forthright and slightly disillusioned spinster.* CHARLES *becomes the plain business man and a little pompous.*

LEONORA.   And then couldn't we ask your dear old Cousin Ermengarde to come and live with us? She's really the self-effacing kind.

CHARLES.   Ask her now. Take her out of the First Grade.

GENEVIEVE.   We only seem to think of it on Christmas day with her Christmas card staring us in the face.

Enter Left, nurse and perambulator. Blue ribbons.

LEONORA.   Another boy! Another boy! Here's a Roderick for you at last.

CHARLES.   Roderick Brandon Bayard. A regular little fighter.

LEONORA.   Goodbye, darling. Don't grow up too fast. Yes, yes. Aië, aië, aië—stay just as you are.—Thank you, nurse.

GENEVIEVE (*who has not left the table, repeats dryly*).   Stay just as you are.

Exit nurse and perambulator. The others return to their places.

LEONORA.   Now I have three children. One, two, three. Two boys and a girl. I'm collecting them. It's very exciting. (*Over her shoulder*) What, Hilda? Oh, Cousin Ermengarde's come! Come in, Cousin.

She goes to the hall and welcomes COUSIN ERMENGARDE *who already wears her white hair.*

ERMENGARDE (*shyly*).   It's such a pleasure to be with you all.

CHARLES (*pulling out her chair for her*).   The twins have taken a great fancy to you already, Cousin.

LEONORA.   The baby went to her at once.

CHARLES.   Exactly how are we related, Cousin Ermengarde?— There, Genevieve, that's your specialty.—First a little more turkey and stuffing, Mother? Cranberry sauce, anybody?

GENEVIEVE.   I can work it out; Grandmother Bayard was your. . . .

ERMENGARDE. Your Grandmother Bayard was a second cousin
of my Grandmother Haskins through the Wainrights.

CHARLES. Well it's all in a book somewhere upstairs. All that
kind of thing is awfully interesting.

GENEVIEVE. Nonsense. There are no such books. I collect my
notes off gravestones, and you have to scrape a good deal of
moss—let me tell you—to find one great-grandparent.

CHARLES. There's a story that my Grandmother Bayard crossed
the Mississippi on a raft before there were any bridges or ferry-
boats. She died before Genevieve or I were born. Time certainly
goes very fast in a great new country like this. Have some more
cranberry sauce, Cousin Ermengarde.

ERMENGARDE (*timidly*). Well, time must be passing very slowly
in Europe with this dreadful, dreadful war going on.

CHARLES. Perhaps an occasional war isn't so bad after all. It clears
up a lot of poisons that collect in nations. It's like a boil.

ERMENGARDE. Oh, dear, oh, dear!

CHARLES (*with relish*). Yes, it's like a boil.—Ho! ho! Here are
your twins.

*The twins appear at the door into the hall. SAM is wearing the
uniform of an ensign. LUCIA is fussing over some detail on it.*

LUCIA. Isn't he wonderful in it, Mother?

CHARLES. Let's get a look at you.

SAM. Mother, don't let Roderick fool with my stamp album
while I'm gone.

LEONORA. Now, Sam, do write a letter once in a while. Do be a
good boy about that, mind.

SAM. You might send some of those cakes of yours once in a
while, Cousin Ermengarde.

ERMENGARDE (*in a flutter*). I certainly will, my dear boy.

CHARLES. If you need any money, we have agents in Paris and
London, remember.

SAM. Well, goodbye. . . .

*SAM goes briskly out through the dark portal, tossing his
unneeded white hair through the door before him.*

LUCIA sits down at the table with lowered eyes.

ERMENGARDE (*after a slight pause, in a low, constrained voice,*

making conversation).   I spoke to Mrs. Fairchild for a moment
coming out of church. Her rheumatism's a little better, she says.
She sends you her warmest thanks for the Christmas present.
The workbasket, wasn't it?—It was an admirable sermon. And
5   our stained-glass window looked so beautiful, Leonora, so beautiful. Everybody spoke of it and so affectionately of Sammy.
(LEONORA's *hand goes to her mouth*.)   Forgive me, Leonora,
but it's better to speak of him than not to speak of him when
we're all thinking of him so hard.

10 LEONORA (*rising, in anguish*).   He was a mere boy. He was a
mere boy, Charles.

CHARLES.   My dear, my dear.

LEONORA.   I want to tell him how wonderful he was. We let him
go so casually. I want to tell him how we all feel about him.—
15   Forgive me, let me walk about a minute.—Yes, of course,
Ermengarde—it's best to speak of him.

LUCIA (*in a low voice to Genevieve*).   Isn't there anything I can
do?

GENEVIEVE.   No, no. Only time, only the passing of time can help
20   in these things.

> LEONORA, *straying about the room finds herself near the door
> to the hall at the moment that her son* RODERICK *enters. He
> links his arm with hers and leads her back to the table.*

RODERICK.   What's the matter, anyway? What are you all so
25   glum about? The skating was fine today.

CHARLES.   Sit down, young man. I have something to say to you.

RODERICK.   Everybody was there. Lucia skated in the corners
with Dan Creighton the whole time. When'll it be, Lucia,
when'll it be?

30 LUCIA.   I don't know what you mean.

RODERICK.   Lucia's leaving us soon, Mother. Dan Creighton, of
all people.

CHARLES (*ominously*).   Roderick, I have something to say to you.

RODERICK.   Yes, Father.

35 CHARLES.   Is it true, Roderick, that you made yourself conspicuous last night at the Country Club—at a Christmas Eve dance,
too?

LEONORA. Not now, Charles, I beg of you. This is Christmas dinner.

RODERICK (*loudly*). No, I didn't.

LUCIA. Really, Father, he didn't. It was that dreadful Johnny Lewis.

CHARLES. I don't want to hear about Johnny Lewis. I want to know whether a son of mine. . . .

LEONORA. Charles, I beg of you. . . .

CHARLES. The first family of this city!

RODERICK (*rising*). I hate this town and everything about it. I always did.

CHARLES. You behaved like a spoiled puppy, sir, an ill-bred spoiled puppy.

RODERICK. What did I do? What did I do that was wrong?

CHARLES. You were drunk and you were rude to the daughters of my best friends.

GENEVIEVE (*striking the table*). Nothing in the world deserves an ugly scene like this. Charles, I'm ashamed of you.

RODERICK. Great God, you gotta get drunk in this town to forget how dull it is. Time passes so slowly here that it stands still, that's what's the trouble.

CHARLES. Well, young man, we can employ your time. You will leave the university and you will come into the Bayard factory on January second.

RODERICK (*at the door into the hall*). I have better things to do than to go into your old factory. I'm going somewhere where time passes, my God!

He goes out into the hall.

LEONORA (*rising*). Roderick, Roderick, come here just a moment.—Charles, where can he go?

LUCIA (*rising*). Sh, Mother. He'll come back. Now I have to go upstairs and pack my trunk.

LEONORA. I won't have any children left!

LUCIA. Sh, Mother. He'll come back. He's only gone to California or somewhere.—Cousin Ermengarde has done most of my packing—thanks a thousand times, Cousin Ermengarde. (*She kisses her mother.*) I won't be long.

She runs out into the hall.

Genevieve *and* Leonora *put on their white hair.*

Ermengarde.   It's a very beautiful day. On the way home from
church I stopped and saw Mrs. Foster a moment. Her arthritis
comes and goes.

Leonora.   Is she actually in pain, dear?

Ermengarde.   Oh, she says it'll all be the same in a hundred
years!

Leonora.   Yes, she's a brave little stoic.

Charles.   Come now, a little white meat, Mother?—Mary, pass
my cousin's plate.

Leonora.   What is it, Mary?—Oh, here's a telegram from them
in Paris! "Love and Christmas greetings to all." I told them we'd
be eating some of their wedding cake and thinking about them
today. It seems to be all decided that they will settle down in
the East, Ermengarde. I can't even have my daughter for a
neighbor. They hope to build before long somewhere on the
shore north of New York.

Genevieve.   There is no shore north of New York.

Leonora.   Well, East or West or whatever it is.

Pause.

Charles.   My, what a dark day.

He puts on his white hair. Pause.

How slowly time passes without any young people in the
house.

Leonora.   I have three children somewhere.

Charles (*blunderingly offering comfort*).   Well, one of them
gave his life for his country.

Leonora (*sadly*).   And one of them is selling aluminum in China.

Genevieve (*slowly working herself up to a hysterical crisis*).   I
can stand everything but this terrible soot everywhere. We
should have moved long ago. We're surrounded by factories.
We have to change the window curtains every week.

Leonora.   Why, Genevieve!

Genevieve.   I can't stand it. I can't stand it any more. I'm going
abroad. It's not only the soot that comes through the very walls
of this house; it's the *thoughts*, it's the thought of what has been

and what might have been here. And the feeling about this house of the years *grinding away*. My mother died yesterday—not twenty-five years ago. Oh, I'm going to live and die abroad! Yes, I'm going to be the American old maid living and dying in a pension in Munich or Florence.

ERMENGARDE. Genevieve, you're tired.

CHARLES. Come, Genevieve, take a good drink of cold water. Mary, open the window a minute.

GENEVIEVE. I'm sorry. I'm sorry.

She hurries tearfully out into the hall.

ERMENGARDE. Dear Genevieve will come back to us, I think.

She rises and starts toward the dark portal.

You should have been out today, Leonora. It was one of those days when everything was encircled with ice. Very pretty indeed.

CHARLES *rises and starts after her.*

CHARLES. Leonora, I used to go skating with Father on mornings like this.—I wish I felt a little better.

LEONORA. What! Have I got two invalids on my hands at once? Now, Cousin Ermengarde, you must get better and help me nurse Charles.

ERMENGARDE. I'll do my best.

ERMENGARDE *turns at the very portal and comes back to the table.*

CHARLES. Well, Leonora, I'll do what you ask. I'll write the puppy a letter of forgiveness and apology. It's Christmas day. I'll cable it. That's what I'll do.

He goes out the dark door.

LEONORA (*drying her eyes*). Ermengarde, it's such a comfort having you here with me. Mary, I really can't eat anything. Well, perhaps, a sliver of white meat.

ERMENGARDE (*very old*). I spoke to Mrs. Keene for a moment coming out of church. She asked after the young people.—At church I felt very proud sitting under our windows, Leonora, and our brass tablets. The Bayard aisle,—it's a regular Bayard aisle and I love it.

LEONORA. Ermengarde, would you be very angry with me if I

went and stayed with the young people a little this Spring?

ERMENGARDE.   Why, no. I know how badly they want you and need you. Especially now that they're about to build a new house.

5 LEONORA.   You wouldn't be angry? This house is yours as long as you want it, remember.

ERMENGARDE.   I don't see why the rest of you dislike it. I like it more than I can say.

LEONORA.   I won't be long. I'll be back in no time and we can

10 have some more of our readings-aloud in the evening.

She kisses her and goes into the hall. ERMENGARDE, *left alone, eats slowly and talks to* MARY.

ERMENGARDE.   Really, Mary, I'll change my mind. If you'll ask Bertha to be good enough to make me a little eggnog. A dear

15 little eggnog.—Such a nice letter this morning from Mrs. Bayard, Mary. Such a nice letter. They're having their first Christmas dinner in the new house. They must be very happy. They call her Mother Bayard, she says, as though she were an old lady. And she says she finds it more comfortable to come and

20 go in a wheel chair.—Such a dear letter. . . . And Mary, I can tell you a secret. It's still a great secret, mind! They're expecting a grandchild. Isn't that good news! Now I'll read a little.

She props a book up before her, still dipping a spoon into a

25 *custard from time to time. She grows from very old to immensely old. She sighs. The book falls down. She finds a cane beside her, and soon totters into the dark portal, murmuring:*

"Dear little Roderick and little Lucia."

———

Wilder, like Barrie, has shown repeatedly in both his plays and his novels a temperamental distaste for literary realism. This play is even less realistic in its conduct than "The Will." Even its setting is less realistic than the one Barrie thought sufficient for his play. The initial stage directions warn us that we are not to expect a play that shall represent the surfaces of life with photographic fidelity. Furthermore, the directions for costuming and for stage business underscore its nonrealistic character.

Here, even more strikingly than in "The Will," time is the most potent of the forces involved, and the success of the play depends on the bold treatment of this element. But Wilder, despite his audacity, has the advantage of Barrie in that he is emphasizing not only what is changed by time but what is left unchanged. The play presents, therefore, a fascinating interplay of elements that change and elements that remain the same; the devices by which Wilder creates this effect of elaborate counterpoint deserve close analysis.

Another indication of the nonrealistic character of this play is its treatment of character. Wilder is not interested in the creation of individuals but of types; the emphasis indeed is on recurrence rather than on novelty or individuality. Yet, though the mothers, for example, exhibit almost identical reactions to events, Wilder differentiates sufficiently the two old maids, Genevieve and Ermengarde, and the two sons, of whom one dies in the service of his country and the other rebels against the family's way of life.

Finally, Wilder is primarily concerned, not with telling a striking story or creating memorable characters but with making an effective pattern of feelings and emotions. He runs the risk of a monotonous repetition of feelings; in order to avoid such an effect, he introduces contrasting emotions. You should define the overall tone of the play, and then investigate the way in which this overall tone is built up out of repeated or contrasted emotions. You should also consider whether the overall tone is sufficiently complex for a faithful representation of the people and life depicted.

Make a genealogical table of the characters who appear or are mentioned in this play. What social implications might be drawn from it?

Why does Wilder not divide his play into scenes as Barrie did? How many Christmas dinners can you distinguish clearly? In how many instances does Wilder indicate the amount of time that has elapsed between one and the next dinner? In how many instances has he left the amount of elapsed time vague?

This play makes constant use of the aesthetic principles of repetition and variation. Make a list of the recurrent motifs. Which of them recur without change? Which of them recur with perceptible variations?

What use does Wilder make of manners and customs to indicate the passage of time?

What enduring human values are emphasized in this play? To what extent do the characters' values change as the play progresses? In this connection, what is the significance of young Roderick's rebellion?

What are the major feelings aroused by this play? Could the play be charged with being sentimental, that is, does it attempt to elicit an amount of emotion that the substance of the play does not warrant? Why or why not?

Beyond the Horizon [1]

EUGENE O'NEILL

CHARACTERS

JAMES MAYO, *a farmer*
KATE MAYO, *his wife*
CAPTAIN DICK SCOTT, *of the bark* Sunda, *her brother*
ANDREW MAYO ⎱ *sons of* JAMES MAYO
ROBERT MAYO ⎰
RUTH ATKINS
MRS. ATKINS, *her widowed mother*
MARY
BEN, *a farm hand*
DOCTOR FAWCETT

ACT I

SCENE I: The Road. Sunset of a day in Spring.
SCENE II: The Farm House. The same night.

ACT II

(*Three years later*)

SCENE I: The Farm House. Noon of a Summer day.
SCENE II: The top of a hill on the farm overlooking the sea. The
following day.

[1] Copyright, 1920, 1947, by Eugene O'Neill. Reprinted by permission of Random House, Inc.

ACT III

(Five years later)

Scene I: The Farm House. Dawn of a day in late Fall.
Scene II: The Road. Sunrise.

ACT ONE

Scene One

*A section of country highway. The road runs diagonally from the
left, forward, to the right, rear, and can be seen in the distance
winding toward the horizon like a pale ribbon between the low,
rolling hills with their freshly plowed fields clearly divided from
each other, checkerboard fashion, by the lines of stone walls and
rough snake fences.*

*The forward triangle cut off by the road is a section of a field from
the dark earth of which myriad bright-green blades of fall-
sown rye are sprouting. A straggling line of piled rocks, too low
to be called a wall, separates this field from the road.*

*To the rear of the road is a ditch with a sloping, grassy bank on
the far side. From the center of this an old, gnarled apple tree,
just budding into leaf, strains its twisted branches heavenwards,
black against the pallor of distance. A snake fence sidles from
left to right along the top of the bank, passing beneath the apple tree.*

*The hushed twilight of a day in May is just beginning. The hori-
zon hills are still rimmed by a faint line of flame, and the sky
above them glows with the crimson flush of the sunset. This
fades gradually as the action of the scene progresses.*

At the rise of the curtain, Robert Mayo *is discovered sitting on
the fence. He is a tall, slender young man of twenty-three.
There is a touch of the poet about him expressed in his high
forehead and wide, dark eyes. His features are delicate and refined, leaning to weakness in the mouth and chin. He is dressed
in gray corduroy trousers pushed into high laced boots, and a
blue flannel shirt with a bright colored tie. He is reading a*

*book by the fading sunset light. He shuts this, keeping a finger
in to mark the place, and turns his head toward the horizon,
gazing out over the fields and hills. His lips move as if he were
reciting something to himself.*

His brother ANDREW *comes along the road from the right, re-
turning from his work in the fields. He is twenty-seven years
old, an opposite type to* ROBERT—*husky, sun-bronzed, hand-
some in a large-featured, manly fashion—a son of the soil, in-
telligent in a shrewd way, but with nothing of the intellectual
about him. He wears overalls, leather boots, a gray flannel
shirt open at the neck, and a soft, mud-stained hat pushed back
on his head. He stops to talk to* ROBERT, *leaning on the hoe he
carries.*

ANDREW (*seeing* ROBERT *has not noticed his presence—in a loud
shout*).   Hey there! (ROBERT *turns with a start. Seeing who it
is, he smiles.*) Gosh, you do take the prize for day-dreaming!
And I see you've toted one of the old books along with you.
(*He crosses the ditch and sits on the fence near his brother.*)   5
What is it this time—poetry, I'll bet. (*He reaches for the
book.*) Let me see.

ROBERT (*handing it to him rather reluctantly*).   Look out you
don't get it full of dirt.

ANDREW (*glancing at his hands*).   That isn't dirt—it's good clean   10
earth. (*He turns over the pages. His eyes read something and
he gives an exclamation of disgust.*) Hump! (*With a provoking
grin at his brother he reads aloud in a doleful, sing-song voice.*)
"I have loved wind and light and the bright sea. But holy and
most sacred night, not as I love and have loved thee." (*He hands   15
the book back.*) Here! Take it and bury it. I suppose it's that
year in college gave you a liking for that kind of stuff. I'm
darn glad I stopped at High School, or maybe I'd been crazy
too. (*He grins and slaps* ROBERT *on the back affectionately.*)
Imagine me reading poetry and plowing at the same time! The   20
team'd run away, I'll bet.

ROBERT (*laughing*).   Or picture me plowing.

ANDREW.   You should have gone back to college last fall, like
I know you wanted to. You're fitted for that sort of thing—
just as I ain't.

ROBERT.   You know why I didn't go back, Andy. Pa didn't like
5   the idea, even if he didn't say so; and I know he wanted the
money to use improving the farm. And besides, I'm not keen
on being a student, just because you see me reading books all
the time. What I want to do now is keep on moving so that I
won't take root in any one place.

10   ANDREW.   Well, the trip you're leaving on tomorrow will keep
you moving all right. (*At this mention of the trip they both
fall silent. There is a pause. Finally* ANDREW *goes on, awk-
wardly, attempting to speak casually.*) Uncle says you'll be
gone three years.

15   ROBERT.   About that, he figures.

ANDREW (*moodily*).   That's a long time.

ROBERT.   Not so long when you come to consider it. You know
the *Sunda* sails around the Horn for Yokohama first, and that's
a long voyage on a sailing ship; and if we go to any of the other
20   places Uncle Dick mentions—India, or Australia, or South
Africa, or South America—they'll be long voyages, too.

ANDREW.   You can have all those foreign parts for all of me.
(*After a pause*) Ma's going to miss you a lot, Rob.

ROBERT.   Yes—and I'll miss her.

25   ANDREW.   And Pa ain't feeling none too happy to have you go
—though he's been trying not to show it.

ROBERT.   I can see how he feels.

ANDREW.   And you can bet that I'm not giving any cheers about
it. (*He puts one hand on the fence near* ROBERT.)

30   ROBERT (*putting one hand on top of* ANDREW's *with a gesture almost of shyness*).   I know that, too, Andy.

ANDREW.   I'll miss you as much as anybody, I guess. You see,
you and I ain't like most brothers—always fighting and separated a lot of the time, while we've always been together—just
35   the two of us. It's different with us. That's why it hits so hard,
I guess.

ROBERT (*with feeling*). It's just as hard for me, Andy—believe that! I hate to leave you and the old folks—but—I feel I've got to. There's something calling me—— (*He points to the horizon.*) Oh, I can't just explain it to you, Andy.

ANDREW. No need to, Rob. (*Angry at himself*) Hell! You want to go—that's all there is to it; and I wouldn't have you miss this chance for the world.

ROBERT. It's fine of you to feel that way, Andy.

ANDREW. Huh! I'd be a nice son-of-a-gun if I didn't, wouldn't I? When I know how you need this sea trip to make a new man of you—in the body, I mean—and give you your full health back.

ROBERT (*a trifle impatiently*). All of you seem to keep harping on my health. You were so used to seeing me lying around the house in the old days that you never will get over the notion that I'm a chronic invalid. You don't realize how I've bucked up in the past few years. If I had no other excuse for going on Uncle Dick's ship but just my health, I'd stay right here and start in plowing.

ANDREW. Can't be done. Farming ain't your nature. There's all the difference shown in just the way us two feel about the farm. You—well, you like the home part of it, I expect; but as a place to work and grow things, you hate it. Ain't that right?

ROBERT. Yes, I suppose it is. For you it's different. You're a Mayo through and through. You're wedded to the soil. You're as much a product of it as an ear of corn is, or a tree. Father is the same. This farm is his life-work, and he's happy in knowing that another Mayo, inspired by the same love, will take up the work where he leaves off. I can understand your attitude, and Pa's; and I think it's wonderful and sincere. But I—well, I'm not made that way.

ANDREW. No, you ain't; but when it comes to understanding, I guess I realize that you've got your own angle of looking at things.

ROBERT (*musingly*). I wonder if you do, really.

ANDREW (*confidently*). Sure I do. You've seen a bit of the

world, enough to make the farm seem small, and you've got the
itch to see it all.

ROBERT.   It's more than that, Andy.

ANDREW.   Oh, of course. I know you're going to learn naviga-
5   tion, and all about a ship, so's you can be an officer. That's
natural, too. There's fair pay in it, I expect, when you consider
that you've always got a home and grub thrown in; and if you're
set on traveling, you can go anywhere you're a mind to without paying fare.

10   ROBERT (*with a smile that is half sad*).   It's more than that, Andy.

ANDREW.   Sure it is. There's always a chance of a good thing
coming your way in some of those foreign ports or other. I've
heard there are great opportunities for a young fellow with
his eyes open in some of those new countries that are just being
15   opened up. (*Jovially*) I'll bet that's what you've been turning
over in your mind under all your quietness! (*He slaps his
brother on the back with a laugh.*) Well, if you get to be a
millionaire all of a sudden, call 'round once in a while and I'll
pass the plate to you. We could use a lot of money right here
20   on the farm without hurting it any.

ROBERT (*forced to laugh*).   I've never considered that practical
side of it for a minute, Andy.

ANDREW.   Well, you ought to.

ROBERT.   No, I oughtn't. (*Pointing to the horizon—dreamily*)
25   Supposing I was to tell you that it's just Beauty that's calling
me, the beauty of the far off and unknown, the mystery and
spell of the East which lures me in the books I've read, the need
of the freedom of great wide spaces, the joy of wandering on
and on—in quest of the secret which is hidden over there, be-
30   yond the horizon? Suppose I told you that was the one and only
reason for my going?

ANDREW.   I should say you were nutty.

ROBERT (*frowning*).   Don't, Andy. I'm serious.

ANDREW.   Then you might as well stay here, because we've
35   got all you're looking for right on this farm. There's wide space
enough, Lord knows; and you can have all the sea you want

by walking a mile down to the beach; and there's plenty of horizon to look at, and beauty enough for anyone, except in the winter. (*He grins*) As for the mystery and spell, I haven't met 'em yet, but they're probably lying around somewheres. I'll have you understand this is a first class farm with all the fixings. (*He laughs*). 5

ROBERT (*joining in the laughter in spite of himself*). It's no use talking to you, you chump!

ANDREW. You'd better not say anything to Uncle Dick about spells and things when you're on the ship. He'll likely chuck you overboard for a Jonah. (*He jumps down from fence.*) 10 I'd better run along. I've got to wash up some as long as Ruth's Ma is coming over for supper.

ROBERT (*pointedly—almost bitterly*). And Ruth.

ANDREW (*confused—looking everywhere except at* ROBERT— *trying to appear unconcerned*). Yes, Ruth'll be staying too. 15 Well, I better hustle, I guess, and—— (*He steps over the ditch to the road while he is talking.*)

ROBERT (*who appears to be fighting some strong inward emotion —impulsively*). Wait a minute, Andy! (*He jumps down from* 20 *the fence.*) There is something I want to—— (*He stops abruptly, biting his lips, his face coloring.*)

ANDREW (*facing him; half-defiantly*). Yes?

ROBERT (*confusedly*). No—— never mind—— it doesn't matter, it was nothing. 25

ANDREW (*after a pause, during which he stares fixedly at* ROBERT'S *averted face*). Maybe I can guess—— what you were going to say—— but I guess you're right not to talk about it. (*He pulls* ROBERT'S *hand from his side and grips it tensely; the two brothers stand looking into each other's eyes for a minute.*) We can't 30 help those things, Rob. (*He turns away, suddenly releasing* ROBERT'S *hand.*) You'll be coming along shortly, won't you?

ROBERT (*dully*). Yes.

ANDREW. See you later, then.

> He walks off down the road to the left. ROBERT *stares after* 35
> *him for a moment; then climbs to the fence rail again, and*

*looks out over the hills, an expression of deep grief on his
face. After a moment or so,* RUTH *enters hurriedly from the
left. She is a healthy, blonde, out-of-door girl of twenty, with
a graceful, slender figure. Her face, though inclined to round-
ness, is undeniably pretty, its large eyes of a deep blue set off
strikingly by the sun-bronzed complexion. Her small, regular
features are marked by a certain strength—an underlying,
stubborn fixity of purpose hidden in the frankly-appealing
charm of her fresh youthfulness. She wears a simple white
dress but no hat.*

RUTH (*seeing him*).   Hello, Rob!

ROBERT (*startled*).   Hello, Ruth!

RUTH (*jumps the ditch and perches on the fence beside him*).   I
was looking for you.

ROBERT (*pointedly*).   Andy just left here.

RUTH.   I know. I met him on the road a second ago. He told me
you were here. (*Tenderly playful*) I wasn't looking for Andy,
Smarty, if that's what you mean. I was looking for *you.*

ROBERT.   Because I'm going away tomorrow?

RUTH.   Because your mother was anxious to have you come
home and asked me to look for you. I just wheeled Ma over
to your house.

ROBERT (*perfunctorily*).   How is your mother?

RUTH (*a shadow coming over her face*).   She's about the same.
She never seems to get any better or any worse. Oh, Rob, I do
wish she'd try to make the best of things that can't be helped.

ROBERT.   Has she been nagging at you again?

RUTH (*nods her head, and then breaks forth rebelliously*).   She
never stops nagging. No matter what I do for her she finds
fault. If only Pa was still living—— (*She stops as if ashamed
of her outburst.*) I suppose I shouldn't complain this way. (*She
sighs*) Poor Ma, Lord knows it's hard enough for her. I suppose
it's natural to be cross when you're not able ever to walk a step.
Oh, I'd like to be going away some place—like you!

ROBERT.   It's hard to stay—and equally hard to go, sometimes.

RUTH. There! If I'm not the stupid body! I swore I wasn't going to speak about your trip—until after you'd gone; and there I go, first thing!

ROBERT. Why didn't you want to speak of it?

RUTH. Because I didn't want to spoil this last night you're here. Oh, Rob, I'm going to—we're all going to miss you so awfully. Your mother is going around looking as if she'd burst out crying any minute. You ought to know how I feel. Andy and you and I—why it seems as if we'd always been together.

ROBERT (*with a wry attempt at a smile*). You and Andy will still have each other. It'll be harder for me without anyone.

RUTH. But you'll have new sights and new people to take your mind off; while we'll be here with the old, familiar place to remind us every minute of the day. It's a shame you're going—just at this time, in spring, when everything is getting so nice. (*With a sigh*) I oughtn't to talk that way when I know going's the best thing for you. You're bound to find all sorts of opportunities to get on, your father says.

ROBERT (*heatedly*). I don't give a damn about that! I wouldn't take a voyage across the road for the best opportunity in the world of the kind Pa thinks of. (*He smiles at his own irritation.*) Excuse me, Ruth, for getting worked up over it; but Andy gave me an overdose of the practical considerations.

RUTH (*slowly, puzzled*). Well, then, if it isn't—— (*With sudden intensity*) Oh, Rob, why *do* you want to go?

ROBERT (*turning to her quickly, in surprise—slowly*). Why do you ask that, Ruth?

RUTH (*dropping her eyes before his searching glance*). Because—— (*Lamely*) It seems such a shame.

ROBERT (*insistently*). Why?

RUTH. Oh, because—everything.

ROBERT. I could hardly back out now, even if I wanted to. And I'll be forgotten before you know it.

RUTH (*indignantly*). You won't! I'll never forget—— (*She stops and turns away to hide her confusion.*)

ROBERT (*softly*).   Will you promise me that?

RUTH (*evasively*).   Of course. It's mean of you to think that any
of us would forget so easily.

ROBERT (*disappointedly*).   Oh!

5   RUTH (*with an attempt at lightness*).   But you haven't told me
your reason for leaving yet?

ROBERT (*moodily*).   I doubt if you'll understand. It's difficult
to explain, even to myself. Either you feel it, or you don't. I
can remember being conscious of it first when I was only a kid

10   —you haven't forgotten what a sickly specimen I was then, in
those days, have you?

RUTH (*with a shudder*).   Let's not think about them.

ROBERT.   You'll have to, to understand. Well, in those days, when
Ma was fixing meals, she used to get me out of the way by

15   pushing my chair to the west window and telling me to look
out and be quiet. That wasn't hard. I guess I was always quiet.

RUTH (*compassionately*).   Yes, you always were—and you suffering so much, too!

ROBERT (*musingly*).   So I used to stare out over the fields to the

20   hills, out there—(*he points to the horizon*) and somehow after a
time I'd forget any pain I was in, and start dreaming. I knew
the sea was over beyond those hills,—the folks had told me—
and I used to wonder what the sea was like, and try to form a
picture of it in my mind. (*With a smile*) There was all the

25   mystery in the world to me then about that—far-off sea—and
there still is! It called to me then just as it does now. (*After a
slight pause*) And other times my eyes would follow this road,
winding off into the distance, toward the hills, as if it, too, was
searching for the sea. And I'd promise myself that when I grew

30   up and was strong, I'd follow that road, and it and I would find
the sea together. (*With a smile*) You see, my making this trip
is only keeping that promise of long ago.

RUTH (*charmed by his low, musical voice telling the dreams of his
childhood*).   Yes, I see.

35   ROBERT.   Those were the only happy moments of my life then,
dreaming there at the window. I liked to be all alone—those

times. I got to know all the different kinds of sunsets by heart. And all those sunsets took place over there—(*he points*) beyond the horizon. So gradually I came to believe that all the wonders of the world happened on the other side of those hills. There was the home of the good fairies who performed beautiful mir- 5 acles. I believed in fairies then. (*With a smile*) Perhaps I still do believe in them. Anyway, in those days they were real enough, and sometimes I could actually hear them calling to me to come out and play with them, dance with them down the road in the dusk in a game of hide-and-seek to find out where 10 the sun was hiding himself. They sang their little songs to me, songs that told of all the wonderful things they had in their home on the other side of the hills; and they promised to show me all of them, if I'd only come, come! But I couldn't come then, and I used to cry sometimes and Ma would think I was 15 in pain. (*He breaks off suddenly with a laugh.*) That's why I'm going now, I suppose. For I can still hear them calling. But the horizon is as far away and as luring as ever. (*He turns to her— softly*) Do you understand now, Ruth?

RUTH (*spellbound, in a whisper*). Yes.   20

ROBERT. You feel it then?

RUTH. Yes, yes, I do! (*Unconsciously she snuggles close against his side. His arm steals about her as if he were not aware of the action.*) Oh, Rob, how could I help feeling it? You tell things so beautifully!   25

ROBERT (*suddenly realizing that his arm is around her, and that her head is resting on his shoulder, gently takes his arm away. RUTH, brought back to herself, is overcome with confusion.*) So now you know why I'm going. It's for that reason—that and one other.   30

RUTH. You've another? Then you must tell me that, too.

ROBERT (*looking at her searchingly. She drops her eyes before his gaze*). I wonder if I ought to! You'll promise not to be angry —whatever it is?

RUTH (*softly, her face still averted*). Yes, I promise.   35

ROBERT (*simply*). I love you. That's the other reason.

RUTH (*hiding her face in her hands*).   Oh, Rob!

ROBERT.   I wasn't going to tell you, but I feel I have to. It can't
matter now that I'm going so far away, and for so long—perhaps forever. I've loved you all these years, but the realization
never came 'til I agreed to go away with Uncle Dick. Then I
thought of leaving you, and the pain of that thought revealed
to me in a flash—that I loved you, had loved you as long as I
could remember. (*He gently pulls one of* RUTH'S *hands away
from her face.*) You mustn't mind my telling you this, Ruth.
I realize how impossible it all is—and I understand; for the revelation of my own love seemed to open my eyes to the love of
others. I saw Andy's love for you—and I knew that you must
love him.

RUTH (*breaking out stormily*).   I don't! I don't love Andy! I
don't! (ROBERT *stares at her in stupid astonishment.* RUTH *weeps
hysterically.*) Whatever—put such a fool notion into—into
your head? (*She suddenly throws her arms about his neck and
hides her head on his shoulder.*) Oh, Rob! Don't go away!
Please! You mustn't, now! You can't! I won't let you! It'd
break my—my heart!

ROBERT. (*The expression of stupid bewilderment giving way to
one of overwhelming joy. He presses her close to him—slowly
and tenderly.*)   Do you mean that—that you love me?

RUTH (*sobbing*).   Yes, yes—of course I do—what d'you s'pose?
(*She lifts up her head and looks into his eyes with a tremulous
smile.*) You stupid thing! (*He kisses her.*) I've loved you right
along.

ROBERT (*mystified*).   But you and Andy were always together!

RUTH.   Because you never seemed to want to go any place with
me. You were always reading an old book, and not paying any
attention to me. I was too proud to let you see I cared because
I thought the year you had away to college had made you
stuck-up, and you thought yourself too educated to waste any
time on me.

ROBERT (*kissing her*).   And I was thinking—— (*With a laugh*)
What fools we've both been!

RUTH (*overcome by a sudden fear*).   You won't go away on the
trip, will you, Rob? You'll tell them you can't go on account of
me, won't you? You can't go now! You can't!

ROBERT (*bewildered*).   Perhaps—you can come too.

RUTH.   Oh, Rob, don't be so foolish. You know I can't. Who'd
take care of Ma? Don't you see I couldn't go—on her account?
(*She clings to him imploringly.*) Please don't go—not now. Tell
them you've decided not to. They won't mind. I know your
mother and father'll be glad. They'll all be. They don't want
you to go so far away from them. Please, Rob! We'll be so
happy here together where it's natural and we know things.
Please tell me you won't go!

ROBERT (*face to face with a definite, final decision, betrays the conflict going on within him*).   But—Ruth—I—Uncle Dick——

RUTH.   He won't mind when he knows it's for your happiness to
stay. How could he? (*As* ROBERT *remains silent she bursts into
sobs again.*) Oh, Rob! And you said—you loved me!

ROBERT (*conquered by this appeal—an irrevocable decision in his
voice*).   I won't go, Ruth. I promise you. There! Don't cry!
(*He presses her to him, stroking her hair tenderly. After a
pause he speaks with happy hopefulness.*) Perhaps after all Andy
was right—righter than he knew—when he said I could find all
the things I was seeking for here, at home on the farm. I think
love must have been the secret—the secret that called to me
from over the world's rim—the secret beyond every horizon;
and when I did not come, it came to me. (*He clasps* RUTH *to
him fiercely.*) Oh, Ruth, our love is sweeter than any distant
dream! (*He kisses her passionately and steps to the ground, lifting* RUTH *in his arms and carrying her to the road where he puts
her down.*)

RUTH (*with a happy laugh*).   My, but you're strong!

ROBERT.   Come! We'll go and tell them at once.

RUTH (*dismayed*).   Oh, no, don't, Rob, not 'til after I've gone.
There'd be bound to be such a scene with them all together.

ROBERT (*kissing her—gayly*).   As you like—little Miss Common
Sense!

RUTH. Let's go, then.

    She takes his hand, and they start to go off left. ROBERT *suddenly stops and turns as though for a last look at the hills and the dying sunset flush.*

5 ROBERT (*looking upward and pointing*). See! The first star. (*He bends down and kisses her tenderly.*) Our star!

RUTH (*in a soft murmur*). Yes. Our very own star. (*They stand for a moment looking up at it, their arms around each other. Then* RUTH *takes his hand again and starts to lead him away.*)

10 Come, Rob, let's go. (*His eyes are fixed again on the horizon as he half turns to follow her.* RUTH *urges*) We'll be late for supper, Rob.

ROBERT (*shakes his head impatiently, as though he were throwing off some disturbing thought—with a laugh*). All right. We'll

15 run then. Come on!

    They run off laughing as

                                 The Curtain Falls

ACT ONE

SCENE TWO

The sitting room of the Mayo farm house about nine o'clock the same night. On the left, two windows looking out on the fields. Against the wall between the windows, an old-fashioned walnut desk. In the left corner, rear, a sideboard with a mirror. In the rear wall to the right of the sideboard, a window looking out on the road. Next to the window a door leading out into the yard. Farther right, a black horse-hair sofa, and another door opening on a bedroom. In the corner, a straight-backed chair. In the right wall, near the middle, an open doorway leading to the kitchen. Farther forward a double-heater stove with coal scuttle, etc. In the center of the newly carpeted floor, an oak dining-room table with a red cover. In the center of the table, a large oil reading lamp. Four chairs, three rockers with crocheted tidies on their backs, and one straight-backed, are placed about

the table. The walls are papered a dark red with a scrolly-
figured pattern.
Everything in the room is clean, well-kept, and in its exact place,
yet there is no suggestion of primness about the whole. Rather
the atmosphere is one of the orderly comfort of a simple, hard-
earned prosperity, enjoyed and maintained by the family as a
unit.
JAMES MAYO, *his wife, her brother,* CAPTAIN DICK SCOTT, *and*
ANDREW *are discovered.* MAYO *is his son* ANDREW *over again in*
body and face—an ANDREW *sixty-five years old with a short,*
square, white beard. MRS. MAYO *is a slight, round-faced, rather*
prim-looking woman of fifty-five who had once been a school
teacher. The labors of a farmer's wife have bent but not broken
her, and she retains a certain refinement of movement and ex-
pression foreign to the MAYO *part of the family. Whatever of*
resemblance ROBERT *has to his parents may be traced to her.*
Her brother, the CAPTAIN, *is short and stocky, with a weather-*
beaten, jovial face and a white mustache—a typical old salt, loud
of voice and given to gesture. He is fifty-eight years old.
JAMES MAYO *sits in front of the table. He wears spectacles, and a*
farm journal which he has been reading lies in his lap. The CAP-
TAIN *leans forward from a chair in the rear, his hands on the*
table in front of him. ANDREW *is tilted back on the straight-*
backed chair to the left, his chin sunk forward on his chest,
staring at the carpet, preoccupied and frowning.
As the Curtain rises the CAPTAIN *is just finishing the relation of*
some sea episode. The others are pretending an interest which
is belied by the absent-minded expressions on their faces.

THE CAPTAIN (*chuckling*). And that mission woman, she hails
me on the dock as I was acomin' ashore, and she says—with her
silly face all screwed up serious as judgment—"Captain," she
says, "would you be so kind as to tell me where the sea-gulls
sleeps at nights?" Blow me if them warn't her exact words! (*He
slaps the table with the palm of his hands and laughs loudly. The
others force smiles.*) Ain't that just like a fool woman's ques-

tion? And I looks at her serious as I could, "Ma'm," says I, "I couldn't rightly answer that question. I ain't never seed a sea-gull in his bunk yet. The next time I hears one snorin'," I says, "I'll make a note of where he's turned in, and write you a letter
5 'bout it." And then she calls me a fool real spiteful and tacks away from me quick. (*He laughs again uproariously.*) So I got rid of her that way. (*The others smile but immediately relapse into expressions of gloom again.*)

MRS. MAYO (*absent-mindedly—feeling that she has to say some-*
10 *thing*). But when it comes to that, where *do* sea-gulls sleep, Dick?

SCOTT (*slapping the table*). Ho! Ho! Listen to her, James. 'Nother one! Well, if that don't beat all hell—'scuse me for cussin', Kate.

15 MAYO (*with a twinkle in his eyes*). They unhitch their wings, Katey, and spreads 'em out on a wave for a bed.

SCOTT. And then they tells the fish to whistle to 'em when it's time to turn out. Ho! Ho!

MRS. MAYO (*with a forced smile*). You men folks are too smart
20 to live, aren't you?

> *She resumes her knitting.* MAYO *pretends to read his paper;* ANDREW *stares at the floor.*

SCOTT (*looks from one to the other of them with a puzzled air. Finally he is unable to bear the thick silence a minute longer,*
25 *and blurts out*). You folks look as if you was settin' up with a corpse. (*With exaggerated concern*) God A'mighty, there ain't anyone dead, be there?

MAYO (*sharply*). Don't play the dunce, Dick! You know as well as we do there ain't no great cause to be feelin' chipper.

30 SCOTT (*argumentatively*). And there ain't no cause to be wearin' mourning, either, I can make out.

MRS. MAYO (*indignantly*). How can you talk that way, Dick Scott, when you're taking our Robbie away from us, in the middle of the night, you might say, just to get on that old boat
35 of yours on time! I think you might wait until morning when he's had his breakfast.

SCOTT (*appealing to the others hopelessly*).   Ain't that a woman's
way o' seein' things for you? God A'mighty, Kate, I can't give
orders to the tide that it's got to be high just when it suits me
to have it. I ain't gettin' no fun out o' missin' sleep and leavin'
here at six bells myself. (*Protestingly*) And the *Sunda* ain't an   5
old ship—leastways, not very old—and she's good's she ever
was.

MRS. MAYO (*her lips trembling*).   I wish Robbie weren't going.

MAYO (*looking at her over his glasses—consolingly*).   There,
Katey!   10

MRS. MAYO (*rebelliously*).   Well, I *do* wish he wasn't!

SCOTT.   You shouldn't be taking it so hard, 's far as I kin see. This
vige'll make a man of him. I'll see to it he learns how to navigate,
'n' study for a mate's c'tificate right off—and it'll give him a
trade for the rest of his life, if he wants to travel.   15

MRS. MAYO.   But I don't want him to travel all his life. You've got
to see he comes home when this trip is over. Then he'll be all
well, and he'll want to—to marry—(ANDREW *sits forward in his
chair with an abrupt movement*)—and settle down right here.
(*She stares down at the knitting in her lap—after a pause*) I   20
never realized how hard it was going to be for me to have Robbie go—or I wouldn't have considered it a minute.

SCOTT.   It ain't no good goin' on that way, Kate, now it's all
settled.

MRS. MAYO (*on the verge of tears*).   It's all right for *you* to talk.   25
You've never had any children. You don't know what it means
to be parted from them—and Robbie my youngest, too.

   ANDREW *frowns and fidgets in his chair.*

ANDREW (*suddenly turning to them*).   There's one thing none of
you seem to take into consideration—that Rob wants to go.   30
He's dead set on it. He's been dreaming over this trip ever since
it was first talked about. It wouldn't be fair to him not to have
him go. (*A sudden uneasiness seems to strike him.*) At least, not
if he still feels the same way about it he did when he was talking
to me this evening.   35

MAYO (*with an air of decision*).   Andy's right, Katey. That ends all argyment, you can see that. (*Looking at his big silver watch*) Wonder what's happened to Robert? He's been gone long enough to wheel the widder to home, certain. He can't be out dreamin' at the stars his last night.

5 MRS. MAYO (*a bit reproachfully*). Why didn't you wheel Mrs. Atkins back tonight, Andy? You usually do when she and Ruth come over.

ANDREW (*avoiding her eyes*). I thought maybe Robert wanted to tonight. He offered to go right away when they were
10 leaving.

MRS. MAYO. He only wanted to be polite.

ANDREW (*gets to his feet*). Well, he'll be right back, I guess. (*He turns to his father.*) Guess I'll go take a look at the black cow, Pa—see if she's ailing any.

15 MAYO. Yes—better had, son.

ANDREW *goes into the kitchen on the right.*

SCOTT (*as he goes out—in a low tone*). There's the boy that would make a good, strong sea-farin' man—if he'd a mind to.

MAYO (*sharply*). Don't you put no such fool notions in Andy's
20 head, Dick—or you 'n' me's goin' to fall out. (*Then he smiles*) You couldn't tempt him, no ways. Andy's a Mayo bred in the bone, and he's a born farmer, and a damn good one, too. He'll live and die right here on this farm, like I expect to. (*With proud confidence*) And he'll make this one of the slickest, best-
25 payin' farms in the state, too, afore he gits through!

SCOTT. Seems to me it's a pretty slick place right now.

MAYO (*shaking his head*). It's too small. We need more land to make it amount to much, and we ain't got the capital to buy it.

ANDREW *enters from the kitchen. His hat is on, and he carries*
30 *a lighted lantern in his hand. He goes to the door in the rear leading out.*

ANDREW (*opens the door and pauses*). Anything else you can think of to be done, Pa?

MAYO. No, nothin' I know of.

35 ANDREW *goes out, shutting the door.*

MRS. MAYO (*after a pause*). What's come over Andy tonight, I
wonder? He acts so strange.

MAYO. He does seem sort o' glum and out of sorts. It's 'count o'
Robert leavin', I s'pose. (*To* SCOTT) Dick, you wouldn't believe
how them boys o' mine sticks together. They ain't like most   5
brothers. They've been thick as thieves all their lives, with nary
a quarrel I kin remember.

SCOTT. No need to tell me that. I can see how they take to each
other.

MRS. MAYO (*pursuing her train of thought*). Did you notice,   10
James, how queer everyone was at supper? Robert seemed
stirred up about something; and Ruth was so flustered and gig-
gly; and Andy sat there dumb, looking as if he'd lost his best
friend; and all of them only nibbled at their food.

MAYO. Guess they was all thinkin' about tomorrow, same as us.   15

MRS. MAYO (*shaking her head*). No. I'm afraid somethin's happened—somethin' else.

MAYO. You mean—'bout Ruth?

MRS. MAYO. Yes.

MAYO (*after a pause—frowning*). I hope her and Andy ain't had 20
a serious fallin'-out. I always sorter hoped they'd hitch up together sooner or later. What d'you say, Dick? Don't you think
them two'd pair up well?

SCOTT (*nodding his head approvingly*). A sweet, wholesome
couple they'd make.   25

MAYO. It'd be a good thing for Andy in more ways than one. I
ain't what you'd call calculatin' generally, and I b'lieve in lettin'
young folks run their affairs to suit themselves; but there's ad-
vantages for both o' them in this match you can't overlook in
reason. The Atkins farm is right next to ourn. Jined together   30
they'd make a jim-dandy of a place, with plenty o' room to
work in. And bein' a widder with only a daughter, and laid up
all the time to boot, Mrs. Atkins can't do nothin' with the place
as it ought to be done. She needs a man, a first-class farmer, to
take hold o' things; and Andy's just the one.   35

MRS. MAYO (*abruptly*). I don't think Ruth loves Andy.

MAYO. You don't? Well, maybe a woman's eyes is sharper in such things, but—they're always together. And if she don't love him now, she'll likely come around to it in time. (*As* MRS. MAYO *shakes her head*) You seem mighty fixed in your opinion, Katey. How d'you know?

MRS. MAYO. It's just—what I feel.

MAYO (*a light breaking over him*). You don't mean to say— (MRS. MAYO *nods.* MAYO *chuckles scornfully.*) Shucks! I'm losin' my respect for your eyesight, Katey. Why, Robert ain't got no time for Ruth, 'cept as a friend!

MRS. MAYO (*warningly*). Sss-h-h!

The door from the yard opens, and ROBERT *enters. He is smiling happily, and humming a song to himself, but as he comes into the room an undercurrent of nervous uneasiness manifests itself in his bearing.*

MAYO. So here you be at last! (ROBERT *comes forward and sits on* ANDY's *chair.* MAYO *smiles slyly at his wife.*) What have you been doin' all this time—countin' the stars to see if they all come out right and proper?

ROBERT. There's only one I'll ever look for any more, Pa.

MAYO (*reproachfully*). You might've even not wasted time lookin' for that one—your last night.

MRS. MAYO (*as if she were speaking to a child*). You ought to have worn your coat a sharp night like this, Robbie.

SCOTT (*disgustedly*). God A'mighty, Kate, you treat Robert as if he was one year old!

MRS. MAYO (*notices* ROBERT's *nervous uneasiness*). You look all worked up over something, Robbie. What is it?

ROBERT (*swallowing hard, looks quickly from one to the other of them—then begins determinedly*). Yes, there *is* something— something I must tell you—all of you. (*As he begins to talk* ANDREW *enters quietly from the rear, closing the door behind him, and setting the lighted lantern on the floor. He remains standing by the door, his arms folded, listening to* ROBERT *with a repressed expression of pain on his face.* ROBERT *is so much*

taken up with what he is going to say that he does not notice
ANDREW'S *presence.*) Something I discovered only this evening
—very beautiful and wonderful—something I did not take into
consideration previously because I hadn't dared to hope that
such happiness could ever come to me. (*Appealingly*) You must   5
all remember that fact, won't you?

MAYO (*frowning*). Let's get to the point, son.

ROBERT (*with a trace of defiance*). Well, the point is this, Pa:
I'm not going—I mean—I can't go tomorrow with Uncle Dick
—or at any future time, either.   10

MRS. MAYO (*with a sharp sigh of joyful relief*). Oh, Robbie, I'm
so glad!

MAYO (*astounded*). You ain't serious, be you, Robert? (*Severely*) Seems to me it's a pretty late hour in the day for you to
be upsettin' all your plans so sudden!   15

ROBERT. I asked you to remember that until this evening I didn't
know myself. I had never dared to dream——

MAYO (*irritably*). What is this foolishness you're talkin' of?

ROBERT (*flushing*). Ruth told me this evening that—she loved
me. It was after I'd confessed I loved her. I told her I hadn't   20
been conscious of my love until after the trip had been arranged, and I realized it would mean—leaving her. That was the
truth. I *didn't* know until then. (*As if justifying himself to the
others*) I hadn't intended telling her anything but—suddenly—I
felt I must. I didn't think it would matter, because I was going   25
away. And I thought she loved—someone else. (*Slowly—his
eyes shining*) And then she cried and said it was I she'd loved all
the time, but I hadn't seen it.

MRS. MAYO (*rushes over and throws her arms about him*). I
knew it! I was just telling your father when you came in—and,   30
oh, Robbie, I'm so happy you're not going!

ROBERT (*kissing her*). I knew you'd be glad, Ma.

MAYO (*bewilderedly*). Well, I'll be damned! You do beat all for
gettin' folks' minds all tangled up, Robert. And Ruth too!
Whatever got into her of a sudden? Why, I was thinkin'——   35

MRS. MAYO (*hurriedly—in a tone of warning*). Never mind

what you were thinking, James. It wouldn't be any use telling
us that now. (*Meaningly*) And what you were hoping for turns
out just the same almost, doesn't it?

MAYO (*thoughtfully—beginning to see this side of the argument*).
Yes; I suppose you're right, Katey. (*Scratching his head in puz-
zlement*) But how it ever come about! It do beat anything ever
I heard. (*Finally he gets up with a sheepish grin and walks over
to* ROBERT.) We're glad you ain't goin', your Ma and I, for we'd
have missed you terrible, that's certain and sure; and we're glad
you've found happiness. Ruth's a fine girl and'll make a good
wife to you.

ROBERT (*much moved*).   Thank you, Pa. (*He grips his father's
hand in his.*)

ANDREW (*his face tense and drawn comes forward and holds out
his hand, forcing a smile*).   I guess it's my turn to offer con-
gratulations, isn't it?

ROBERT (*with a startled cry when his brother appears before him
so suddenly*).   Andy! (*Confused*) Why—I—I didn't see you.
Were you here when——

ANDREW.   I heard everything you said; and here's wishing you
every happiness, you and Ruth. You both deserve the best
there is.

ROBERT (*taking his hand*).   Thanks, Andy, it's fine of you to——
(*His voice dies away as he sees the pain in* ANDREW's *eyes.*)

ANDREW (*giving his brother's hand a final grip*).   Good luck to
you both!
      *He turns away and goes back to the rear where he bends over
      the lantern, fumbling with it to hide his emotion from the
      others.*

MRS. MAYO (*to the* CAPTAIN, *who has been too flabbergasted by*
ROBERT's *decision to say a word*).   What's the matter, Dick?
Aren't you going to congratulate Robbie?

SCOTT (*embarrassed*).   Of course I be! (*He gets to his feet and
shakes* ROBERT's *hand, muttering a vague*) Luck to you, boy.
      He stands beside ROBERT *as if he wanted to say something
      more but doesn't know how to go about it.*

ROBERT. Thanks, Uncle Dick.

SCOTT. So you're not acomin' on the *Sunda* with me? (*His voice indicates disbelief.*)

ROBERT. I can't, Uncle—not now. I wouldn't miss it for anything else in the world under any other circumstances. (*He sighs unconsciously.*) But you see I've found—a bigger dream. (*Then with joyous high spirits*) I want you all to understand one thing—I'm not going to be a loafer on your hands any longer. This means the beginning of a new life for me in every way. I'm going to settle right down and take a real interest in the farm, and do my share. I'll prove to you, Pa, that I'm as good a Mayo as you are—or Andy, when I want to be.

MAYO (*kindly but skeptically*). That's the right spirit, Robert. Ain't none of us doubts your willin'ness, but you ain't never learned——

ROBERT. Then I'm going to start learning right away, and you'll teach me, won't you?

MAYO (*mollifyingly*). Of course I will, boy, and be glad to, only you'd best go easy at first.

SCOTT (*who has listened to this conversation in mingled consternation and amazement*). You don't mean to tell me you're goin' to let him stay, do you, James?

MAYO. Why, things bein' as they be, Robert's free to do as he's a mind to.

MRS. MAYO. *Let him!* The very idea!

SCOTT (*more and more ruffled*). Then all I got to say is, you're a soft, weak-willed critter to be permittin' a boy—and women, too—to be layin' your course for you wherever they damn pleases.

MAYO (*slyly amused*). It's just the same with me as 'twas with you, Dick. You can't order the tides on the seas to suit you, and I ain't pretendin' I can reg'late love for young folks.

SCOTT (*scornfully*). Love! They ain't old enough to know love when they sight it! Love! I'm ashamed of you, Robert, to go lettin' a little huggin' and kissin' in the dark spile your chances to make a man out o' yourself. It ain't common sense—no siree, it ain't—not by a hell of a sight!

He pounds the table with his fists in exasperation.

MRS. MAYO (*laughing provokingly at her brother*). A fine one you are to be talking about love, Dick—an old cranky bachelor like you. Goodness sakes!

SCOTT (*exasperated by their joking*). I've never been a damn fool like most, if that's what you're steerin' at.

MRS. MAYO (*tauntingly*). Sour grapes, aren't they, Dick? (*She laughs. ROBERT and his father chuckle. SCOTT sputters with annoyance.*) Good gracious, Dick, you do act silly, flying into a temper over nothing.

SCOTT (*indignantly*). Nothin'! You talk as if I wasn't concerned nohow in this here business. Seems to me I've got a right to have my say. Ain't I made all arrangements with the owners and stocked up with some special grub all on Robert's account?

ROBERT. You've been fine, Uncle Dick; and I appreciate it. Truly.

MAYO. 'Course; we all does, Dick.

SCOTT (*unplacated*). I've been countin' sure on havin' Robert for company on this vige—to sorta talk to and show things to, and teach, kinda, and I got my mind so set on havin' him I'm goin' to be double lonesome this vige. (*He pounds on the table, attempting to cover up this confession of weakness.*) Darn all this silly lovin' business, anyway. (*Irritably*) But all this talk ain't tellin' me what I'm to do with that sta'b'd cabin I fixed up. It's all painted white, an' a bran new mattress on the bunk, 'n' new sheets 'n' blankets 'n' things. And Chips built in a bookcase so's Robert could take his books along—with a slidin' bar fixed across't it, mind, so's they couldn't fall out no matter how she rolled. (*With excited consternation*) What d'you suppose my officers is goin' to think when there's no one comes aboard to occupy that sta'b'd cabin? And the men what did the work on it—what'll *they* think? (*He shakes his finger indignantly.*) They're liable as not to suspicion it was a *woman* I'd planned to ship along, and that she gave me the go-by at the last moment! (*He wipes his perspiring brow in anguish at this thought.*) Gawd A'mighty! They're only lookin' to have the laugh on me for something like that. They're liable to b'lieve anything, those fellers is!

MAYO (*with a wink*). Then there's nothing to it but for you to get right out and hunt up a wife somewheres for that spick 'n' span cabin. She'll have to be a pretty one, too, to match it. (*He looks at his watch with exaggerated concern.*) You ain't got much time to find her, Dick.

SCOTT (*as the others smile—sulkily*). You kin go to thunder, Jim Mayo!

ANDREW (*comes forward from where he has been standing by the door, rear, brooding. His face is set in a look of grim determination*). You needn't worry about that spare cabin, Uncle Dick, if you've a mind to take me in Robert's place.

ROBERT (*turning to him quickly*). Andy! (*He sees at once the fixed resolve in his brother's eyes, and realizes immediately the reason for it—in consternation*) Andy, you mustn't!

ANDREW. You've made your decision, Rob, and now I've made mine. You're out of this, remember.

ROBERT (*hurt by his brother's tone*). But Andy——

ANDREW. Don't interfere, Rob—that's all I ask. (*Turning to his uncle*) You haven't answered my question, Uncle Dick.

SCOTT (*clearing his throat, with an uneasy side glance at* JAMES MAYO *who is staring at his elder son as if he thought he had suddenly gone mad*). O' course, I'd be glad to have you, Andy.

ANDREW. It's settled then. I can pack the little I want to take in a few minutes.

MRS. MAYO. Don't be a fool, Dick. Andy's only joking you.

SCOTT (*disgruntledly*). It's hard to tell who's jokin' and who's not in this house.

ANDREW (*firmly*). I'm not joking, Uncle Dick. (*As* SCOTT *looks at him uncertainly*) You needn't be afraid I'll go back on my word.

ROBERT (*hurt by the insinuation he feels in* ANDREW's *tone*). Andy! That isn't fair!

MAYO (*frowning*). Seems to me this ain't no subject to joke over —not for Andy.

ANDREW (*facing his father*). I agree with you, Pa, and I tell you again, once and for all, that I've made up my mind to go.

MAYO (*dumbfounded—unable to doubt the determination in* ANDREW's *voice—helplessly*). But why, son? Why?

5   ANDREW (*evasively*). I've always wanted to go.

ROBERT. Andy!

ANDREW (*half angrily*). You shut up, Rob! (*Turning to his father again*) I didn't ever mention it because as long as Rob was going I knew it was no use; but now Rob's staying on here,

10   there isn't any reason for me not to go.

MAYO (*breathing hard*). No reason? Can you stand there and say that to me, Andrew?

MRS. MAYO (*hastily—seeing the gathering storm*). He doesn't mean a word of it, James.

15   MAYO (*making a gesture to her to keep silence*). Let me talk, Katey. (*In a more kindly tone*) What's come over you so sudden, Andy? You know's well as I do that it wouldn't be fair o' you to run off at a moment's notice right now when we're up to our necks in hard work.

20   ANDREW (*avoiding his eyes*). Rob'll hold his end up as soon as he learns.

MAYO. Robert was never cut out for a farmer, and you was.

ANDREW. You can easily get a man to do my work.

MAYO (*restraining his anger with an effort*). It sounds strange

25   to hear you, Andy, that I always thought had good sense, talkin' crazy like that. (*Scornfully*) Get a man to take your place! You ain't been workin' here for no hire, Andy, that you kin give me your notice to quit like you've done. The farm is your'n as well as mine. You've always worked on it with that under-

30   standing; and what you're sayin' you intend doin' is just skulkin' out o' your rightful responsibility.

ANDREW (*looking at the floor—simply*). I'm sorry, Pa. (*After a slight pause*) It's no use talking any more about it.

MRS. MAYO (*in relief*). There! I knew Andy'd come to his

35   senses!

ANDREW. Don't get the wrong idea, Ma. I'm not backing out.

Mayo. You mean you're goin' in spite of—everythin'?

Andrew. Yes. I'm going. I've got to. (*He looks at his father defiantly*) I feel I oughtn't to miss this chance to go out into the world and see things, and—I want to go.

Mayo (*with bitter scorn*). So—you want to go out into the world and see thin's! (*His voice raised and quivering with anger*) I never thought I'd live to see the day when a son o' mine'd look me in the face and tell a bare-faced lie! (*Bursting out*) You're a liar, Andy Mayo, and a mean one to boot!

Mrs. Mayo. James!

Robert. Pa!

Scott. Steady there, Jim!

Mayo (*waving their protests aside*). He is and he knows it.

Andrew (*his face flushed*). I won't argue with you, Pa. You can think as badly of me as you like.

Mayo (*shaking his finger at* Andy, *in a cold rage*). You know I'm speakin' truth—that's why you're afraid to argy! You lie when you say you want to go 'way—and see thin's! You ain't got no likin' in the world to go. I've watched you grow up, and I know your ways, and they're my ways. You're runnin' against your own nature, and you're goin' to be a'mighty sorry for it if you do. 'S if I didn't know your real reason for runnin' away! And runnin' away's the only words to fit it. You're runnin' away 'cause you're put out and riled 'cause your own brother's got Ruth 'stead o' you, and——

Andrew (*his face crimson—tensely*). Stop, Pa! I won't stand hearing that—not even from you!

Mrs. Mayo (*rushing to* Andy *and putting her arms about him protectingly*). Don't mind him, Andy dear. He don't mean a word he's saying!

    Robert *stands rigidly, his hands clenched, his face contracted by pain.* Scott *sits dumbfounded and open-mouthed.* Andrew *soothes his mother who is on the verge of tears.*

Mayo (*in angry triumph*). It's the truth, Andy Mayo! And you ought to be bowed in shame to think of it!

Robert (*protestingly*). Pa!

MRS. MAYO (*coming from* ANDREW *to his father; puts her hands on his shoulders as though to try and push him back in the chair from which he has risen*). Won't you be still, James? Please won't you?

5 MAYO (*looking at* ANDREW *over his wife's shoulder—stubbornly*). The truth—God's truth!

MRS. MAYO. Sh-h-h! (*She tries to put a finger across his lips, but he twists his head away.*)

ANDREW (*who has regained control over himself*). You're wrong,
10 Pa, it isn't truth. (*With defiant assertiveness*) I don't love Ruth. I never loved her, and the thought of such a thing never entered my head.

MAYO (*with an angry snort of disbelief*). Hump! You're pilin' lie on lie!

15 ANDREW (*losing his temper—bitterly*). I suppose it'd be hard for you to explain anyone's wanting to leave this blessed farm except for some outside reason like that. But I'm sick and tired of it—whether you want to believe me or not—and that's why I'm glad to get a chance to move on.

20 ROBERT. Andy! Don't! You're only making it worse.

ANDREW (*sulkily*). I don't care. I've done my share of work here. I've earned my right to quit when I want to. (*Suddenly overcome with anger and grief; with rising intensity*) I'm sick and tired of the whole damn business. I hate the farm and every
25 inch of ground in it. I'm sick of digging in the dirt and sweating in the sun like a slave without getting a word of thanks for it. (*Tears of rage starting to his eyes—hoarsely*) I'm through, through for good and all; and if Uncle Dick won't take me on his ship, I'll find another. I'll get away somewhere, somehow.

30 MRS. MAYO (*in a frightened voice*). Don't you answer him, James. He doesn't know what he's saying. Don't say a word to him 'til he's in his right senses again. Please James, don't——

MAYO (*pushes her away from him; his face is drawn and pale with the violence of his passion. He glares at* ANDREW *as if he hated*
35 *him*). You dare to—you dare to speak like that to me? You talk like that 'bout this farm—the Mayo farm—where you was

born—you—you—— (*He clenches his fist above his head and advances threateningly on* ANDREW) You damned whelp!

MRS. MAYO (*with a shriek*). James!
> *She covers her face with her hands and sinks weakly into* MAYO's *chair.* ANDREW *remains standing motionless, his face pale and set.*

SCOTT (*starting to his feet and stretching his arms across the table toward* MAYO). Easy there, Jim!

ROBERT (*throwing himself between father and brother*). Stop! Are you mad?

MAYO (*grabs* ROBERT's *arm and pushes him aside—then stands for a moment gasping for breath before* ANDREW. *He points to the door with a shaking finger*). Yes—go!—go!—You're no son o' mine—no son o' mine! You can go to hell if you want to! Don't let me find you here—in the mornin'—or—or—I'll *throw* you out!

ROBERT. Pa! For God's sake! (MRS. MAYO *bursts into noisy sobbing.*)

MAYO. (*He gulps convulsively and glares at* ANDREW.) You go —tomorrow mornin'—and by God—don't come back—don't dare come back—by God, not while I'm livin'—or I'll—I'll——
> *He shakes over his muttered threat and strides toward the door rear, right.*

MRS. MAYO (*rising and throwing her arms around him—hysterically*). James! James! Where are you going?

MAYO (*incoherently*). I'm goin'—to bed, Katey. It's late, Katey —it's late. (*He goes out.*)

MRS. MAYO (*following him, pleading hysterically*). James! Take back what you've said to Andy. James!
> *She follows him out.* ROBERT *and the* CAPTAIN *stare after them with horrified eyes.* ANDREW *stands rigidly looking straight in front of him, his fists clenched at his sides.*

SCOTT (*the first to find his voice—with an explosive sigh*). Well, if he ain't the devil himself when he's roused! You oughtn't to have talked to him that way, Andy, 'bout the damn farm, knowin' how touchy he is about it. (*With another sigh*) Well, you won't mind what he's said in anger. He'll be sorry for it when he's calmed down a bit.

ANDREW (*in a dead voice*). You don't know him. (*Defiantly*) What's said is said and can't be unsaid; and I've chosen.

5 ROBERT (*with violent protest*). Andy! You can't go! This is all so stupid—and terrible!

ANDREW (*coldly*). I'll talk to you in a minute, Rob.

Crushed by his brother's attitude ROBERT *sinks down into a chair, holding his head in his hands.*

10 SCOTT (*comes and slaps* ANDREW *on the back*). I'm damned glad you're shippin' on, Andy. I like your spirit, and the way you spoke up to him. (*Lowering his voice to a cautious whisper*) The sea's the place for a young feller like you that isn't half dead 'n' alive. (*He gives* ANDY *a final approving slap.*) You 'n'

15 me'll get along like twins, see if we don't. I'm goin' aloft to turn in. Don't forget to pack your dunnage. And git some sleep, if you kin. We'll want to sneak out extra early b'fore they're up. It'll do away with more argyments. Robert can drive us down to the town, and bring back the team. (*He goes*

20 *to the door in the rear, left.*) Well, good night.

ANDREW. Good night. (SCOTT *goes out. The two brothers remain silent for a moment. Then* ANDREW *comes over to his brother and puts a hand on his back. He speaks in a low voice, full of feeling.*) Buck up, Rob. It ain't any use crying over spilt

25 milk; and it'll all turn out for the best—let's hope. It couldn't be helped—what's happened.

ROBERT (*wildly*). But it's a lie, Andy, a lie!

ANDREW. Of course it's a lie. You know it and I know it,—but that's all ought to know it.

30 ROBERT. Pa'll never forgive you. Oh, the whole affair is so senseless—and tragic. Why did you think you must go away?

ANDREW. You know better than to ask that. You know why. (*Fiercely*) I can wish you and Ruth all the good luck in the world, and I do, and I mean it; but you can't expect me to stay

35 around here and watch you two together, day after day—and me alone. I couldn't stand it—not after all the plans I'd made to

happen on this place thinking—— (*his voice breaks*) thinking
she cared for me.

ROBERT (*putting a hand on his brother's arm*).   God! It's horrible!
I feel so guilty—to think that I should be the cause of your
suffering, after we've been such pals all our lives. If I could have   5
foreseen what'd happen, I swear to you I'd have never said a
word to Ruth. I swear I wouldn't have, Andy!

ANDREW.   I know you wouldn't; and that would've been worse,
for Ruth would've suffered then. (*He pats his brother's shoulder.*) It's best as it is. It had to be, and I've got to stand the gaff,   10
that's all. Pa'll see how I felt—after a time. (*As* ROBERT *shakes
his head*)—and if he don't—well, it can't be helped.

ROBERT.   But think of Ma! God, Andy, you can't go! You can't!

ANDREW (*fiercely*).   I've got to go—to get away! I've got to, I
tell you. I'd go crazy here, bein' reminded every second of the   15
day what a fool I'd made of myself. I've got to get away and try
and forget, if I can. And I'd hate the farm if I stayed, hate it for
bringin' things back. I couldn't take interest in the work any
more, work with no purpose in sight. Can't you see what a hell
it'd be? You love her too, Rob. Put yourself in my place, and   20
remember I haven't stopped loving her, and couldn't if I was
to stay. Would that be fair to you or to her? Put yourself in my
place. (*He shakes his brother fiercely by the shoulder.*) What'd
you do then? Tell me the truth! You love her. What'd you do?

ROBERT (*Chokingly*).   I'd—I'd go, Andy! (*He buries his face in*   25
his hands with a shuddering sob.) God!

ANDREW (*seeming to relax suddenly all over his body—in a low,
steady voice*).   Then you know why I got to go; and there's
nothing more to be said.

ROBERT (*in a frenzy of rebellion*).   Why did this have to happen   30
to us? It's damnable! (*He looks about him wildly, as if his
vengeance were seeking the responsible fate.*)

ANDREW (*soothingly—again putting his hands on his brother's
shoulder*).   It's no use fussing any more, Rob. It's done. (*Forcing a smile*) I guess Ruth's got a right to have who she likes.   35
She made a good choice—and God bless her for it!

ROBERT. Andy! Oh, I wish I could tell you half I feel of how fine you are!

ANDREW (*interrupting him quickly*) Shut up! Let's go to bed. I've got to be up long before sun-up. You, too, if you're going to drive us down.

ROBERT. Yes. Yes.

ANDREW (*turning down the lamp*). And I've got to pack yet. (*He yawns with utter weariness.*) I'm as tired as if I'd been plowing twenty-four hours at a stretch. (*Dully*) I feel—dead. (ROBERT *covers his face again with his hands.* ANDREW *shakes his head as if to get rid of his thoughts, and continues with a poor attempt at cheery briskness.*) I'm going to douse the light. Come on. (*He slaps his brother on the back.* ROBERT *does not move.* ANDREW *bends over and blows out the lamp. His voice comes from the darkness*) Don't sit there mourning, Rob. It'll all come out in the wash. Come on and get some sleep. Everything'll turn out all right in the end.

> ROBERT *can be heard stumbling to his feet, and the dark figures of the two brothers can be seen groping their way toward the doorway in the rear as*
>
> > *The Curtain Falls*

ACT TWO

SCENE ONE

Same as Act One, Scene Two. Sitting room of the farm house about half past twelve in the afternoon of a hot, sun-baked day in mid-summer, three years later. All the windows are open, but no breeze stirs the soiled white curtains. A patched screen door is in the rear. Through it the yard can be seen, its small stretch of lawn divided by the dirt path leading to the door from the gate in the white picket fence which borders the road.

The room has changed, not so much in its outward appearance as in its general atmosphere. Little significant details give evidence of carelessness, of inefficiency, of an industry gone to seed. The chairs appear shabby from lack of paint; the table cover is spotted and askew; holes show in the curtains; a child's doll, with one arm gone, lies under the table; a hoe stands in a corner; a man's coat is flung on the couch in the rear; the desk is cluttered up with odds and ends; a number of books are piled carelessly on the sideboard. The noon enervation of the sultry, scorching day seems to have penetrated indoors, causing even inanimate objects to wear an aspect of despondent exhaustion. A place is set at the end of the table, left, for someone's dinner. Through the open door to the kitchen comes the clatter of dishes being washed, interrupted at intervals by a woman's irritated voice and the peevish whining of a child.

At the rise of the curtain MRS. MAYO *and* MRS. ATKINS *are discovered sitting facing each other,* MRS. MAYO *to the rear,* MRS. ATKINS *to the right of the table.* MRS. MAYO'*s face has lost all character, disintegrated, become a weak mask wearing a helpless, doleful expression of being constantly on the verge of comfortless tears. She speaks in an uncertain voice, without assertiveness, as if all power of willing had deserted her.* MRS. ATKINS *is in her wheel chair. She is a thin, pale-faced, unintelligent looking woman of about forty-eight, with hard, bright eyes. A victim of partial paralysis for many years, condemned to be pushed from day to day of her life in a wheel chair, she has developed the selfish, irritable nature of the chronic invalid. Both women are dressed in black.* MRS. ATKINS *knits nervously as she talks. A ball of unused yarn, with needles stuck through it, lies on the table before* MRS. MAYO.

MRS. ATKINS (*with a disapproving glance at the place set on the table*).   Robert's late for his dinner again, as usual. I don't see why Ruth puts up with it, and I've told her so. Many's the time I've said to her "It's about time you put a stop to his nonsense. Does he suppose you're runnin' a hotel—with no one to help with things?" But she don't pay no attention. She's as bad as he is, a'most—thinks she knows better than an old, sick body like me.

Mrs. Mayo (*dully*).   Robbie's always late for things. He can't
help it, Sarah.

Mrs. Atkins (*with a snort*).   Can't help it! How you do go on,
Kate, findin' excuses for him! Anybody can help anything
5   they've a mind to—as long as they've got health, and ain't
rendered helpless like me—(*she adds as a pious afterthought*)—
through the will of God.

Mrs. Mayo.   Robbie can't.

Mrs. Atkins.   Can't! It do make me mad, Kate Mayo, to see folks
10   that God gave all the use of their limbs to potterin' round and
wastin' time doin' everything the wrong way—and me power-
less to help and at their mercy, you might say. And it ain't that
I haven't pointed the right way to 'em. I've talked to Robert
thousands of times and told him how things ought to be done.
15   You know that, Kate Mayo. But d'you s'pose he takes any notice of what I say? Or Ruth, either—my own daughter? No,
they think I'm a crazy, cranky old woman, half dead a'ready,
and the sooner I'm in the grave and out o' their way the better
it'd suit them.

20   Mrs. Mayo.   You mustn't talk that way, Sarah. They're not as
wicked as that. And you've got years and years before you.

Mrs. Atkins.   You're like the rest, Kate. You don't know how
near the end I am. Well, at least I can go to my eternal rest with
a clear conscience. I've done all a body could do to avert ruin
25   from this house. On their heads be it!

Mrs. Mayo (*with hopeless indifference*).   Things might be
worse. Robert never had any experience in farming. You can't
expect him to learn in a day.

Mrs. Atkins (*snappily*).   He's had three years to learn, and he's
30   gettin' worse 'stead of better. Not on'y your place but mine
too is driftin' to rack and ruin, and I can't do nothin' to prevent.

Mrs. Mayo (*with a spark of assertiveness*).   You can't say but
Robbie works hard, Sarah.

Mrs. Atkins.   What good's workin' hard if it don't accomplish
35   anythin', I'd like to know?

Mrs. Mayo.   Robbie's had bad luck against him.

MRS. ATKINS.   Say what you've a mind to, Kate, the proof of the
puddin's in the eatin'; and you can't deny that things have been
goin' from bad to worse ever since your husband died two years
back.

MRS. MAYO (*wiping tears from her eyes with her handkerchief*).   5
It was God's will that he should be taken.

MRS. ATKINS (*triumphantly*).   It was God's punishment on James
Mayo for the blasphemin' and denyin' of God he done all his
sinful life! (MRS. MAYO *begins to weep softly*.) There, Kate, I
shouldn't be remindin' you, I know. He's at peace, poor man,   10
and forgiven, let's pray.

MRS. MAYO (*wiping her eyes—simply*).   James was a good man.

MRS. ATKINS (*ignoring this remark*).   What I was sayin' was
that since Robert's been in charge things've been goin' down
hill steady. You don't know *how* bad they are. Robert don't   15
let on to you what's happenin'; and you'd never see it yourself
if 'twas under your nose. But, thank the Lord, Ruth still comes
to me once in a while for advice when she's worried near out of
her senses by his goin's-on. Do you know what she told me last
night? But I forgot, she said not to tell you—still I think you've   20
got a right to know, and it's my duty not to let such things go
on behind your back.

MRS. MAYO (*wearily*).   You can tell me if you want to.

MRS. ATKINS (*bending over toward her—in a low voice*).   Ruth
was almost crazy about it. Robert told her he'd have to mort-   25
gage the farm—said he didn't know how he'd pull through 'til
harvest without it, and he can't get money any other way. (*She
straightens up—indignantly*) Now what do you think of your
Robert?

MRS. MAYO (*resignedly*).   If it has to be——   30

MRS. ATKINS.   You don't mean to say you're goin' to sign away
your farm, Kate Mayo—after me warnin' you?

MRS. MAYO.   —I'll do what Robbie says is needful.

MRS. ATKINS (*holding up her hands*).   Well, of all the foolishness!—well, it's your farm, not mine, and I've nothin' more to   35
say.

MRS. MAYO.   Maybe Robbie'll manage till Andy gets back and
sees to things. It can't be long now.

MRS. ATKINS (*with keen interest*).   Ruth says Andy ought to
turn up any day. When does Robert figger he'll get here?

5   MRS. MAYO.   He says he can't calculate exactly on account o' the
Sunda being a sail boat. Last letter he got was from England,
the day they were sailing for home. That was over a month ago,
and Robbie thinks they're overdue now.

MRS. ATKINS.   We can give praise to God then that he'll be back
10   in the nick o' time. He ought to be tired of travelin' and anxious
to get home and settle down to work again.

MRS. MAYO.   Andy *has* been working. He's head officer on Dick's
boat, he wrote Robbie. You know that.

MRS. ATKINS.   That foolin' on ships is all right for a spell, but he
15   must be right sick of it by this.

MRS. MAYO (*musingly*).   I wonder if he's changed much. He
used to be so fine-looking and strong. (*With a sigh*) Three
years! It seems more like three hundred. (*Her eyes filling—
piteously*) Oh, if James could only have lived 'til he came back
20   —and forgiven him!

MRS. ATKINS.   He never would have—not James Mayo! Didn't
he keep his heart hardened against him till the last in spite of all
you and Robert did to soften him?

MRS. MAYO (*with a feeble flash of anger*).   Don't you dare say
25   that! (*Brokenly*) Oh, I know deep down in his heart he forgave
Andy, though he was too stubborn ever to own up to it. It was
that brought on his death—breaking his heart just on account
of his stubborn pride. (*She wipes her eyes with her handkerchief and sobs.*)

30   MRS. ATKINS (*piously*).   It was the will of God. (*The whining
crying of the child sounds from the kitchen.* MRS. ATKINS
frowns irritably.) Drat that young one! Seems as if she cries all
the time on purpose to set a body's nerves on edge.

MRS. MAYO (*wiping her eyes*).   It's the heat upsets her. Mary
35   doesn't feel any too well these days, poor little child!

MRS. ATKINS.   She gets it right from her Pa—bein' sickly all the time. You can't deny Robert was always ailin' as a child. (*She sighs heavily.*) It was a crazy mistake for them two to get married. I argyed against it at the time, but Ruth was so spelled with Robert's wild poetry notions she wouldn't listen to sense. Andy was the one would have been the match for her.

MRS. MAYO. I've often thought since it might have been better the other way. But Ruth and Robbie seem happy enough together.

MRS. ATKINS. At any rate it was God's work—and His will be done.

The two women sit in silence for a moment. RUTH *enters from the kitchen, carrying in her arms her two year old daughter,* MARY, *a pretty but sickly and ænemic looking child with a tear-stained face.* RUTH *has aged appreciably. Her face has lost its youth and freshness. There is a trace in her expression of something hard and spiteful. She sits in the rocker in front of the table and sighs wearily. She wears a gingham dress with a soiled apron tied around her waist.*

RUTH. Land sakes, if this isn't a scorcher! That kitchen's like a furnace. Phew! (*She pushes the damp hair back from her forehead.*)

MRS. MAYO. Why didn't you call me to help with the dishes?

RUTH (*shortly*). No. The heat in there'd kill you.

MARY (*sees the doll under the table and struggles on her mother's lap*). Dolly, Mama! Dolly!

RUTH (*pulling her back*). It's time for your nap. You can't play with Dolly now.

MARY (*commencing to cry whiningly*). Dolly!

MRS. ATKINS (*irritably*). Can't you keep that child still? Her racket's enough to split a body's ears. Put her down and let her play with the doll if it'll quiet her.

RUTH (*lifting* MARY *to the floor*). There! I hope you'll be satisfied and keep still. (MARY *sits down on the floor before the table and plays with the doll in silence.* RUTH *glances at the place set on the table.*) It's a wonder Rob wouldn't try to get to meals on time once in a while.

MRS. MAYO (*dully*).   Something must have gone wrong again.

RUTH (*wearily*).   I s'pose so. Something's always going wrong these days, it looks like.

MRS. ATKINS (*snappily*).   It wouldn't if you possessed a bit of
5   spunk. The idea of you permittin' him to come in to meals at all hours—and you doin' the work! I never heard of such a thin'. You're too easy goin', that's the trouble.

RUTH.   Do stop your nagging at me, Ma! I'm sick of hearing you. I'll do as I please about it; and thank you for not interfering.
10   (*She wipes her moist forehead—wearily*) Phew! It's too hot to argue. Let's talk of something pleasant. (*Curiously*) Didn't I hear you speaking about Andy a while ago?

MRS. MAYO.   We were wondering when he'd get home.

RUTH (*brightening*).   Rob says any day now he's liable to drop
15   in and surprise us—him and the Captain. It'll certainly look natural to see him around the farm again.

MRS. ATKINS.   Let's hope the farm'll look more natural, too, when he's had a hand at it. The way thin's are now!

RUTH (*irritably*).   Will you stop harping on that, Ma? We all
20   know things aren't as they might be. What's the good of your complaining all the time?

MRS. ATKINS.   There, Kate Mayo! Ain't that just what I told you? I can't say a word of advice to my own daughter even, she's that stubborn and self-willed.

25 RUTH (*putting her hands over her ears—in exasperation*).   For goodness sakes, Ma!

MRS. MAYO (*dully*).   Never mind. Andy'll fix everything when he comes.

RUTH (*hopefully*).   Oh, yes, I know he will. He always did know
30   just the right thing ought to be done. (*With weary vexation*) It's a shame for him to come home and have to start in with things in such a topsy-turvy.

MRS. MAYO.   Andy'll manage.

RUTH (*sighing*).   I s'pose it isn't Rob's fault things go wrong
35   with him.

MRS. ATKINS (*scornfully*). Hump! (*She fans herself nervously.*)
Land o' Goshen, but it's bakin' in here! Let's go out in under
the trees in back where there's a breath of fresh air. Come, Kate.
(MRS. MAYO *gets up obediently and starts to wheel the invalid's
chair toward the screen door.*) You better come too, Ruth. It'll   5
do you good. Learn him a lesson and let him get his own
dinner. Don't be such a fool.

RUTH (*going and holding the screen door open for them—listlessly*). He wouldn't mind. He doesn't eat much. But I can't
go anyway. I've got to put baby to bed.   10

MRS. ATKINS. Let's go, Kate. I'm boilin' in here.

   MRS. MAYO *wheels her out and off left.* RUTH *comes back and
   sits down in her chair.*

RUTH (*mechanically*). Come and let me take off your shoes and
stockings, Mary, that's a good girl. You've got to take your nap   15
now.

   *The child continues to play as if she hadn't heard, absorbed
   in her doll. An eager expression comes over* RUTH's *tired face.
   She glances toward the door furtively—then gets up and
   goes to the desk. Her movements indicate a guilty fear of*   20
   *discovery. She takes a letter from a pigeonhole and retreats
   swiftly to her chair with it. She opens the envelope and reads
   the letter with great interest, a flush of excitement coming to
   her cheeks.* ROBERT *walks up the path and opens the screen
   door quietly and comes into the room. He, too, has aged. His*   25
   *shoulders are stooped as if under too great a burden. His eyes
   are dull and lifeless, his face burned by the sun and unshaven
   for days. Streaks of sweat have smudged the layer of dust on
   his cheeks. His lips drawn down at the corners, give him a
   hopeless, resigned expression. The three years have accentu-*   30
   *ated the weakness of his mouth and chin. He is dressed in
   overalls, laced boots, and a flannel shirt open at the neck.*

ROBERT (*throwing his hat over on the sofa—with a great sigh of
exhaustion*). Phew! The sun's hot today!

   RUTH *is startled. At first she makes an instinctive motion as if*   35

*to hide the letter in her bosom. She immediately thinks better
of this and sits with the letter in her hands looking at him
with defiant eyes. He bends down and kisses her.*

RUTH (*feeling of her cheek—irritably*). Why don't you shave?
5   You look awful.

ROBERT (*indifferently*). I forgot—and it's too much trouble this
weather.

MARY (*throwing aside her doll, runs to him with a happy cry*).
Dada! Dada!

10 ROBERT (*swinging her up above his head—lovingly*). And how's
this little girl of mine this hot day, eh?

MARY (*screeching happily*). Dada! Dada!

RUTH (*in annoyance*). Don't do that to her! You know it's time
for her nap and you'll get her all waked up; then I'll be the one
15   that'll have to sit beside her till she falls asleep.

ROBERT (*sitting down in the chair on the left of table and cuddling
MARY on his lap*). You needn't bother. I'll put her to bed.

RUTH (*shortly*). You've got to get back to your work, I s'pose.

ROBERT (*with a sigh*). Yes, I was forgetting. (*He glances at the
20   open letter on RUTH's lap.*) Reading Andy's letter again? I
should think you'd know it by heart by this time.

RUTH (*coloring as if she'd been accused of something—defiantly*).
I've got a right to read it, haven't I? He says it's meant for all
of us.

25 ROBERT (*with a trace of irritation*). Right? Don't be so silly.
There's no question of right. I was only saying that you must
know all that's in it after so many readings.

RUTH. Well, I don't. (*She puts the letter on the table and gets
wearily to her feet.*) I s'pose you'll be wanting your dinner
30   now.

ROBERT (*listlessly*). I don't care. I'm not hungry.

RUTH. And here I been keeping it hot for you!

ROBERT (*irritably*). Oh, all right then. Bring it in and I'll try to
eat.

35 RUTH. I've got to get her to bed first. (*She goes to lift MARY off*

his lap.) Come, dear. It's after time and you can hardly keep
your eyes open now.

MARY (*crying*). No, no! (*Appealing to her father*) Dada! No!

RUTH (*accusingly to* ROBERT). There! Now see what you've
done! I told you not to——

ROBERT (*shortly*). Let her alone, then. She's all right where she
is. She'll fall asleep on my lap in a minute if you'll stop bothering her.

RUTH (*hotly*). She'll not do any such thing! She's got to learn
to mind me! (*Shaking her finger at* MARY) You naughty child!
Will you come with Mama when she tells you for your own
good?

MARY (*clinging to her father*). No, Dada!

RUTH (*losing her temper*). A good spanking's what you need,
my young lady—and you'll get one from me if you don't mind
better, d'you hear?

MARY *starts to whimper frightenedly.*

ROBERT (*with sudden anger*). Leave her alone! How often have
I told you not to threaten her with whipping? I won't have it.
(*Soothing the wailing* MARY) There! There, little girl! Baby
mustn't cry. Dada won't like you if you do. Dada'll hold you
and you must promise to go to sleep like a good little girl. Will
you when Dada asks you?

MARY (*cuddling up to him*). Yes, Dada.

RUTH (*looking at them, her pale face set and drawn*). A fine one
you are to be telling folks how to do things! (*She bites her lips.
Husband and wife look into each other's eyes with something
akin to hatred in their expressions; then* RUTH *turns away with
a shrug of affected indifference.*) All right, take care of her then,
if you think it's so easy. (*She walks away into the kitchen.*)

ROBERT (*smoothing* MARY's *hair—tenderly*). We'll show Mama
you're a good little girl, won't we?

MARY (*crooning drowsily*). Dada, Dada.

ROBERT. Let's see: Does your mother take off your shoes and
stockings before your nap?

MARY (*nodding with half-shut eyes*). Yes, Dada.

ROBERT (*taking off her shoes and stockings*). We'll show Mama we know how to do those things, won't we? There's one old shoe off—and there's the other old shoe—and here's one old stocking—and there's the other old stocking. There we are, all nice and cool and comfy. (*He bends down and kisses her.*) And now will you promise to go right to sleep if Dada takes you to bed? (MARY *nods sleepily.*) That's the good little girl.

> *He gathers her up in his arms carefully and carries her into the bedroom. His voice can be heard faintly as he lulls the child to sleep.* RUTH *comes out of the kitchen and gets the plate from the table. She hears the voice from the room and tiptoes to the door to look in. Then she starts for the kitchen but stands for a moment thinking, a look of ill-concealed jealousy on her face. At a noise from inside she hurriedly disappears into the kitchen. A moment later* ROBERT *re-enters. He comes forward and picks up the shoes and stockings which he shoves carelessly under the table. Then, seeing no one about, he goes to the sideboard and selects a book. Coming back to his chair, he sits down and immediately becomes absorbed in reading.* RUTH *returns from the kitchen bringing his plate heaped with food, and a cup of tea. She sets those before him and sits down in her former place.* ROBERT *continues to read, oblivious to the food on the table.*

RUTH (*after watching him irritably for a moment*). For heaven's sakes, put down that old book! Don't you see your dinner's getting cold?

ROBERT (*closing his book*). Excuse me, Ruth. I didn't notice. (*He picks up his knife and fork and begins to eat gingerly, without appetite.*)

RUTH. I should think you might have some feeling for me, Rob, and not always be late for meals. If you think it's fun sweltering in that oven of a kitchen to keep things warm for you, you're mistaken.

ROBERT. I'm sorry, Ruth, really I am. Something crops up every day to delay me. I mean to be here on time.

RUTH (*with a sigh*).   Mean-tos don't count.

ROBERT (*with a conciliating smile*).   Then punish me, Ruth. Let the food get cold and don't bother about me.

RUTH.   I'd have to wait just the same to wash up after you.

ROBERT.   But I can wash up.

RUTH.   A nice mess there'd be then!

ROBERT (*with an attempt at lightness*).   The food is lucky to be able to get cold this weather.

> As RUTH *doesn't answer or smile he opens his book and resumes his reading, forcing himself to take a mouthful of food every now and then.* RUTH *stares at him in annoyance.*

RUTH.   And besides, you've got your own work that's got to be done.

ROBERT (*absent-mindedly, without taking his eyes from the book*).   Yes, of course.

RUTH (*spitefully*).   Work you'll never get done by reading books all the time.

ROBERT (*shutting the book with a snap*).   Why do you persist in nagging at me for getting pleasure out of reading? Is it because—— (*He checks himself abruptly.*)

RUTH (*coloring*).   Because I'm too stupid to understand them, I s'pose you were going to say.

ROBERT (*shame-facedly*).   No—no. (*In exasperation*) Why do you goad me into saying things I don't mean? Haven't I got my share of troubles trying to work this cursed farm without your adding to them? You know how hard I've tried to keep things going in spite of bad luck——

RUTH (*scornfully*).   Bad luck!

ROBERT.   And my own very apparent unfitness for the job, I was going to add; but you can't deny there's been bad luck to it, too. Why don't you take things into consideration? Why can't we pull together? We used to. I know it's hard on you also. Then why can't we help each other instead of hindering?

RUTH (*sullenly*).   I do the best I know how.

ROBERT (*gets up and puts his hand on her shoulder*).   I know you do. But let's both of us try to do better. We can both improve. Say a word of encouragement once in a while when things go wrong, even if it is my fault. You know the odds I've been up against since Pa died. I'm not a farmer. I've never claimed to be one. But there's nothing else I can do under the circumstances, and I've got to pull things through somehow. With your help, I can do it. With you against me—— (*He shrugs his shoulders. There is a pause. Then he bends down and kisses her hair—with an attempt at cheerfulness.*) So you promise that; and I'll promise to be here when the clock strikes —and anything else you tell me to. Is it a bargain?

RUTH (*dully*)   I s'pose so. (*They are interrupted by the sound of a loud knock at the kitchen door.*) There's someone at the kitchen door. (*She hurries out. A moment later she reappears.*) It's Ben.

ROBERT (*frowning*).   What's the trouble now, I wonder? (*In a loud voice*) Come on in here, Ben. (BEN *slouches in from the kitchen. He is a hulking, awkward young fellow with a heavy, stupid face and shifty, cunning eyes. He is dressed in overalls, boots, etc., and wears a broad-brimmed hat of coarse straw pushed back on his head.*) Well, Ben, what's the matter?

BEN (*drawlingly*).   The mowin' machine's bust.

ROBERT.   Why, that can't be. The man fixed it only last week.

BEN.   It's bust just the same.

ROBERT.   And can't you fix it?

BEN.   No. Don't know what's the matter with the goll-darned thing. 'Twon't work, anyhow.

ROBERT (*getting up and going for his hat*).   Wait a minute and I'll go look it over. There can't be much the matter with it.

BEN (*impudently*).   Don't make no diff'rence t' me whether there be or not. I'm quittin'.

ROBERT (*anxiously*).   You don't mean you're throwing up your job here?

BEN.   That's what! My month's up today and I want what's owin' t' me.

ROBERT.   But why are you quitting now, Ben, when you know

I've so much work on hand? I'll have a hard time getting another man at such short notice.

BEN.   That's for you to figger. I'm quittin'.

ROBERT.   But what's your reason? You haven't any complaint to
make about the way you've been treated, have you?   5

BEN.   No. 'Tain't that. (*Shaking his finger*) Look-a-here. I'm
sick o' being made fun at, that's what; an' I got a job up to
Timms' place; an' I'm quittin' here.

ROBERT.   Being made fun of? I don't understand you. Who's
making fun of you?   10

BEN.   They all do. When I drive down with the milk in the
mornin' they all laughs and jokes at me—that boy up to Harris'
and the new feller up to Slocum's, and Bill Evans down to
Meade's, and all the rest on 'em.

ROBERT.   That's a queer reason for leaving me flat. Won't they   15
laugh at you just the same when you're working for Timms?

BEN.   They wouldn't dare to. Timms is the best farm hereabouts.
They was laughin' at me for workin' for *you*, that's what!
"How're things up to the Mayo place?" they hollers every
mornin'. "What's Robert doin' now—pasturin' the cattle in the   20
cornlot? Is he seasonin' his hay with rain this year, same as
last?" they shouts. "Or is he inventin' some 'lectrical milkin' en-
gine to fool them dry cows o' his into givin' hard cider?"
(*Very much ruffled*) That's like they talks; and I ain't goin' to
put up with it no longer. Everyone's always knowed me as a   25
first-class hand hereabouts, and I ain't wantin' 'em to get no different notion. So I'm quittin' you. And I wants what's comin'
to me.

ROBERT (*coldly*).   Oh, if that's the case, you can go to the devil.
You'll get your money tomorrow when I get back from town   30
—not before!

BEN (*turning to doorway to kitchen*).   That suits me. (*As he
goes out he speaks back over his shoulder.*) And see that I do
get it, or there'll be trouble.

   He disappears and the slamming of the kitchen door is heard.   35

ROBERT (*as* RUTH *comes from where she has been standing by the doorway and sits down dejectedly in her old place*). The stupid damn fool! And now what about the haying? That's an example of what I'm up against. No one can say I'm responsible
5   for that.

RUTH.   He wouldn't dare act that way with anyone else! (*Spitefully, with a glance at* ANDREW'S *letter on the table*) It's lucky Andy's coming back.

ROBERT (*without resentment*).   Yes, Andy'll see the right thing
10   to do in a jiffy. (*With an affectionate smile*) I wonder if the old chump's changed much? He doesn't seem to from his letters, does he? (*Shaking his head*) But just the same I doubt if he'll want to settle down to a hum-drum farm life, after all he's been through.

15   RUTH (*resentfully*).   Andy's not like you. He likes the farm.

ROBERT (*immersed in his own thoughts—enthusiastically*).   Gad, the things he's seen and experienced! Think of the places he's been! All the wonderful far places I used to dream about! God, how I envy him! What a trip! (*He springs to his feet and in-
20   stinctively goes to the window and stares out at the horizon.*)

RUTH (*bitterly*).   I s'pose you're sorry now you didn't go?

ROBERT (*too occupied with his own thoughts to hear her—vindictively*).   Oh, those cursed hills out there that I used to think promised me so much! How I've grown to hate the sight
25   of them! They're like the walls of a narrow prison yard shutting me in from all the freedom and wonder of life! (*He turns back to the room with a gesture of loathing.*) Sometimes I think if it wasn't for you, Ruth, and—(*his voice softening*)—little Mary, I'd chuck everything up and walk down the road with
30   just one desire in my heart—to put the whole rim of the world between me and those hills, and be able to breathe freely once more! (*He sinks down into his chair and smiles with bitter self-scorn*) There I go dreaming again—my old fool dreams.

RUTH (*in a low, repressed voice—her eyes smoldering*).   You're
35   not the only one!

ROBERT (*buried in his own thoughts—bitterly*).   And Andy,

who's had the chance—what has he got out of it? His letters
read like the diary of a—of a farmer! "We're in Singapore now.
It's a dirty hole of a place and hotter than hell. Two of the
crew are down with fever and we're short-handed on the work.
I'll be damn glad when we sail again, although tacking back and 5
forth in these blistering seas is a rotten job too!" (*Scornfully*)
That's about the way he summed up his impressions of the
East.

RUTH (*her repressed voice trembling*). You needn't make fun
of Andy. 10

ROBERT. When I think—but what's the use? You know I wasn't
making fun of Andy personally, but his attitude toward things
is——

RUTH (*her eyes flashing—bursting into uncontrollable rage*).
You was too making fun of him! And I ain't going to stand for 15
it! You ought to be ashamed of yourself! (ROBERT *stares at her
in amazement. She continues furiously.*) A fine one to talk
about anyone else—after the way you've ruined everything
with your lazy loafing!—and the stupid way you do things!

ROBERT (*angrily*). Stop that kind of talk, do you hear? 20

RUTH. You findin' fault—with your own brother who's ten
times the man you ever was or ever will be! You're jealous,
that's what! Jealous because he's made a man of himself, while
you're nothing but a—but a—— (*She stutters incoherently,
overcome by rage.*) 25

ROBERT. Ruth! Ruth! You'll be sorry for talking like that.

RUTH. I won't! I won't never be sorry! I'm only saying what
I've been thinking for years.

ROBERT (*aghast*). Ruth! You can't mean that!

RUTH. What do you think—living with a man like you—having 30
to suffer all the time because you've never been man enough to
work and do things like other people. But no! You never own
up to that. You think you're so much better than other folks,
with your college education, where you never learned a thing,
and always reading your stupid books instead of working. I 35
s'pose you think I ought to be *proud* to be your wife—a poor,

ignorant thing like me! (*Fiercely*) But I'm not. I hate it! I hate the sight of you. Oh, if I'd only known! If I hadn't been such a fool to listen to your cheap, silly, poetry talk that you learned out of books! If I could have seen how you were in your true

5   self—like you are now—I'd have killed myself before I'd have married you! I was sorry for it before we'd been together a month. I knew what you were really like—when it was too late.

ROBERT (*his voice raised loudly*).   And now—I'm finding out what you're really like—what a—a creature I've been living

10   with. (*With a harsh laugh*) God! It wasn't that I haven't guessed how mean and small you are—but I've kept on telling myself that I must be wrong—like a fool!—like a damned fool!

RUTH.   You were saying you'd go out on the road if it wasn't for me. Well, you can go, and the sooner the better! I don't care!

15   I'll be glad to get rid of you! The farm'll be better off too. There's been a curse on it ever since you took hold. So go! Go and be a tramp like you've always wanted. It's all you're good for. I can get along without you, don't you worry. (*Exulting fiercely*) Andy's coming back, don't forget that! He'll attend

20   to things like they should be. He'll show what a man can do! I don't need you. Andy's coming!

ROBERT (*they are both standing.* ROBERT *grabs her by the shoulders and glares into her eyes*).   What do you mean? (*He shakes her violently.*) What are you thinking of? What's in

25   your evil mind, you—you—— (*His voice is a harsh shout*).

RUTH (*in a defiant scream*).   Yes I do mean it! I'd say it if you was to kill me! I do love Andy. I do! I do! I always loved him. (*Exultantly*) And he loves me! He loves me! I know he does. He always did! And you know he did, too! So go! Go if you

30   want to!

ROBERT (*throwing her away from him. She staggers back against the table—thickly*).   You—you slut!

He stands glaring at her as she leans back, supporting herself by the table, gasping for breath. A loud frightened whimper

35   *sounds from the awakened child in the bedroom. It continues. The man and woman stand looking at one another in*

horror, the extent of their terrible quarrel suddenly brought home to them. A pause. The noise of a horse and carriage comes from the road before the house. The two, suddenly struck by the same premonition, listen to it breathlessly, as to a sound heard in a dream. It stops. They hear ANDY's *voice from the road shouting a long hail—"Ahoy there!"*   5

RUTH (*with a strangled cry of joy*).   Andy! Andy!

She rushes and grabs the knob of the screen door, about to fling it open.

ROBERT (*in a voice of command that forces obedience*).   Stop!   10
(*He goes to the door and gently pushes the trembling* RUTH *away from it. The child's crying rises to a louder pitch.*) I'll meet Andy. You better go in to Mary, Ruth.

She looks at him defiantly for a moment, but there is some-thing in his eyes that makes her turn and walk slowly into   15
the bedroom.

ANDY's VOICE (*in a louder shout*).   Ahoy there, Rob!

ROBERT (*in an answering shout of forced cheeriness*).   Hello, Andy!

He opens the door and walks out as   20

The Curtain Falls

ACT TWO

SCENE TWO

The top of a hill on the farm. It is about eleven o'clock the next morning. The day is hot and cloudless. In the distance the sea can be seen.

The top of the hill slopes downward slightly toward the left. A big boulder stands in the center toward the rear. Further right, a large oak tree. The faint trace of a path leading upward to it from the left foreground can be detected through the bleached, sun-scorched grass.

ROBERT *is discovered sitting on the boulder, his chin resting on his hands, staring out toward the horizon seaward. His face is*

pale and haggard, his expression one of utter despondency.
MARY *is sitting on the grass near him in the shade, playing with*
her doll, singing happily to herself. Presently she casts a curious
glance at her father, and, propping her doll up against the tree,
comes over and clambers to his side.

MARY (*pulling at his hand—solicitously*).   Dada sick?
ROBERT (*looking at her with a forced smile*).   No, dear. Why?
MARY.   Play wif Mary.
ROBERT (*gently*).   No, dear, not today. Dada doesn't feel like
5   playing today.
MARY (*protestingly*).   Yes, Dada!
ROBERT.   No, dear. Dada does feel sick—a little. He's got a bad
      headache.
MARY.   Mary see. (*He bends his head. She pats his hair.*) Bad
10   head.
ROBERT (*kissing her—with a smile*).   There! It's better now,
      dear, thank you. (*She cuddles up close against him. There is a*
      pause during which each of them looks out seaward. Finally
      ROBERT *turns to her tenderly.*) Would you like Dada to go
15   away?—far, far away?
MARY (*tearfully*).   No! No! No, Dada, no!
ROBERT.   Don't you like Uncle Andy—the man that came yes-
      terday—not the old man with the white mustache—the other?
MARY.   Mary loves Dada.
20 ROBERT (*with fierce determination*)   He won't go away, baby.
      He was only joking. He couldn't leave his little Mary.
          He presses the child in his arms.
MARY (*with an exclamation of pain*).   Oh! Hurt!
ROBERT.   I'm sorry, little girl. (*He lifts her down to the grass*)
25   Go play with Dolly, that's a good girl; and be careful to keep
      in the shade.
          She reluctantly leaves him and takes up her doll again. A mo-
          ment later she points down the hill to the left.
MARY.   Mans, Dada.
30 ROBERT (*looking that way*).   It's your Uncle Andy.

A moment later ANDREW *comes up from the left, whistling
cheerfully. He has changed but little in appearance, except
for the fact that his face has been deeply bronzed by his years
in the tropics; but there is a decided change in his manner.
The old easy-going good-nature seems to have been partly*   5
*lost in a breezy, business-like briskness of voice and gesture.
There is an authoritative note in his speech as though he were
accustomed to give orders and have them obeyed as a matter
of course. He is dressed in the simple blue uniform and cap
of a merchant ship's officer.*   10

ANDREW.   Here you are, eh?

ROBERT.   Hello, Andy.

ANDREW (*going over to* MARY).   And who's this young lady I
find you all alone with, eh? Who's this pretty young lady? (*He
tickles the laughing, squirming* MARY, *then lifts her up at arm's*   15
length over his head.) Upsy—daisy! (*He sets her down on the
ground again.*) And there you are! (*He walks over and sits
down on the boulder beside* ROBERT *who moves to one side to
make room for him.*) Ruth told me I'd probably find you up
top-side here; but I'd have guessed it, anyway. (*He digs his*   20
brother in the ribs affectionately.) Still up to your old tricks,
you old beggar! I can remember how you used to come up
here to mope and dream in the old days.

ROBERT (*with a smile*).   I come up here now because it's the
coolest place on the farm. I've given up dreaming.   25

ANDREW (*grinning*).   I don't believe it. You can't have changed
that much. (*After a pause—with boyish enthusiasm*) Say, it
sure brings back old times to be up here with you having a chin
all by our lonesomes again. I feel great being back home.

ROBERT.   It's great for us to have you back.   30

ANDREW (*after a pause—meaningly*).   I've been looking over the
old place with Ruth. Things don't seem to be——

ROBERT (*his face flushing—interrupts his brother shortly*).
Never mind the damn farm! Let's talk about something interesting. This is the first chance I've had to have a word with you   35
alone. Tell me about your trip.

ANDREW. Why, I thought I told you everything in my letters.

ROBERT (*smiling*). Your letters were—sketchy, to say the least.

ANDREW. Oh, I know I'm no author. You needn't be afraid of hurting my feelings. I'd rather go through a typhoon again
5 than write a letter.

ROBERT (*with eager interest*). Then you were through a typhoon?

ANDREW. Yes—in the China Sea. Had to run before it under bare poles for two days. I thought we were bound down for
10 Davy Jones, sure. Never dreamed waves could get so big or the wind blow so hard. If it hadn't been for Uncle Dick being such a good skipper we'd have gone to the sharks, all of us. As it was we came out minus a main top-mast and had to beat back to Hong-Kong for repairs. But I must have written you all this.

15 ROBERT. You never mentioned it.

ANDREW. Well, there was so much dirty work getting things ship-shape again I must have forgotten about it.

ROBERT (*looking at* ANDREW—*marveling*). Forget a typhoon? (*With a trace of scorn*) You're a strange combination, Andy.
20 And is what you've told me all you remember about it?

ANDREW. Oh, I could give you your bellyful of details if I wanted to turn loose on you. It was all-wool-and-a-yard-wide—Hell, I'll tell you. You ought to have been there. I remember thinking about you at the worst of it, and saying to myself:
25 "This'd cure Rob of them ideas of his about the beautiful sea, if he could see it." And it would have too, you bet! (*He nods emphatically.*)

ROBERT (*dryly*). The sea doesn't seem to have impressed you very favorably.

30 ANDREW. I should say it didn't! I'll never set foot on a ship again if I can help it—except to carry me some place I can't get to by train.

ROBERT. But you studied to become an officer!

ANDREW. Had to do something or I'd gone mad. The days were
35 like years. (*He laughs*) And as for the East you used to rave about—well, you ought to see it, and *smell* it! One walk down

one of their filthy narrow streets with the tropic sun beating on
it would sicken you for life with the "wonder and mystery"
you used to dream of.

ROBERT (*shrinking from his brother with a glance of aversion*).
So all you found in the East was a stench?   5

ANDREW.   *A* stench! Ten thousand of them!

ROBERT.   But you did like some of the places, judging from your
letters—Sydney, Buenos Aires——

ANDREW.   Yes, Sydney's a good town. (*Enthusiastically*) But
Buenos Aires—there's the place for you. Argentine's a country   10
where a fellow has a chance to make good. You're right I like
it. And I'll tell you, Rob, that's right where I'm going just as
soon as I've seen you folks a while and can get a ship. I can get
a berth as second officer, and I'll jump the ship when I get
there. I'll need every cent of the wages Uncle's paid me to   15
get a start at something in B. A.

ROBERT (*staring at his brother—slowly*).   So you're not going to
stay on the farm?

ANDREW.   Why sure not! Did you think I was? There wouldn't
be any sense. One of us is enough to run this little place.   20

ROBERT.   I suppose it does seem small to you now.

ANDREW (*not noticing the sarcasm in* ROBERT'S *tone*).   You've
no idea, Rob, what a splendid place Argentine is. I had a letter
from a marine insurance chap that I'd made friends with in
Hong-Kong to his brother, who's in the grain business in   25
Buenos Aires. He took quite a fancy to me, and what's more
important, he offered me a job if I'd come back there. I'd have
taken it on the spot, only I couldn't leave Uncle Dick in the
lurch, and I'd promised you folks to come home. But I'm going
back there, you bet, and then you watch me get on! (*He slaps*   30
ROBERT *on the back*) But don't you think it's a big chance,
Rob?

ROBERT.   It's fine—for you, Andy.

ANDREW.   We call this a farm—but you ought to hear about the
farms down there—ten square miles where we've got an acre.   35
It's a new country where big things are opening up—and I

want to get in on something big before I die. I'm no fool when it comes to farming, and I know something about grain. I've been reading up a lot on it, too, lately. (*He notices* ROBERT's *absent-minded expression and laughs.*) Wake up, you old po-
5   etry book worm, you! I know my talking about business makes you want to choke me, doesn't it?

ROBERT (*with an embarrassed smile*). No, Andy, I—I just hap-pened to think of something else. (*Frowning*) There've been lots of times lately that I've wished I had some of your faculty
10   for business.

ANDREW (*soberly*). There's something I want to talk about, Rob,—the farm. You don't mind, do you?

ROBERT. No.

ANDREW. I walked over it this morning with Ruth—and she told
15   me about things—— (*Evasively*) I could see the place had run down; but you mustn't blame yourself. When luck's against anyone——

ROBERT. Don't, Andy! It *is* my fault. You know it as well as I do. The best I've ever done was to make ends meet.

20   ANDREW (*after a pause*). I've got over a thousand saved, and you can have that.

ROBERT (*firmly*). No. You need that for your start in Buenos Aires.

ANDREW. I don't. I can——

25   ROBERT (*determinedly*). No, Andy! Once and for all, no! I won't hear of it!

ANDREW (*protestingly*). You obstinate old son of a gun!

ROBERT. Oh, everything'll be on a sound footing after harvest. Don't worry about it.

30   ANDREW (*doubtfully*). Maybe. (*After a pause*) It's too bad Pa couldn't have lived to see things through. (*With feeling*) It cut me up a lot—hearing he was dead. He never—softened up, did he—about me, I mean?

ROBERT. He never understood, that's a kinder way of putting it.
35   He does now.

ANDREW (*after a pause*). You've forgotten all about what—

caused me to go, haven't you, Rob? (ROBERT *nods but keeps his face averted.*) I was a slushier damn fool in those days than you were. But it was an act 'of Providence I did go. It opened my eyes to how I'd been fooling myself. Why, I'd forgotten all about—that—before I'd been at sea six months.   5

ROBERT (*turns and looks into* ANDREW's *eyes searchingly*). You're speaking of—Ruth?

ANDREW (*confused*).   Yes. I didn't want you to get false notions in your head, or I wouldn't say anything. (*Looking* ROBERT *squarely in the eyes*) I'm telling you the truth when I say I'd   10
forgotten long ago. It don't sound well for me, getting over things so easy, but I guess it never really amounted to more than a kid idea I was letting rule me. I'm certain now I never was in love—I was getting fun out of thinking I was—and being a hero to myself. (*He heaves a great sigh of relief.*) There!   15
Gosh, I'm glad that's off my chest. I've been feeling sort of awkward ever since I've been home, thinking of what you two might think. (*A trace of appeal in his voice*) You've got it all straight now, haven't you, Rob?

ROBERT (*in a low voice*).   Yes, Andy.   20

ANDREW.   And I'll tell Ruth, too, if I can get up the nerve. She must feel kind of funny having me round—after what used to be—and not knowing how I feel about it.

ROBERT (*slowly*).   Perhaps—for her sake—you'd better not tell her.   25

ANDREW.   For her sake? Oh, you mean she wouldn't want to be reminded of my foolishness? Still, I think it'd be worse if——

ROBERT (*breaking out—in an agonized voice*).   Do as you please, Andy; but for God's sake, let's not talk about it! (*There is a pause.* ANDREW *stares at* ROBERT *in hurt stupefaction.* ROBERT   30
continues after a moment in a voice which he vainly attempts to keep calm.) Excuse me, Andy. This rotten headache has my nerves shot to pieces.

ANDREW (*mumbling*).   It's all right, Rob—long as you're not sore at me.   35

ROBERT.   Where did Uncle Dick disappear to this morning?

ANDREW.   He went down to the port to see to things on the *Sunda*. He said he didn't know exactly when he'd be back. I'll have to go down and tend to the ship when he comes. That's why I dressed up in these togs.

5 MARY (*pointing down the hill to the left*).   See! Mama! Mama! *She struggles to her feet.* RUTH *appears at left. She is dressed in white, shows she has been fixing up. She looks pretty, flushed and full of life.*

MARY (*running to her mother*).   Mama!

10 RUTH (*kissing her*).   Hello, dear! (*She walks toward the rock and addresses* ROBERT *coldly.*) Jake wants to see you about something. He finished working where he was. He's waiting for you at the road.

ROBERT (*getting up—wearily*).   I'll go down right away.

15 *As he looks at* RUTH, *noting her changed appearance, his face darkens with pain.*

RUTH.   And take Mary with you, please. (*To* MARY) Go with Dada, that's a good girl. Grandma has your dinner most ready for you.

20 ROBERT (*shortly*).   Come, Mary!

MARY (*taking his hand and dancing happily beside him*).   Dada! Dada!
They go down the hill to the left. RUTH *looks after them for a moment, frowning—then turns to* ANDY *with a smile.*

25 RUTH.   I'm going to sit down. Come on, Andy. It'll be like old times. (*She jumps lightly to the top of the rock and sits down.*) It's so fine and cool up here after the house.

ANDREW (*half-sitting on the side of the boulder*).   Yes. It's great.

RUTH.   I've taken a holiday in honor of your arrival. (*Laughing*
30 *excitedly*) I feel so free I'd like to have wings and fly over the sea. You're a man. You can't know how awful and stupid it is —cooking and washing dishes all the time.

ANDREW (*making a wry face*).   I can guess.

RUTH.   Besides, your mother just insisted on getting your first
35 dinner to home, she's that happy at having you back. You'd think I was planning to poison you the flurried way she shooed me out of the kitchen.

ANDREW.   That's just like Ma, bless her!

RUTH.   She's missed you terrible. We all have. And you can't deny the farm has, after what I showed you and told you when we was looking over the place this morning.

ANDREW (*with a frown*).   Things are run down, that's a fact! It's too darn hard on poor old Rob.

RUTH (*scornfully*).   It's his own fault. He never takes any interest in things.

ANDREW (*reprovingly*).   You can't blame him. He wasn't born for it; but I know he's done his best for your sake and the old folks and the little girl.

RUTH (*indifferently*).   Yes, I suppose he has. (*Gayly*) But thank the Lord, all those days are over now. The "hard luck" Rob's always blaming won't last long when you take hold, Andy. All the farm's ever needed was someone with the knack of looking ahead and preparing for what's going to happen.

ANDREW.   Yes, Rob hasn't got that. He's frank to own up to that himself. I'm going to try and hire a good man for him—an experienced farmer—to work the place on a salary and percentage. That'll take it off of Rob's hands, and he needn't be worrying himself to death any more. He looks all worn out, Ruth. He ought to be careful.

RUTH (*absent-mindedly*).   Yes, I s'pose. (*Her mind is filled with premonitions by the first part of his statement.*) Why do you want to hire a man to oversee things? Seems as if now that you're back it wouldn't be needful.

ANDREW.   Oh, of course I'll attend to everything while I'm here. I mean after I'm gone.

RUTH (*as if she couldn't believe her ears*).   Gone!

ANDREW.   Yes. When I leave for the Argentine again.

RUTH (*aghast*).   You're going away to sea!

ANDREW.   Not to sea, no; I'm through with the sea for good as a job. I'm going down to Buenos Aires to get in the grain business.

RUTH.   But—that's far off—isn't it?

ANDREW (*easily*).   Six thousand miles more or less. It's quite a trip. (*With enthusiasm*) I've got a peach of a chance down

there, Ruth. Ask Rob if I haven't. I've just been telling him all
about it.

RUTH (*a flush of anger coming over her face*).   And didn't he
try to stop you from going?

5 ANDREW (*in surprise*).   No, of course not. Why?

RUTH (*slowly and vindictively*).   That's just like him—not to.

ANDREW (*resentfully*).   Rob's too good a chum to try and stop
me when he knows I'm set on a thing. And he could see just as
soon's I told him what a good chance it was.

10 RUTH (*dazedly*). And you're bound on going?

ANDREW.   Sure thing. Oh, I don't mean right off. I'll have to wait
for a ship sailing there for quite a while, likely. Anyway, I
want to stay to home and visit with you folks a spell before
I go.

15 RUTH (*dumbly*).   I s'pose. (*With sudden anguish*) Oh, Andy,
you can't go! You can't. Why we've all thought—we've all
been hoping and praying you was coming home to stay, to
settle down on the farm and see to things. You mustn't go!
Think of how your Ma'll take on if you go—and how the
20 farm'll be ruined if you leave it to Rob to look after. You can
see that.

ANDREW (*frowning*).   Rob hasn't done so bad. When I get a
man to direct things the farm'll be safe enough.

RUTH (*insistently*).   But your Ma—think of her.

25 ANDREW.   She's used to me being away. She won't object when
she knows it's best for her and all of us for me to go. You ask
Rob. In a couple of years down there I'll make my pile, see if
I don't; and then I'll come back and settle down and turn this
farm into the crackiest place in the whole state. In the mean-
30 time, I can help you both from down there. (*Earnestly*) I tell
you, Ruth, I'm going to make good right from the minute I
land, if working hard and a determination to get on can do it;
and I *know* they can! (*Excitedly—in a rather boastful tone*) I
tell you, I feel ripe for bigger things than settling down here.
35 The trip did that for me, anyway. It showed me the world is a
larger proposition than ever I thought it was in the old days.

I couldn't be content any more stuck here like a fly in molasses.
It all seems trifling, somehow. You ought to be able to understand what I feel.

RUTH (*dully*).   Yes—I s'pose I ought. (*After a pause—a sudden
suspicion forming in her mind*) What did Rob tell you—
about me?

ANDREW.   Tell? About you? Why, nothing.

RUTH (*staring at him intensely*).   Are you telling me the truth,
Andy Mayo? Didn't he say—I—— (*She stops confusedly*).

ANDREW (*surprised*).   No, he didn't mention you, I can remember. Why? What made you think he did?

RUTH (*wringing her hands*).   Oh, I wish I could tell if you're
lying or not!

ANDREW (*indignantly*).   What're you talking about? I didn't
used to lie to you, did I? And what in the name of God is there
to lie for?

RUTH (*still unconvinced*).   Are you sure—will you swear—it
isn't the reason—— (*She lowers her eyes and half turns away
from him.*) The same reason that made you go last time that's
driving you away again? 'Cause if it is—I was going to say—
you mustn't go—on that account. (*Her voice sinks to a tremulous, tender whisper as she finishes.*)

ANDREW (*confused—forces a laugh*).   Oh, is *that* what you're
driving at? Well, you needn't worry about that no more——
(*Soberly*) I don't blame you, Ruth, feeling embarrassed having
me around again, after the way I played the dumb fool about
going away last time.

RUTH (*her hope crushed—with a gasp of pain*).   Oh, Andy!

ANDREW (*misunderstanding*).   I know I oughtn't to talk about
such foolishness to you. Still I figure it's better to get it out of
my system so's we three can be together same's years ago, and
not be worried thinking one of us might have the wrong notion.

RUTH.   Andy! Please! Don't!

ANDREW.   Let me finish now that I've started. It'll help clear
things up. I don't want you to think once a fool always a fool,
and be upset all the time I'm here on my fool account. I want

you to believe I put all that silly nonsense back of me a long
time ago—and now—it seems—well—as if you'd always been
my sister, that's what, Ruth.

RUTH (*at the end of her endurance—laughing hysterically*). For
5   God's sake, Andy—won't you please stop talking! (*She again
hides her face in her hands, her bowed shoulders trembling.*)

ANDREW (*ruefully*). Seem's if I put my foot in it whenever I
open my mouth today. Rob shut me up with almost the same
words when I tried speaking to him about it.

10 RUTH (*fiercely*). You told him—what you've told me?

ANDREW (*astounded*). Why sure! Why not?

RUTH (*shuddering*). Oh, my God!

ANDREW (*alarmed*). Why? Shouldn't I have?

RUTH (*hysterically*). Oh, I don't care what you do! I don't care!
15 Leave me alone!

ANDREW *gets up and walks down the hill to the left, embarrassed, hurt, and greatly puzzled by her behavior.*

ANDREW (*after a pause—pointing down the hill*). Hello! Here
they come back—and the Captain's with them. How'd he come
20 to get back so soon, I wonder? That means I've got to hustle
down to the port and get on board. Rob's got the baby with
him. (*He comes back to the boulder.* RUTH *keeps her face
averted from him.*) Gosh, I never saw a father so tied up in a
kid as Rob is! He just watches every move she makes. And I
25 don't blame him. You both got a right to feel proud of her.
She's surely a little winner. (*He glances at* RUTH *to see if this
very obvious attempt to get back in her good graces is having
any effect.*) I can see the likeness to Rob standing out all over
her, can't you? But there's no denying she's your young one,
30 either. There's something about her eyes——

RUTH (*piteously*). Oh, Andy, I've a headache! I don't want to
talk! Leave me alone, won't you please?

ANDREW (*stands staring at her for a moment—then walks away
saying in a hurt tone*): Everybody hereabouts seems to be on
35 edge today. I begin to feel as if I'm not wanted around.

He stands near the path, left, kicking at the grass with the toe of his shoe. A moment later CAPTAIN DICK SCOTT *enters, followed by* ROBERT *carrying* MARY. *The* CAPTAIN *seems scarcely to have changed at all from the jovial, booming person he was three years before. He wears a uniform similar to* ANDREW'S. *He is puffing and breathless from his climb and mops wildly at his perspiring countenance.* ROBERT *casts a quick glance at* ANDREW, *noticing the latter's discomfited look, and then turns his eyes on* RUTH *who, at their approach, has moved so her back is toward them, her chin resting on her hands as she stares out seaward.*

MARY.   Mama! Mama!

ROBERT *puts her down and she runs to her mother.* RUTH *turns and grabs her up in her arms with a sudden fierce tenderness, quickly turning away again from the others. During the following scene she keeps* MARY *in her arms.*

SCOTT (*wheezily*).   Phew! I got great news for you, Andy. Let me get my wind first. Phew! God A'mighty, mountin' this damned hill is worser'n goin' aloft to the skys'l yard in a blow. I got to lay to a while.

He sits down on the grass, mopping his face.

ANDREW.   I didn't look for you this soon, Uncle.

SCOTT.   I didn't figger it, neither; but I run across a bit o' news down to the Seamen's Home made me 'bout ship and set all sail back here to find you.

ANDREW (*eagerly*).   What is it, Uncle?

SCOTT.   Passin' by the Home I thought I'd drop in an' let 'em know I'd be lackin' a mate next trip count o' your leavin'. Their man in charge o' the shippin' asked after you 'special curious. "Do you think he'd consider a berth as Second on a steamer, Captain?" he asks. I was goin' to say no when I thinks o' you wantin' to get back down south to the Plate agen; so I asks him: "What is she and where's she bound?" "She's the *El Paso*, a brand new tramp," he says, "and she's bound for Buenos Aires."

ANDREW (*his eyes lighting up—excitedly*).   Gosh, that is luck! When does she sail?

SCOTT.   Tomorrow mornin'. I didn't know if you'd want to ship away agen so quick an' I told him so. "Tell him I'll hold the berth open for him until late this afternoon," he says. So there you be, an' you can make your own choice.

ANDREW. I'd like to take it. There may not be another ship for Buenos Aires with a vacancy in months. (*His eyes roving from* ROBERT *to* RUTH *and back again—uncertainly*) Still—damn it all—tomorrow morning *is* soon. I wish she wasn't leaving for a week or so. That'd give me a chance—it seems hard to go right away again when I've just got home. And yet it's a chance in a thousand—— (*Appealing to* ROBERT) What do you think, Rob? What would you do?

ROBERT (*forcing a smile*). He who hesitates, you know. (*Frowning*) It's a piece of good luck thrown in your way—and—I think you owe it to yourself to jump at it. But don't ask me to decide for you.

RUTH (*turning to look at* ANDREW—*in a tone of fierce resentment*). Yes, go, Andy!
      She turns quickly away again. There is a moment of embarrassed silence.

ANDREW (*thoughtfully*). Yes, I guess I will. It'll be the best thing for all of us in the end, don't you think so, Rob?
      ROBERT *nods but remains silent.*

SCOTT (*getting to his feet*). Then, that's settled.

ANDREW. (*Now that he has definitely made a decision his voice rings with hopeful strength and energy.*) Yes, I'll take the berth. The sooner I go the sooner I'll be back, that's a certainty; and I won't come back with empty hands next time. You bet I won't!

SCOTT. You ain't got so much time, Andy. To make sure you'd best leave here soon's you kin. I got to get right back aboard. You'd best come with me.

ANDREW. I'll go to the house and repack my bag right away.

ROBERT (*quietly*). You'll both be here for dinner, won't you?

ANDREW (*worriedly*). I don't know. Will there be time? What time is it now, I wonder?

ROBERT (*reproachfully*). Ma's been getting dinner especially for you, Andy.

ANDREW (*flushing—shamefacedly*). Hell! And I was forgetting! Of course I'll stay for dinner if I missed every damned ship in the world. (*He turns to the* CAPTAIN—*briskly*) Come on, Uncle. Walk down with me to the house and you can tell me more about this berth on the way. I've got to pack before dinner. 5 (*He and the* CAPTAIN *start down to the left.* ANDREW *calls back over his shoulder.*) You're coming soon, aren't you, Rob?

ROBERT. Yes. I'll be right down.

> ANDREW *and the* CAPTAIN *leave.* RUTH *puts* MARY *on the ground and hides her face in her hands. Her shoulders shake* 10 *as if she were sobbing.* ROBERT *stares at her with a grim, somber expression.* MARY *walks backward toward* ROBERT, *her wondering eyes fixed on her mother.*

MARY (*her voice vaguely frightened, taking her father's hand*). Dada, Mama's cryin', Dada. 15

ROBERT (*bending down and stroking her hair—in a voice he endeavors to keep from being harsh*). No, she isn't, little girl. The sun hurts her eyes, that's all. Aren't you beginning to feel hungry, Mary?

MARY (*decidedly*). Yes, Dada. 20

ROBERT (*meaningly*). It must be your dinner time now.

RUTH (*in a muffled voice*). I'm coming, Mary. (*She wipes her eyes quickly and, without looking at* ROBERT, *comes and takes* MARY'S *hand—in a dead voice*) Come on and I'll get your dinner for you. 25

> *She walks out left, her eyes fixed on the ground, the skipping* MARY *tugging at her hand.* ROBERT *waits a moment for them to get ahead and then slowly follows as*

The Curtain Falls

ACT THREE

SCENE ONE

Same as Act Two, Scene One—The sitting room of the farm house about six o'clock in the morning of a day toward the end of October five years later. It is not yet dawn, but as the action

*progresses the darkness outside the windows gradually fades to
gray.*

*The room, seen by the light of the shadeless oil lamp with a
smoky chimney which stands on the table, presents an appearance of decay, of dissolution. The curtains at the windows are
torn and dirty and one of them is missing. The closed desk is
gray with accumulated dust as if it had not been used in years.
Blotches of dampness disfigure the wall paper. Threadbare
trails, leading to the kitchen and outer doors, show in the faded
carpet. The top of the coverless table is stained with the imprints of hot dishes and spilt food. The rung of one rocker has
been clumsily mended with a piece of plain board. A brown
coating of rust covers the unblacked stove. A pile of wood is
stacked up carelessly against the wall by the stove.*

*The whole atmosphere of the room, contrasted with that of
former years, is one of an habitual poverty too hopelessly resigned to be any longer ashamed or even conscious of itself.*

At the rise of the curtain RUTH *is discovered sitting by the stove,
with hands outstretched to the warmth as if the air in the room
were damp and cold. A heavy shawl is wrapped about her
shoulders, half-concealing her dress of deep mourning. She has
aged horribly. Her pale, deeply lined face has the stony lack
of expression of one to whom nothing more can ever happen,
whose capacity for emotion has been exhausted. When she
speaks her voice is without timbre, low and monotonous. The
negligent disorder of her dress, the slovenly arrangement of
her hair, now streaked with gray, her muddied shoes run down
at the heel, give full evidence of the apathy in which she lives.*

*Her mother is asleep in her wheel chair beside the stove toward
the rear, wrapped up in a blanket.*

*There is a sound from the open bedroom door in the rear as if
someone were getting out of bed.* RUTH *turns in that direction
with a look of dull annoyance. A moment later* ROBERT *appears
in the doorway, leaning weakly against it for support. His hair
is long and unkempt, his face and body emaciated. There are
bright patches of crimson over his cheek bones and his eyes are*

burning with fever. He is dressed in corduroy pants, a flannel shirt, and wears worn carpet slippers on his bare feet.

RUTH (*dully*).   S-s-s-h-! Ma's asleep.

ROBERT (*speaking with an effort*).   I won't wake her.
   He walks weakly to a rocker by the side of the table and sinks down in it exhausted.

RUTH (*staring at the stove*).   You better come near the fire where   5
   it's warm.

ROBERT.   No. I'm burning up now.

RUTH.   That's the fever. You know the doctor told you not to get up and move round.

ROBERT (*iritably*).   That old fossil! He doesn't know anything.   10
   Go to bed and stay there—that's his only prescription.

RUTH (*indifferently*).   How are you feeling now?

ROBERT (*buoyantly*).   Better! Much better than I've felt in ages.
   Really I'm fine now—only very weak. It's the turning point,
   I guess. From now on I'll pick up so quick I'll surprise you—and   15
   no thanks to that old fool of a country quack, either.

RUTH.   He's always tended to us.

ROBERT.   Always helped us to die, you mean! He "tended" to
   Pa and Ma and—(*his voice breaks*)—and to—Mary.

RUTH (*dully*).   He did the best he knew, I s'pose. (*After a pause*)   20
   Well, Andy's bringing a specialist with him when he comes.
   That ought to suit you.

ROBERT (*bitterly*).   Is that why you're waiting up all night?

RUTH.   Yes.

ROBERT.   For Andy?   25

RUTH (*without a trace of feeling*).   Somebody had got to. It's
   only right for someone to meet him after he's been gone five
   years.

ROBERT (*with bitter mockery*).   Five years! It's a long time.

RUTH.   Yes.   30

ROBERT (*meaningly*).   To *wait!*

RUTH (*indifferently*).   It's past now.

ROBERT.   Yes, it's past. (*After a pause*) Have you got his two telegrams with you? (RUTH *nods.*) Let me see them, will you? My head was so full of fever when they came I couldn't make head or tail to them. (*Hastily*) But I'm feeling fine now. Let me read them again.

5   RUTH *takes them from the bosom of her dress and hands them to him.*

RUTH. Here. The first one's on top.

ROBERT (*opening it*). New York. "Just landed from steamer. Have important business to wind up here. Will be home as soon as deal is completed." (*He smiles bitterly.*) Business first was always Andy's motto. (*He reads.*) "Hope you are all well. Andy." (*He repeats ironically.*) "Hope you are all well!"

RUTH (*dully*). He couldn't know you'd been took sick till I answered that and told him.

15   ROBERT (*contritely*). Of course he couldn't. I'm a fool. I'm touchy about nothing lately. Just what did you say in your reply?

RUTH (*inconsequentially*). I had to send it collect.

ROBERT (*irritably*). What did you say was the matter with me?

20   RUTH. I wrote you had lung trouble.

ROBERT (*flying into a petty temper*). You *are* a fool! How often have I explained to you that it's *pleurisy* is the matter with me. You can't seem to get it in your head that the pleura is outside the lungs, not in them!

25   RUTH (*callously*). I only wrote what Doctor Smith told me.

ROBERT (*angrily*). He's a damned ignoramus!

RUTH (*dully*). Makes no difference. I had to tell Andy something, didn't I?

ROBERT (*after a pause, opening the other telegram*). He sent this last evening. Let's see. (*He reads.*) "Leave for home on midnight train. Just received your wire. Am bringing specialist to see Rob. Will motor to farm from Port." (*He calculates.*) What time is it now?

RUTH. Round six, must be.

35   ROBERT. He ought to be here soon. I'm glad he's bringing a

doctor who knows something. A specialist will tell you in a
second that there's nothing the matter with my lungs.

RUTH (*stolidly*).   You've been coughing an awful lot lately.

ROBERT (*irritably*).   What nonsense! For God's sake, haven't you
ever had a bad cold yourself? (RUTH *stares at the stove in silence.* ROBERT *fidgets in his chair. There is a pause. Finally*
ROBERT'S *eyes are fixed on the sleeping* MRS. ATKINS.) Your
mother is lucky to be able to sleep so soundly.

RUTH.   Ma's tired. She's been sitting up with me most of the
night.

ROBERT (*mockingly*).   Is she waiting for Andy, too? (*There is a
pause.* ROBERT *sighs.*) I couldn't get to sleep to save my soul.
I counted ten million sheep if I counted one. No use! I gave up
trying finally and just laid there in the dark thinking. (*He
pauses, then continues in a tone of tender sympathy.*) I was
thinking about you, Ruth—of how hard these last years must
have been for you. (*Appealingly*) I'm sorry, Ruth.

RUTH (*in a dead voice*).   I don't know. They're past now. They
were hard on all of us.

ROBERT.   Yes; on all of us but Andy. (*With a flash of sick jeal-
ousy*) Andy's made a big success of himself—the kind he
wanted. (*Mockingly*) And now he's coming home to let us
admire his greatness. (*Frowning—irritably*) What am I talking
about? My brain must be sick, too. (*After a pause*) Yes, these
years have been terrible for both of us. (*His voice is lowered
to a trembling whisper.*) Especially the last eight months since
Mary—died. (*He forces back a sob with a convulsive shudder
—then breaks out in a passionate agony.*) Our last hope of happiness! I could curse God from the bottom of my soul—if there
was a God!

> He is racked by a violent fit of coughing and hurriedly puts
> his handkerchief to his lips.

RUTH (*without looking at him*).   Mary's better off—being dead.

ROBERT (*gloomily*).   We'd all be better off for that matter.
(*With a sudden exasperation*) You tell that mother of yours

she's got to stop saying that Mary's death was due to a weak
constitution inherited from me. (*On the verge of tears of weakness*) It's got to stop, I tell you!

RUTH (*sharply*).   S-h-h! You'll wake her; and then she'll nag at
5   me—not you.

ROBERT (*coughs and lies back in his chair weakly—a pause*).   It's
all because your mother's down on me for not begging Andy
for help.

RUTH (*resentfully*).   You might have. He's got plenty.

10   ROBERT.   How can *you* of all people think of taking money from
him?

RUTH (*dully*).   I don't see the harm. He's your own brother.

ROBERT (*shrugging his shoulders*).   What's the use of talking to
you? Well, *I* couldn't. (*Proudly*) And I've managed to keep
15   things going, thank God. You can't deny that without help
I've succeeded in—— (*He breaks off with a bitter laugh.*) My
God, what am I boasting of? Debts to this one and that, taxes,
interest unpaid! I'm a fool! (*He lies back in his chair closing his
eyes for a moment, then speaks in a low voice.*) I'll be frank,
20   Ruth. I've been an utter failure, and I've dragged you with me.
I couldn't blame you in all justice—for hating me.

RUTH (*without feeling*).   I don't hate you. It's been my fault too,
I s'pose.

ROBERT.   No. You couldn't help loving—Andy.

25   RUTH (*dully*). I don't love anyone.

ROBERT (*waving her remark aside*).   You needn't deny it. It
doesn't matter. (*After a pause—with a tender smile*) Do you
know, Ruth, what I've been dreaming back there in the dark?
(*With a short laugh*) I was planning our future when I get well.
30   (*He looks at her with appealing eyes as if afraid she will sneer
at him. Her expression does not change. She stares at the stove.
His voice takes on a note of eagerness.*) After all, why shouldn't
we have a future? We're young yet. If we can only shake off
the curse of this farm! It's the farm that's ruined our lives, damn
35   it! And now that Andy's coming back—I'm going to sink my
foolish pride, Ruth! I'll borrow the money from him to give us

a good start in the city. We'll go where people live instead of
stagnating, and start all over again. (*Confidently*) I won't be
the failure there that I've been here, Ruth. You won't need to
be ashamed of me there. I'll prove to you the reading I've done
can be put to some use. (*Vaguely*) I'll write, or something of   5
that sort. I've always wanted to write. (*Pleadingly*) You'll want
to do that, won't you, Ruth?

RUTH (*dully*).   There's Ma.

ROBERT.   She can come with us.

RUTH.   She wouldn't.   10

ROBERT (*angrily*).   So that's your answer! (*He trembles with
violent passion. His voice is so strange that* RUTH *turns to look
at him in alarm*) You're lying, Ruth! Your mother's just an
excuse. You want to stay here. You think that because Andy's
coming back that——   15

    He chokes and has an attack of coughing.

RUTH (*getting up—in a frightened voice*).   What's the matter?
(*She goes to him.*) I'll go with you, Rob. Stop that coughing
for goodness' sake! It's awful bad for you. (*She soothes him in
dull tones.*) I'll go with you to the city—soon's you're well   20
again. Honest I will, Rob, I promise! (ROB *lies back and closes
his eyes. She stands looking down at him anxiously.*) Do you
feel better now?

ROBERT.   Yes. (RUTH *goes back to her chair. After a pause he
opens his eyes and sits up in his chair. His face is flushed and*   25
happy.) Then you *will* go, Ruth?

RUTH.   Yes.

ROBERT (*excitedly*).   We'll make a new start, Ruth—just you
and I. Life owes us some happiness after what we've been
through. (*Vehemently*) It must! Otherwise our suffering would   30
be meaningless—and that is unthinkable.

RUTH (*worried by his excitement*).   Yes, yes, of course, Rob, but
you mustn't——

ROBERT.   Oh, don't be afraid. I feel completely well, really I do
—now that I can hope again. Oh, if you knew how glorious it   35
feels to have something to look forward to! Can't you feel the

thrill of it, too—the vision of a new life opening up after all the horrible years?

RUTH. Yes, yes, but do be——

ROBERT. Nonsense! I won't be careful. I'm getting back all my strength. (*He gets lightly to his feet.*) See! I feel light as a feather. (*He walks to her chair and bends down to kiss her smilingly.*) One kiss—the first in years, isn't it?—to greet the dawn of a new life together.

RUTH (*submitting to his kiss—worriedly*). Sit down, Rob, for goodness' sake!

ROBERT (*with tender obstinacy—stroking her hair*). I won't sit down. You're silly to worry. (*He rests one hand on the back of her chair.*) Listen. All our suffering has been a test through which we had to pass to prove ourselves worthy of a finer realization. (*Exultingly*) And we did pass through it! It hasn't broken us! And now the dream is to come true! Don't you see?

RUTH (*looking at him with frightened eyes as if she thought he had gone mad*). Yes, Rob, I see; but won't you go back to bed now and rest?

ROBERT. No. I'm going to see the sun rise. It's an augury of good fortune. (*He goes quickly to the window in the rear left, and pushing the curtains aside, stands looking out.* RUTH *springs to her feet and comes quickly to the table, left, where she remains watching* ROBERT *in a tense, expectant attitude. As he peers out his body seems gradually to sag, to grow limp and tired. His voice is mournful as he speaks.*) No sun yet. It isn't time. All I can see is the black rim of the damned hills outlined against a creeping grayness. (*He turns around; letting the curtains fall back, stretching a hand out to the wall to support himself. His false strength of a moment has evaporated leaving his face drawn and hollow-eyed. He makes a pitiful attempt to smile.*) That's not a very happy augury, is it? But the sun'll come— soon. (*He sways weakly.*)

RUTH (*hurrying to his side and supporting him*). Please go to bed, won't you, Rob? You don't want to be all wore out when the specialist comes, do you?

ROBERT (*quickly*).   No. That's right. He mustn't think I'm sicker than I am. And I feel as if I could sleep now—(*cheerfully*)—a good, sound, restful sleep.

RUTH (*helping him to the bedroom door*).   That's what you need most. (*They go inside. A moment later she reappears calling back.*) I'll shut this door so's you'll be quiet. (*She closes the door and goes quickly to her mother and shakes her by the shoulder.*) Ma! Ma! Wake up!

MRS. ATKINS (*coming out of her sleep with a start*).   Glory be! What's the matter with you?

RUTH.   It was Rob. He's just been talking to me out here. I put him back to bed. (*Now that she is sure her mother is awake her fear passes and she relapses into dull indifference. She sits down in her chair and stares at the stove—dully.*) He acted—funny; and his eyes looked so—so wild like.

MRS. ATKINS (*with asperity*).   And is that all you woke me out of a sound sleep for, and scared me near out of my wits?

RUTH.   I was afraid. He talked so crazy. I couldn't quiet him. I didn't want to be alone with him that way. Lord knows what he might do.

MRS. ATKINS (*scornfully*).   Humph! A help I'd be to you and me not able to move a step! Why didn't you run and get Jake?

RUTH (*dully*).   Jake isn't here. He quit last night. He hasn't been paid in three months.

MRS. ATKINS (*indignantly*).   I can't blame him. What decent person'd want to work on a place like this? (*With sudden exasperation*) Oh, I wish you'd never married that man!

RUTH (*wearily*).   You oughn't to talk about him now when he's sick in his bed.

MRS. ATKINS (*working herself into a fit of rage*).   You know very well, Ruth Mayo, if it wasn't for me helpin' you on the sly out of my savin's, you'd both been in the poor house—and all 'count of his pigheaded pride in not lettin' Andy know the state thin's were in. A nice thin' for me to have to support him out of what I'd saved for my last days—and me an invalid with no one to look to!

RUTH.   Andy'll pay you back, Ma. I can tell him so's Rob'll never know.

MRS. ATKINS (*with a snort*).   What'd Rob think you and him was livin' on, I'd like to know?

5 RUTH (*dully*).   He didn't think about it, I s'pose. (*After a slight pause*) He said he'd made up his mind to ask Andy for help when he comes. (*As a clock in the kitchen strikes six*) Six o'clock. Andy ought to get here directly.

MRS. ATKINS.   D'you think this special doctor'll do Rob any
10 good?

RUTH (*hopelessly*).   I don't know.

The two women remain silent for a time staring dejectedly at the stove.

MRS. ATKINS (*shivering irritably*).   For goodness' sake put some
15 wood on that fire. I'm most freezin'!

RUTH (*pointing to the door in the rear*).   Don't talk so loud. Let him sleep if he can. (*She gets wearily from the chair and puts a few pieces of wood in the stove.*) This is the last of the wood. I don't know who'll cut more now that Jake's left. (*She sighs
20 and walks to the window in the rear, left, pulls the curtains aside, and looks out.*) It's getting gray out. (*She comes back to the stove.*) Looks like it'd be a nice day. (*She stretches out her hands to warm them.*) Must've been a heavy frost last night. We're paying for the spell of warm weather we've been having.

25   *The throbbing whine of a motor sounds from the distance outside.*

MRS. ATKINS (*sharply*).   S-h-h! Listen! Ain't that an auto I hear?

RUTH (*without interest*).   Yes. It's Andy, I s'pose.

MRS. ATKINS (*with nervous irritation*).   Don't sit there like a
30 silly goose. Look at the state of this room! What'll this strange doctor think of us? Look at that lamp chimney all smoke! Gracious sakes, Ruth——

RUTH (*indifferently*).   I've got a lamp all cleaned up in the kitchen.

35 MRS. ATKINS (*peremptorily*).   Wheel me in there this minute. I don't want him to see me looking a sight. I'll lay down in the

room the other side. You don't need me now and I'm dead for
sleep.

RUTH *wheels her mother off right. The noise of the motor
grows louder and finally ceases as the car stops on the road
before the farmhouse.* RUTH *returns from the kitchen with a*   5
*lighted lamp in her hand which she sets on the table beside
the other. The sound of footsteps on the path is heard—then
a sharp rap on the door.* RUTH *goes and opens it.* ANDREW
enters, followed by DOCTOR FAWCETT *carrying a small black
bag.* ANDREW *has changed greatly. His face seems to have*   10
*grown highstrung, hardened by the look of decisiveness
which comes from being constantly under a strain where
judgments on the spur of the moment are compelled to be
accurate. His eyes are keener and more alert. There is even a
suggestion of ruthless cunning about them. At present, how-*   15
ever, his expression is one of tense anxiety. DOCTOR FAWCETT
*is a short, dark, middle-aged man with a Vandyke beard. He
wears glasses.*

RUTH. Hello, Andy! I've been waiting——

ANDREW *(kissing her hastily)*. I got here as soon as I could. *(He*   20
throws off his cap and heavy overcoat on the table, introducing
RUTH *and the* DOCTOR *as he does so. He is dressed in an expen-
sive business suit and appears stouter.)* My sister-in-law, Mrs.
Mayo—Doctor Fawcett. *(They bow to each other silently.*
ANDREW *casts a quick glance about the room.)* Where's Rob?   25

RUTH *(pointing)*. In there.

ANDREW. I'll take your coat and hat, Doctor. *(As he helps the*
DOCTOR *with his things)* Is he very bad, Ruth?

RUTH *(dully)*. He's been getting weaker.

ANDREW. Damn! This way, Doctor. Bring the lamp, Ruth.   30
He goes into the bedroom, followed by the DOCTOR *and* RUTH
carrying the clean lamp. RUTH *reappears almost immediately
closing the door behind her, and goes slowly to the outside
door, which she opens, and stands in the doorway looking
out. The sound of* ANDREW's *and* ROBERT's *voices comes from*   35
the bedroom. A moment later ANDREW *re-enters, closing the*

*door softly. He comes forward and sinks down in the rocker
on the right of table, leaning his head on his hand. His face is
drawn in a shocked expression of great grief. He sighs heavily,
staring mournfully in front of him. RUTH turns and stands*
5 *watching him. Then she shuts the door and returns to her
chair by the stove, turning it so she can face him.*

ANDREW (*glancing up quickly—in a harsh voice*). How long
has this been going on?

RUTH. You mean—how long has he been sick?

10 ANDREW (*shortly*). Of course! What else?

RUTH. It was last summer he had a bad spell first, but he's been
ailin' ever since Mary died—eight months ago.

ANDREW (*harshly*). Why didn't you let me know—cable me?
Do you want him to die, all of you? I'm damned if it doesn't

15 look that way! (*His voice breaking*) Poor old chap! To be sick
in this out-of-the-way hole without anyone to attend to him
but a country quack! It's a damned shame!

RUTH (*dully*). I wanted to send you word once, but he only got
mad when I told him. He was too proud to ask anything, he

20 said.

ANDREW. Proud? To ask *me?* (*He jumps to his feet and paces
nervously back and forth.*) I can't understand the way you've
acted. Didn't you see how sick he was getting? Couldn't you
realize—why, I nearly dropped in my tracks when I saw him!

25 He looks—(*He shudders.*)—terrible! (*With fierce scorn*) I
suppose you're so used to the idea of his being delicate that you
took his sickness as a matter of course. God, if I'd only known!

RUTH (*without emotion*). A letter takes so long to get where
you were—and we couldn't afford to telegraph. We owed

30 everyone already, and I couldn't ask Ma. She'd been giving me
money out of her savings till she hadn't much left. Don't say
anything to Rob about it. I never told him. He'd only be mad
at me if he knew. But I had to, because—God knows how we'd
have got on if I hadn't.

35 ANDREW. You mean to say—— (*His eyes seem to take in the
poverty-stricken appearance of the room for the first time.*)

You sent that telegram to me collect. Was it because—— (RUTH *nods silently.* ANDREW *pounds on the table with his fist.*) Good God! And all this time I've been—why I've had everything! (*He sits down in his chair and pulls it close to* RUTH's—*impulsively.*) But—I can't get it through my head. Why? Why? What has happened? How did it ever come about? Tell me!

RUTH (*dully*). There's nothing much to tell. Things kept getting worse, that's all—and Rob didn't seem to care. He never took any interest since way back when your Ma died. After that he got men to take charge, and they nearly all cheated him —he couldn't tell—and left one after another. Then after Mary died he didn't pay no heed to anything any more—just stayed indoors and took to reading books again. So I had to ask Ma if she wouldn't help us some.

ANDREW (*surprised and horrified*). Why, damn it, this is frightful! Rob must be mad not to have let me know. Too proud to ask help of *me!* What's the matter with him in God's name? (*A sudden, horrible suspicion entering his mind*) Ruth! Tell me the truth. His mind hasn't gone back on him, has it?

RUTH (*dully*). I don't know. Mary's dying broke him up terrible—but he's used to her being gone by this, I s'pose.

ANDREW (*looking at her queerly*). Do you mean to say *you're* used to it?

RUTH (*in a dead tone*). There's a time comes—when you don't mind any more—anything.

ANDREW (*looks at her fixedly for a moment—with great pity*). I'm sorry, Ruth—if I seemed to blame you. I didn't realize—— The sight of Rob lying in bed there, so gone to pieces—it made me furious at everyone. Forgive me, Ruth.

RUTH. There's nothing to forgive. It doesn't matter.

ANDREW (*springing to his feet again and pacing up and down*). Thank God I came back before it was too late. This doctor will know exactly what to do. That's the first thing to think of. When Rob's on his feet again we can get the farm working on a sound basis once more. I'll see to that—before I leave.

RUTH. You're going away again?

ANDREW. I've got to.

RUTH. You wrote Rob you was coming back to stay this time.

ANDREW. I expected to—until I got to New York. Then I learned
certain facts that make it necessary. (*With a short laugh*) To be
candid, Ruth, I'm not the rich man you've probably been led
to believe by my letters—not now. I was when I wrote them.
I made money hand over fist as long as I stuck to legitimate trad-
ing; but I wasn't content with that. I wanted it to come easier,
so like all the rest of the idiots, I tried speculation. Oh, I won
all right! Several times I've been almost a millionaire—on paper
—and then come down to earth again with a bump. Finally the
strain was too much. I got disgusted with myself and made up
my mind to get out and come home and forget it and really
live again. (*He gives a harsh laugh.*) And now comes the funny
part. The day before the steamer sailed I saw what I thought
was a chance to become a millionaire again. (*He snaps his fingers.*) That easy! I plunged. Then, before things broke, I left
—I was so confident I couldn't be wrong. But when I landed in
New York—I wired you I had business to wind up, didn't I?
Well, it was the business that wound me up! (*He smiles grimly,
pacing up and down, his hands in his pockets.*)

RUTH (*dully*). You found—you'd lost everything?

ANDREW (*sitting down again*). Practically. (*He takes a cigar
from his pocket, bites the end off, and lights it.*) Oh, I don't
mean I'm dead broke. I've saved ten thousand from the wreck-
age, maybe twenty. But that's a poor showing for five years'
hard work. That's why I'll have to go back. (*Confidently*) I can
make it up in a year or so down there—and I don't need but a
shoestring to start with. (*A weary expression comes over his
face and he sighs heavily.*) I wish I didn't have to. I'm sick of it
all.

RUTH. It's too bad—things seem to go wrong so.

ANDREW (*shaking off his depression—briskly*). They might be
much worse. There's enough left to fix the farm O. K. before
I go. I won't leave 'til Rob's on his feet again. In the meantime
I'll make things fly around here. (*With satisfaction*) I need a

rest, and the kind of rest I need is hard work in the open—just
like I used to do in the old days. (*Stopping abruptly and lowering his voice cautiously*) Not a word to Rob about my losing
money! Remember that, Ruth! You can see why. If he's grown
so touchy he'd never accept a cent if he thought I was hard up;   5
see?

RUTH.   Yes, Andy.

After a pause, during which ANDREW *puffs at his cigar ab-
stractedly, his mind evidently busy with plans for the future,
the bedroom door is opened and* DOCTOR FAWCETT *enters,*   10
*carrying a bag. He closes the door quietly behind him and
comes forward, a grave expression on his face.* ANDREW
springs out of his chair.

ANDREW.   Ah, Doctor! (*He pushes a chair between his own and*
RUTH'S.) Won't you have a chair?   15

FAWCETT (*glancing at his watch*).   I must catch the nine o'clock
back to the city. It's imperative. I have only a moment. (*Sitting
down and clearing his throat—in a perfunctory, impersonal
voice*) The case of your brother, Mr. Mayo, is—— (*He stops
and glances at* RUTH *and says meaningly to* ANDREW) Perhaps   20
it would be better if you and I——

RUTH (*with dogged resentment*).   I know what you mean, Doctor. (*Dully*) Don't be afraid I can't stand it. I'm used to bearing
trouble by this; and I can guess what you've found out. (*She
hesitates for a moment—then continues in a monotonous voice.*)   25
Rob's going to die.

ANDREW (*angrily*).   Ruth!

FAWCETT (*raising his hand as if to command silence*).   I am afraid
my diagnosis of your brother's condition forces me to the same
conclusion as Mrs. Mayo's.   30

ANDREW (*groaning*).   But, Doctor, surely——

FAWCETT (*calmly*).   Your brother hasn't long to live—perhaps
a few days, perhaps only a few hours. It's a marvel that he's
alive at this moment. My examination revealed that both of his
lungs are terribly affected.   35

ANDREW (*brokenly*).   Good God!

RUTH *keeps her eyes fixed on her lap in a trance-like stare.*

FAWCETT.   I am sorry I have to tell you this. If there was anything that could be done——

ANDREW.   There isn't anything?

5 FAWCETT (*shaking his head*).   It's too late. Six months ago there
might have——

ANDREW (*in anguish*).   But if we were to take him to the moun-
tains—or to Arizona—or——

FAWCETT.   That might have prolonged his life six months ago.

10 (ANDREW *groans*.) But now—— (*He shrugs his shoulders
significantly.*)

ANDREW (*appalled by a sudden thought*).   Good heavens, you
haven't told him this, have you, Doctor?

FAWCETT.   No. I lied to him. I said a change of climate—— (*He

15 looks at his watch again nervously.*) I must leave you. (*He gets
up.*)

ANDREW (*getting to his feet—insistently*).   But there must still
be some chance——

FAWCETT (*as if he were reassuring a child*).   There is always that

20 last chance—the miracle. (*He puts on his hat and coat—bowing
to* RUTH.) Good-by, Mrs. Mayo.

RUTH (*without raising her eyes—dully*).   Good-by.

ANDREW (*mechanically*).   I'll walk to the car with you, Doctor.
(*They go out of the door.* RUTH *sits motionlessly. The motor

25 is heard starting and the noise gradually recedes into the distance.* ANDREW *re-enters and sits down in his chair, holding his
head in his hands*) Ruth! (*She lifts her eyes to his*) Hadn't we
better go in and see him? God! I'm afraid to! I know he'll read
it in my face. (*The bedroom door is noiselessly opened and*

30 ROBERT *appears in the doorway. His cheeks are flushed with
fever, and his eyes appear unusually large and brilliant.* ANDREW
continues with a groan.) It can't be, Ruth. It can't be as hopeless as he said. There's always a fighting chance. We'll take Rob
to Arizona. He's *got* to get well. There *must* be a chance!

35 ROBERT (*in a gentle tone*).   Why must there, Andy?

RUTH *turns and stares at him with terrified eyes.*

ANDREW (*whirling around*). Rob! (*Scoldingly*) What are you
doing out of bed? (*He gets up and goes to him.*) Get right
back now and obey the Doc, or you're going to get a licking
from me!

ROBERT (*ignoring these remarks*). Help me over to the chair,   5
please, Andy.

ANDREW.   Like hell I will! You're going right back to bed, that's
where you're going, and stay there! (*He takes hold of* ROBERT's
arm.)

ROBERT (*mockingly*). Stay there 'til I die, eh, Andy? (*Coldly*)   10
Don't behave like a child. I'm sick of lying down. I'll be more
rested sitting up. (*As* ANDREW *hesitates—violently*) I swear I'll
get out of bed every time you put me there. You'll have to sit
on my chest, and that wouldn't help my health any. Come on,
Andy. Don't play the fool. I want to talk to you, and I'm going   15
to. (*With a grim smile*) A dying man has some rights, hasn't he?

ANDREW (*with a shudder*).   Don't talk that way, for God's sake!
I'll only let you sit down if you'll promise that. Remember.
(*He helps* ROBERT *to the chair between his own and* RUTH's)
Easy now! There you are! Wait, and I'll get a pillow for you.   20
(*He goes into the bedroom.* ROBERT *looks at* RUTH *who shrinks
away from him in terror.* ROBERT *smiles bitterly.* ANDREW
comes back with the pillow which he places behind ROBERT's
back.) How's that?

ROBERT (*with an affectionate smile*). Fine! Thank you! (*As*   25
ANDREW *sits down*) Listen, Andy. You've asked me not to
talk—and I won't after I've made my position clear. (*Slowly*)
In the first place I know I'm dying.

> RUTH *bows her head and covers her face with her hands.*
> *She remains like this all during the scene between the two*   30
> *brothers.*

ANDREW.   Rob! That isn't so!

ROBERT (*wearily*). It *is* so! Don't lie to me. After Ruth put me
to bed before you came, I saw it clearly for the first time.
(*Bitterly*) I'd been making plans for our future—Ruth's and   35
mine—so it came hard at first—the realization. Then when the

doctor examined me, I knew—although he tried to lie about it. And then to make sure I listened at the door to what he told you. So don't mock me with fairy tales about Arizona, or any such rot as that. Because I'm dying is no reason you should

5 treat me as an imbecile or a coward. Now that I'm sure what's happening I can say Kismet to it with all my heart. It was only the silly uncertainty that hurt.

There is a pause. ANDREW *looks around in impotent anguish, not knowing what to say.* ROBERT *regards him with an af-*

10 *fectionate smile.*

ANDREW (*finally blurts out*). It isn't foolish. You *have* got a chance. If you heard all the Doctor said that ought to prove it to you.

ROBERT.   Oh, you mean when he spoke of the miracle? (*Dryly*)

15 I don't believe in miracles—in my case. Besides, I know more than any doctor on earth *could* know—because I *feel* what's coming. (*Dismissing the subject*) But we've agreed not to talk of it. Tell me about yourself, Andy. That's what I'm interested in. Your letters were too brief and far apart to be illuminating.

20 ANDREW.   I meant to write oftener.

ROBERT (*with a faint trace of irony*).   I judge from them you've accomplished all you set out to do five years ago?

ANDREW.   That isn't much to boast of.

ROBERT (*surprised*).   Have you really, honestly reached that

25 conclusion?

ANDREW.   Well, it doesn't seem to amount to much now.

ROBERT.   But you're rich, aren't you?

ANDREW (*with a quick glance at* RUTH).   Yes, I s'pose so.

ROBERT.   I'm glad. You can do to the farm all I've undone. But

30 what did you do down there? Tell me. You went in the grain business with that friend of yours?

ANDREW.   Yes. After two years I had a share in it. I sold out last year.

He is answering ROBERT'S *questions with great reluctance.*

35 ROBERT.   And then?

ANDREW. I went in on my own.

ROBERT. Still in grain?

ANDREW. Yes.

ROBERT. What's the matter? You look as if I were accusing you of something.

ANDREW. I'm proud enough of the first four years. It's after that I'm not boasting of. I took to speculating.

ROBERT. In wheat?

ANDREW. Yes.

ROBERT. And you made money—gambling?

ANDREW. Yes.

ROBERT (*thoughtfully*). I've been wondering what the great change was in you. (*After a pause*) You—a farmer—to gamble in a wheat pit with scraps of paper. There's a spiritual significance in that picture, Andy. (*He smiles bitterly.*) I'm a failure, and Ruth's another—but we can both justly lay some of the blame for our stumbling on God. But you're the deepest-dyed failure of the three, Andy. You've spent eight years running away from yourself. Do you see what I mean? You used to be a creator when you loved the farm. You and life were in harmonious partnership. And now—— (*He stops as if seeking vainly for words*) My brain is muddled. But part of what I mean is that your gambling with the thing you used to love to create proves how far astray—— So you'll be punished. You'll have to suffer to win back—— (*His voice grows weaker and he sighs wearily.*) It's no use. I can't say it. (*He lies back and closes his eyes, breathing pantingly.*)

ANDREW (*slowly*). I think I know what you're driving at, Rob —and it's true, I guess.

ROBERT *smiles gratefully and stretches out his hand, which* ANDREW *takes in his.*

ROBERT. I want you to promise me to do one thing, Andy, after——

ANDREW. I'll promise anything, as God is my Judge!

ROBERT. Remember, Andy, Ruth has suffered double her share.

(*His voice faltering with weakness*) Only through contact with suffering, Andy, will you—awaken. Listen. You must marry Ruth—afterwards.

RUTH (*with a cry*).   Rob!

ROBERT *lies back, his eyes closed, gasping heavily for breath.*

ANDREW (*making signs to her to humor him—gently*) You're tired out, Rob. You better lie down and rest a while, don't you think? We can talk later on.

ROBERT (*with a mocking smile*).   Later on! You always were an optimist, Andy! (*He sighs with exhaustion.*) Yes, I'll go and rest a while. (*As* ANDREW *comes to help him*) It must be near sunrise, isn't it?

ANDREW.   It's after six.

ROBERT (*as* ANDREW *helps him into the bedroom*).   Shut the door, Andy. I want to be alone.

ANDREW *reappears and shuts the door softly. He comes and sits down on his chair again, supporting his head on his hands. His face is drawn with the intensity of his dry-eyed anguish.*

RUTH (*glancing at him—fearfully*).   He's out of his mind now, isn't he?

ANDREW.   He may be a little delirious. The fever would do that. (*With impotent rage*) God, what a shame! And there's nothing we can do but sit and—wait! (*He springs from his chair and walks to the stove.*)

RUTH (*dully*).   He was talking—wild—like he used to—only this time it sounded—unnatural, don't you think?

ANDREW.   I don't know. The things he said to me had truth in them—even if he did talk them way up in the air, like he always sees things. Still—— (*He glances down at* RUTH *keenly.*) Why do you suppose he wanted us to promise we'd—— (*Confusedly*) You know what he said.

RUTH (*dully*).   His mind was wandering, I s'pose.

ANDREW (*with conviction*).   No—there was something back of it.

RUTH.   He wanted to make sure I'd be all right—after he'd gone, I expect.

ANDREW.   No, it wasn't that. He knows very well I'd naturally look after you without—anything like that.

RUTH.   He might be thinking of—something happened five years back, the time you came home from the trip.

ANDREW.   What happened? What do you mean?   5

RUTH (*dully*).   We had a fight.

ANDREW.   A fight? What has that to do with me?

RUTH.   It was about you—in a way.

ANDREW (*amazed*).   About *me?*

RUTH.   Yes, mostly. You see I'd found out I'd made a mistake   10
about Rob soon after we were married—when it was too late.

ANDREW.   Mistake? (*Slowly*) You mean—you found out you didn't love Rob?

RUTH.   Yes.

ANDREW.   Good God!   15

RUTH.   And then I thought that when Mary came it'd be dif-
ferent, and I'd love him; but it didn't happen that way. And I couldn't bear with his blundering and book-reading—and I grew to hate him, almost.

ANDREW.   Ruth!   20

RUTH.   I couldn't help it. No woman could. It had to be because I loved someone else, I'd found out. (*She sighs wearily.*) It can't do no harm to tell you now—when it's all past and gone —and dead. *You* were the one I really loved—only I didn't come to the knowledge of it 'til too late.   25

ANDREW (*stunned*).   Ruth! Do you know what you're saying?

RUTH.   It was true—then. (*With sudden fierceness*) How could I help it? No woman could.

ANDREW.   Then—you loved me—that time I came home?

RUTH (*doggedly*).   I'd known your real reason for leaving home   30
the first time—everybody knew it—and for three years I'd been thinking——

ANDREW.   That I loved you?

RUTH.   Yes. Then that day on the hill you laughed about what a fool you'd been for loving me once—and I knew it was all   35
over.

ANDREW.   Good God, but I never thought—— (*He stops, shud-*
dering at his remembrance.) And did Rob——

RUTH.   That was what I'd started to tell. We'd had a fight just
before you came and I got crazy mad—and I told him all I've
5   told you.

ANDREW (*gaping at her speechlessly for a moment*).   You told
Rob—you loved me?

RUTH.   Yes.

ANDREW (*shrinking away from her in horror*).   You—you—you
10   mad fool, you! How could you do such a thing?

RUTH.   I couldn't help it. I'd got to the end of bearing things—
without talking.

ANDREW.   Then Rob must have known every moment I stayed
here! And yet he never said or showed—God, how he must
15   have suffered! Didn't you know how much he loved you?

RUTH (*dully*).   Yes. I knew he liked me.

ANDREW.   Liked you! What kind of a woman are you? Couldn't
you have kept silent? Did you have to torture him? No wonder
he's dying! And you've lived together for five years with this
20   between you?

RUTH.   We've lived in the same house.

ANDREW.   Does he still think——

RUTH.   I don't know. We've never spoke a word about it since
that day. Maybe, from the way he went on, he s'poses I care for
25   you yet.

ANDREW.   But you don't. It's outrageous. It's stupid! You don't
love me!

RUTH (*slowly*).   I wouldn't know how to feel love, even if I
tried, any more.

30   ANDREW (*brutally*).   And I don't love you, that's sure! (*He sinks
into his chair, his head between his hands.*) It's damnable such
a thing should be between Rob and me. Why, I love Rob
better'n anybody in the world and always did. There isn't
a thing on God's green earth I wouldn't have done to keep
35   trouble away from him. And I have to be the very one—it's
damnable! How am I going to face him again? What can I say

to him now? (*He groans with anguished rage. After a pause*)
He asked me to promise—what am I going to do?

RUTH.   You can promise—so's it'll ease his mind—and not mean
anything.

ANDREW.   What? Lie to him now—when he's dying? (*Deter-*
minedly) No! It's *you* who'll have to do the lying, since it
must be done. You've got a chance now to undo some of all
the suffering you've brought on Rob. Go in to him! Tell him
you never loved me—it was all a mistake. Tell him you only
said so because you were mad and didn't know what you were
saying! Tell him something, anything, that'll bring him peace!

RUTH (*dully*).   He wouldn't believe me.

ANDREW (*furiously*).   You've got to make him believe you, do
you hear? You've got to—now—hurry—you never know
when it may be too late. (*As she hesitates—imploringly*) For
God's sake, Ruth! Don't you see you owe it to him? You'll
never forgive yourself if you don't.

RUTH (*dully*).   I'll go. (*She gets wearily to her feet and walks*
slowly toward the bedroom.) But it won't do any good. (*AN-*
DREW's eyes are fixed on her anxiously. She opens the door
and steps inside the room. She remains standing there for a
minute. Then she calls in a frightened voice.) Rob! Where are
you? (*Then she hurries back, trembling with fright.*) Andy!
Andy! He's gone!

ANDREW (*misunderstanding her—his face pale with dread*).   He's
not——

RUTH (*interrupting him—hysterically*).   He's gone! The bed's
empty. The window's wide open. He must have crawled out
into the yard!

ANDREW. (*Springing to his feet. He rushes into the bedroom*
and returns immediately with an expression of alarmed amaze-
ment on his face.)   Come! He can't have gone far! (*Grabbing*
his hat he takes RUTH's *arm and shoves her toward the door.*)
Come on! (*Opening the door*) Let's hope to God——

The door closes behind them, cutting off his words as

The Curtain Falls

ACT THREE
SCENE TWO

*Same as Act One, Scene One—A section of country highway.
The sky to the east is already alight with bright color and a thin,
quivering line of flame is spreading slowly along the horizon rim
of the dark hills. The roadside, however, is still steeped in the
grayness of the dawn, shadowy and vague. The field in the foreground has a wild uncultivated appearance as if it had been
allowed to remain fallow the preceding summer. Parts of the
snake-fence in the rear have been broken down. The apple tree
is leafless and seems dead.*

ROBERT *staggers weakly in from the left. He stumbles into the
ditch and lies there for a moment; then crawls with a great
effort to the top of the bank where he can see the sun rise, and
collapses weakly.* RUTH *and* ANDREW *come hurriedly along the
road from the left.*

ANDREW (*stopping and looking about him*).   There he is! I knew
it! I knew we'd find him here.

ROBERT (*trying to raise himself to a sitting position as they hasten
to his side—with a wan smile*).   I thought I'd given you the
5   slip.

ANDREW (*with kindly bullying*).   Well you didn't, you old
scoundrel, and we're going to take you right back where you
belong—in bed.

He makes a motion to lift ROBERT.

10   ROBERT.   Don't, Andy. Don't, I tell you!

ANDREW.   You're in pain?

ROBERT (*simply*).   No. I'm dying. (*He falls back weakly.* RUTH
*sinks down beside him with a sob and pillows his head on her
lap.* ANDREW *stands looking down at him helplessly.* ROBERT
15   *moves his head restlessly on* RUTH'S *lap.*) I couldn't stand it
back there in the room. It seemed as if all my life—I'd been
cooped in a room. So I thought I'd try to end as I might have
—if I'd had the courage—alone—in a ditch by the open road
—watching the sun rise.

ANDREW.   Rob! Don't talk. You're wasting your strength. Rest
a while and then we'll carry you——

ROBERT.   Still hoping, Andy? Don't. I know. (*There is a pause
during which he breathes heavily, straining his eyes toward the
horizon.*) The sun comes so slowly. (*With an ironical smile*)   5
The doctor told me to go to the far-off places—and I'd be
cured. He was right. That was always the cure for me. It's too
late—for this life—but—— (*He has a fit of coughing which
racks his body.*)

ANDREW (*with a hoarse sob*).   Rob! (*He clenches his fists in an*   10
impotent rage against Fate.) God! God!

  RUTH *sobs brokenly and wipes* ROBERT'S *lips with her handkerchief.*

ROBERT (*in a voice which is suddenly ringing with the happiness
of hope*).   You musn't feel sorry for me. Don't you see I'm   15
happy at last—free—free!—freed from the farm—free to
wander on and on—eternally! (*He raises himself on his elbow,
his face radiant, and points to the horizon.*) Look! Isn't it beautiful beyond the hills? I can hear the old voices calling me to
come—— (*Exultantly*) And this time I'm going! It isn't the   20
end. It's a free beginning—the start of my voyage! I've won
to my trip—the right of release—beyond the horizon! Oh,
you ought to be glad—glad—for my sake! (*He collapses
weakly.*) Andy! (ANDREW *bends down to him.*) Remember
Ruth——   25

ANDREW.   I'll take care of her, I swear to you, Rob!   '

ROBERT.   Ruth has suffered—remember, Andy—only through
sacrifice—the secret beyond there—— (*He suddenly raises
himself with his last remaining strength and points to the horizon where the edge of the sun's disc is rising from the rim of the*   30
hills.) The sun! (*He remains with his eyes fixed on it for a
moment. A rattling noise throbs from his throat. He mumbles.*)
Remember! (*And falls back and is still.*)

  RUTH *gives a cry of horror and springs to her feet, shuddering, her hands over her eyes.* ANDREW *bends on one knee*   35
  beside the body, placing a hand over ROBERT'S *heart, then he*

kisses his brother reverentially on the forehead and stands up.

ANDREW (*facing* RUTH, *the body between them—in a dead voice*). He's dead. (*With a sudden burst of fury*) God damn you, you
5   never told him!

RUTH (*piteously*).   He was so happy without my lying to him.

ANDREW (*pointing to the body—trembling with the violence of his rage*).   This is your doing, you damn woman, you coward, you murderess!

10 RUTH (*sobbing*).   Don't, Andy! I couldn't help it—and he knew how I'd suffered, too. He told you—to remember.

ANDREW. (*Stares at her for a moment, his rage ebbing away, an expression of deep pity gradually coming over his face. Then he glances down at his brother and speaks brokenly in a com-*
15 *passionate voice.*)   Forgive me, Ruth—for his sake—and I'll remember—— (RUTH *lets her hands fall from her face and looks at him uncomprehendingly. He lifts his eyes to hers and forces out falteringly.*) I—you—we've both made a mess of things! We must try to help each other—and—in time—we'll
20 come to know what's right—— (*Desperately*) And perhaps we——

But RUTH, *if she is aware of his words, gives no sign. She remains silent, gazing at him dully with the sad humility of exhaustion, her mind already sinking back into that spent*
25 *calm beyond the further troubling of any hope.*

                                                   The Curtain Falls

————————

Although this full-length play raises no really new problems in an-alysis, it will give the student an opportunity to study a full-bodied plot as well as characterizations more elaborate than those likely to be found in a one-act play. The plot of this play embodies all the struc-tural elements we have distinguished in our discussion of plot: exposi-tion, development—both simplifying and complicating—turning point, climax, further development—both simplifying and complicating—and denouement. Answering the questions that follow this commentary should clarify the large-scale use of the structural elements that constitute plot.

This play also offers an opportunity to study more elaborate characterization than one is likely to find in the one-act play. The methods are the same, but their application is extended. All the methods available to the dramatist are utilized here: what the characters look like; what they say; how they express themselves; what they do; how they look at life; what they think of each other; what—to a degree—the dramatist thinks of them. As for the results of this elaborate process of character creation, the reader must judge for himself. To what extent are the characters individuals? To what extent are they types? Are they painted in broad or minute strokes? Do they embody coherent and credible personality patterns?

A full-length play such as this likewise raises sharply the important problem of the relationship between character and action. The life histories of three major characters are exhibited here, and, if the play is to be aesthetically satisfying, the reader must come to feel that there is a close and constant relationship between what the characters are and what they do, and that their development is an intelligible result of what they do, and what other characters do to them. This particular play, moreover, raises the question as to whether the tragic fate of the characters is or is not in excess of what we might reasonably expect. Are the final incidents in the action commensurate or incommensurate with the characters that the playwright has created?

Certain other problems arise from the fact that this play is not a comedy but a tragedy. The curious reader might consider whether or not this play illustrates the conception of tragedy held by Aristotle or a different conception. And he should decide whether its hero does or does not conform to Aristotle's conception of the ideal hero for tragedy, as quoted in the questions on Synge's "Riders to the Sea."

Finally, the play invites questioning with regard to the overall tone that results from the author's attitude toward his subject and his characters. Is the tone appropriate to the action and the characters involved in it, or is the tone sentimental? In other words, are the feelings and emotions of the characters appropriate to themselves and the situation in which they find themselves, or are the feelings and emotions in excess of those the characters might reasonably be expected to feel in the situations in which they are exhibited?

ACT I

Almost half of Scene I is devoted to exposition. What do we learn about the history of the family and of the two brothers in particular? What do we learn of the characters of the brothers? In the second half of Scene I, what complicating development takes place? Is Robert's decision psychologically plausible? Why or why not? What do we know of the character of Ruth by the end of this scene? Is she seen more or less clearly than the two brothers? Why?

Scene II introduces us to three more characters in the play. What do we learn about them in the part of the scene before Robert enters? What light does the Captain's attitude toward Robert throw on his own character? On Robert's? What additional complications does Robert's announcement of his decision make? Is the father's reaction to Andrew's decision credible or incredible? Give the reasons for your answer. Is Andrew's treatment of his brother after the other characters leave in character? Why or why not?

ACT II

What portion of Scene I in Act II is devoted to exposition of what has happened in the time that has elapsed since the end of Act I? What is the first method by which O'Neill brings out the changes that have taken place? By what means does he attempt to arouse and sustain interest in the long exposition that opens the scene? Is he successful? Why or why not? What advance in the action takes place in the remainder of the scene? What complicating developments occur? Why does O'Neill have Ben "give notice" at this point? Is the return of Andrew at the end of the scene a simplifying or a complicating development, or both? Give the reasons for your answer. Is Mrs. Atkins a character or a caricature? Give the reasons for your answer.

How much of Scene II is devoted to exposition and how much to development of the action? Of what value is the expository passage that opens the scene? What effect does Andrew's decision not to stay on the farm have on Robert? On Ruth? On their relations to each other? Is Andrew's announcement of his decision to leave the turning point in the play? Give the reasons for your answer. Why does O'Neill contrive Andrew's almost immediate departure? Is his decision to accept the chance to leave adequately motivated? Why or why not?

ACT III

Would the following details from the stage directions of Scene I be effective in the theater? "The closed desk is gray with accumulated dust as if it had not been used for years. Blotches of dampness disfigure the wall paper. Threadbare trails, leading to the kitchen and outer doors, show in the faded carpet. The top of the coverless table is stained with the imprints of hot dishes and spilt food. The rung of one rocker has been clumsily mended with a piece of plain board."

Of how many distinct parts is Scene I composed? Which of them are devoted to exposition of past action and which to the advancement of the action? Is the arrangement of expository passages and passages of action effective? Why or why not?

What changes have taken place in the character of Ruth in the five years that have elapsed since the end of Act II? How do you know?

Is Robert's dream of a new life for Ruth and himself made to seem psychologically plausible? Does Robert's refusal to inform Andrew of his plight seem to be in character? Why or why not?

What light does Andrew's reaction to his discovery of what happened during his preceding visit throw on his character? Is his insistence that Ruth shall assure Robert that she has always loved him and not Andrew in character? Why or why not?

What developments of the plot take place in this Act? Which of them are complicating and which simplifying developments?

Are there any further developments in Scene II of this Act or is it devoted entirely to the denouement? Give the reasons for your answer.

Does the climax, the scene of greatest emotional intensity, occur in the second or the third Act? In which part of which scene? Give the reasons for your choice.

What is the pattern of feeling and emotions through which Andrew passes in the final scene of the play? Is this pattern made to seem psychologically plausible? Why or why not?

Appendixes

APPENDIX A

The Study of Literature

No one who has ever read an absorbing novel or play or poem would doubt that he had had a vivid and exciting experience. Many addicts of literature, however, never give a thought to the nature of such an experience or the means by which it has been made possible.

When we begin to analyze what happens when we read a compelling piece of imaginative narrative, we discover that the experience is both like and unlike one in real life. Reading and living both involve something happening, an incident, an event, the rise and fall of a feeling or emotion, the coming and passing of a mood. Both experiences, therefore, involve the psychological elements of sensation, feeling, and emotion. Both imply a sense of duration, since any happening, whether objective or subjective, implies a beginning, a going on, and an ending, and each of these terms implies a relationship in time. But the differences between reading and living are as important as their resemblances. Only the most naïve or highly suggestible reader would ever confuse one experience with the other. Reading belongs to the realm of imagination; living belongs to the realm of actuality. The distance between art and life is, and always will be, immeasurable. Art indeed finds its values, not merely in its resemblance to life, but in its inevitable and insuperable divergence from it.

Art is the work of man; man is the work of God. The artist's relation to his handiwork resembles God's relation to His. The artist's powers mirror—on a smaller scale—the creative powers of God. A work of art is a "construct," a structure built, in literature, of words; in sculpture, of bronze or marble or wood; in painting, of paint and canvas; in music, of sounds. In this book, we have been concerned solely with "constructs" made of words, but the method of analyzing such "constructs" has relevance and utility to persons who are more easily moved by painting or sculpture or music than by literature.

To deal at all justly with the problem of why thousands of gifted men have devoted their lives to building constructs of words would lead us into an extended and perhaps irrelevant discussion. Two of the most famous answers to the problem were made centuries ago, and volumes have since been written in discussion of these answers. Aristotle suggested in the *Poetics* that men create works of imaginative literature for two reasons, first, because they love rhythm and harmony and, second, because they love to "imitate." These reasons are only apparently simple; a discussion of the concept of imitation alone would involve writing a history of aesthetics from Aristotle's time to our own. The terms "rhythm" and "harmony," although they belong primarily to the art of music, are elements common to all the arts; their application to painting, sculpture, and architecture, however illuminating, is actually metaphorical. The Aristotelian term "imitation," the most famous term in the history of aesthetics, is taken here to mean "presentation in an aesthetic medium." The term "representation" is deliberately avoided, since it might be defined—as some aestheticians have assumed—as the presentation of objects or events in a realistic aesthetic medium; this definition carries the erroneous implication that realism is the only defensible mode of imaginative literature or of pictorial art.

If we push the investigation a little further and ask why certain men love to "imitate," love to present real or imagined events or objects in an aesthetic medium, a second ancient writer, Horace, in his *Art of Poetry* has given us a time-honored answer:

> Aut prodesse volunt aut delectare poetae,
> Aut simul et iucunda et idonea dicere vitae,

or, as Ben Jonson translated the lines,

> Poets would either profit or delight,
> Or mixing sweet and fit, teach life the right.

Around these two words, "profit" and "delight," the discussion of the purposes of art has revolved, and, if we were surveying the history of aesthetics, we should discover that in some periods the didactic function of literature has been stressed and in other periods the pleasure function, but that in no period has either of them been entirely ignored.

It is easier for the modern reader to accept the pleasure-giving function of literature than the didactic. Writers of imaginative literature or painters or musicians or sculptors get some kind of pleasure (as well as pain, perhaps) out of the process of creation, just as children of all ages get pleasure from making snowmen, baking mudpies, or playing with dolls. And people who read imaginative literature or look at pictures or listen to music, get a more or less complex pleasure from the process, although most of them may not be able to give any very convincing reasons why art in general gives them pleasure or why a given work of art pleases them particularly.

If most modern readers shy away from the notion of the didactic function of imaginative literature, it is the word rather than the idea at which they boggle. No one who takes his reading with becoming seriousness will deny that reading imaginative literature is not only a pleasurable but somehow a profitable experience. The problem is the nature of the profit. Naïve readers find profit in the explicit moral that some great and some not so great literature embodies. More fastidious readers, although they shrink from an overt or over-simplified didacticism, would agree that they find profit in the power of imaginative literature to vivify life and to illuminate its meaning. To persons who find literature the most rewarding of the arts, it may indeed seem the clearest guide to the intricacies of the human heart and mind, the most powerful light cast upon the darkness with which human existence is encompassed.

This volume has set forth a method for the intensive analysis of imaginative literature in the form of the drama. Three ways of approaching literature are open, and an enumeration of those ways may serve to make clear what this book has attempted and what it has not attempted to do. These three approaches are the historical-biographical; the philosophical-ethical and the aesthetic-critical. Of these, the first is concerned with the relation between the work of art and the period in which it was produced or between the work of art and the man who produced it. The second considers the philosophical or ethical ideas embodied in the literary work or suggested by it. The third interprets and evaluates the work of art—a verbal-symbolic construct—as a work of art.

The aesthetic-critical approach to literature is, and should remain, primary. Works of art are, to be sure, produced by men living in a specific period of history, but, if such works of art have a more than historical value, they speak directly to readers of other times and ages through the signs and symbols out of which they are constructed. The study of the historical period in which a work is produced or of the man who produced the work may throw light on a literary work, but if the literary work has intrinsic worth, if it is more than raw material for the construction of literary history, it will, if read properly, yield its essential significance to the reader, without the aid of historical or biographical information. Thus, a play by James M. Barrie or Thornton Wilder will, if properly read, communicate its essence to the reader, become an absorbing and memorable and illuminating experience for him, even though the reader does not know that Barrie was known as the father of the Kailyard School of Scottish fiction or that Wilder won the Pulitzer Prize for a novel, *The Bridge of San Luis Rey.* The *excellence of a play does not consist of, or depend upon, its historical, biographical, or philosophical underpinning.*

APPENDIX B

The Values of Drama

A work of art is not the result of the imposition of technique upon subject matter; it is the *offspring of the union of substance and form,* of subject matter and technique. This offspring, like every human being, is a unique organism. It cannot properly be considered as the addition of form to substance, or of technique to subject matter. If this were the case, the form and substance, technique and subject matter, would be separable. But since a work of art is an organism, is the product of the complex fusion of substance and form, of subject matter and technique, it has an indestructible uniqueness. There is, besides, a functional relationship between form and substance, between subject matter and technique, just as there is a functional relationship between mind and body. Destroy the vital connection between mind and body, and you destroy a living human being. Ignore the vital connection between substance and form, between the subject matter and the technique of a work of art, and you destroy the living work of art.

There is a common critical heresy that analyzing a piece of literature destroys any pleasure it might give, if it were not analyzed. But just as the uncritical life, in Socrates' phrase, is the life of a beast, so the unanalyzed pleasure induced by a work of art is crude and coarse. The pleasure such heretics lose is that which arises from their fantasies concerning a work they have imperfectly comprehended. That such fantasies have their psychological utility cannot be denied, but the use of a literary work as a stimulus to egocentric day-dreaming is a perversion

of its real function. The method of intensive analysis set forth in this
book is intended to bring about, first, the student's accurate and detailed comprehension of the work under analysis and, second, an understanding of the means by which the artist has achieved the effect that
the student has, through the process of analysis, really grasped. There
is no comparison between the rewards of casual reading accompanied
by vague personal associations and the rewards of attentive reading
free from illegitimate associations.

What, then, are the values that the reader may derive from the
aesthetic-critical approach to the drama and from the process of intensive analysis?

If we make a thoroughgoing analysis of our experience when we
really read a play, we shall discover in it a number of distinct elements,
any one of which it may be agreeable or instructive to experience. These
elements may be designated as "factual," psychological, technical, symbolical, and ideational. They constitute the different values that are
inherent in the aesthetic experience of literature. To define and illustrate
them may make clear how the study of drama can be both pleasant
and profitable.

"FACTUAL" VALUES[1]

"Factual" values are the values of the raw material of the work.
They are evident in a simple prose summary of the substance of a work.
These are the most elementary of literary values, because they arise
from the substance forcibly separated from the form. For instance, the
"factual" values of The Merchant of Venice or of Hamlet are those that
might be felt if one read an accurate summary of the action of these
works. But these values, though elementary, are not, for that reason,
unimportant. They are the base on which the more subtle pleasures
that the work may give are built.

Now, how is it that we can get pleasure from even a summary of a
drama? Such a summary can give us one of two kinds of pleasure, or
a pleasure that involves both kinds. One kind of pleasure is the pleasure
of recognition. The pleasure of recognition arises from our finding ele-

[1] Quotation marks are used around the word, factual, to distinguish a "fact" in a
literary work from a fact in life. They do no more than hint at the philosophical implications of this distinction.

ments in the substance of a drama familiar to us either because they are part and parcel of our personal experience or because they echo our literary experiences. The possible intensity of the pleasure of recognition may explain the behavior of persons who select their reading on the basis of its subject matter, for example, Westerns, mysteries, or stories of horror and the supernatural. They would feel unhappy if forced to read stories the subject matter of which they had not encountered repeatedly.

But pleasure is quite as likely to come to us because the substance of a drama is unfamiliar. The strange, the unknown, the exotic may be much more alluring than that which has become familiar to us in either our daily lives or our habitual reading. The history of literature furnishes numerous examples of the vogue of exotic subject matters and their exploitation. Italy at the time of the English Renaissance, the American Indian in the late eighteenth and nineteenth centuries, the South Sea Islands in the late nineteenth and early twentieth centuries are instances of exotic material that stirred the imagination and excited the feelings of both writers and audiences.

Most dramas blend familiar and unfamiliar elements. In dramas about life with which the reader is most familiar, some novel observation or fresh insight prevents their being disappointingly banal. On the other hand, dramas of the most fantastic sort—if they are to be acceptable —must have something in common with life as we know it or they will be well-nigh unintelligible to us.

These "factual" values are implicit in the raw material of the drama, the condensed prose meaning of its content. The other values—psychological, technical, symbolical, and ideational—all grow out of the fusion of substance and form in a unique organism; they cannot properly be experienced apart from the total effect of that product.

PSYCHOLOGICAL VALUES

The psychological values of a drama may be classified as sensory, emotional, empathetic, and analytical.

By the sensory values in a drama we mean the experience of a rich and vivid series of images. Some words evoke images (in the reader endowed with a normal apparatus of sense perception), and others do not evoke specific images. Words like *red, hot, saline, soft, crunch, bludgeon* are image-making words; words like *thought, soul, enumerate, sociological,* or *ideal* may evoke associations that involve images but they do not evoke images directly. Psychologists distinguish six types of images: visual (sight), auditory (sound), tactile (touch), gustatory (taste), olfactory (smell), and kinesthetic (the sensation of tension or relaxation in muscles, tendons, or joints).

In any play it is possible to discover the words that make images, the words that do not, and the proportion of image-making to non-image-making words. Dialogue in which the proportion of image-making words is high makes an impact on our senses only slightly less sharp and distinct than actual sense perceptions. Dialogue in which the proportion of nonimage-making words is high obviously has a limited sensory appeal and makes considerable demands on the reader's power to conceive of abstract terms easily and clearly. For these reasons most readers agree that the reading of dramas is easy and that the reading of philosophical works is hard. On the other hand, the reader addicted to philosophy may find the reading of philosophical works easy and the reading of plays hard.

Words have other powers, however, than those of evoking images and denoting abstract ideas. They also have the power of arousing feelings and emotions. Feelings can be roughly distinguished from emotions by their vagueness and lack of intensity. Love and hate are emotions; anxiety, serenity, melancholy, lassitude are feelings. Words that represent universal elements in simple human experience—words like *home, mother, war, death*—arouse emotional responses that are practically identical for persons conditioned by the same culture. It is on the power of such words that writers—both popular and sophisticated—rely to manipulate the emotions of the reader. (The cold-blooded exploitation of such emotions is obvious in the American commercialization of "Mother's Day.") Not all words that arouse feelings, however, arouse the same feelings in all readers; such a common word as "cat" evokes very different emotions from those who "love" cats and those who are afraid of them. Although the word "snake" evokes in most readers a feeling of vague distaste, if not of fear, there are persons who devote their lives to a study of the genus, and a snake-charmer hardly shares the normal distaste for this creature. Lovers of dogs might very well resent the fact—if they were aware of it—that Shakespeare never mentions a dog except to attach a disagreeable or distasteful feeling to this usually unobjectionable animal.

One particular complex feeling, that of empathy, may be distinguished from simple feelings of distaste or fondness. Empathy, as the root of the word indicates, means the experience of "feeling oneself into" a character or emotion or situation. It is brought about in literature by the accumulation of a complex series of images and feelings that lure the reader into identifying himself with a character or emotion or situation. Probably any drama which we experience intimately gives us the beginnings of the feeling of empathy, but some works manifest the power of empathy to a very high degree. Any situation that arouses basic human emotions is likely to lure even the experienced reader into feeling, temporarily, one or more of the emotions appropriate to the situation. But the experience of empathy depends on the nature and experience of the reader. Some readers whose feelings and emotions are easily stirred will experience empathy much more rapidly and vividly than readers whose feelings and emotions are sluggish and who have a strong sense of their own identity. Naïve or relatively inexperienced readers certainly achieve empathy more easily than experienced or sophisticated readers. Probably every adult reader can recall the time when it was easy for him to become so completely absorbed in reading an engrossing story that he lost contact for the time being with his immediate surroundings. A book is so accessible a means of escaping the pressures of actuality that for many apparently mature readers the consumption of novels is not to be distinguished psychologically, if it may be ethically, from addiction to drugs or liquor. Genuinely adult readers, however, will feel that the loss of the power to identify themselves with the hero or the heroine of a work is offset by the subtler and more dependable experience of analyzing the work objectively and appreciating it for other reasons than its power to produce a transient orgy of wish-fulfillment.

The final kind of psychological value to be defined and discussed is the analytical. It is the most complex and, therefore, perhaps the least tangible of the psychological values that inhere in drama, but its presence is essential to all drama of quality. It is the power manifested by the author in his analysis of character and his understanding of the motivation of human beings. The analysis of character may be made explicitly, or the results of the analysis may be presented and the analysis itself left implicit. Older writers were inclined to make explicit analyses of their characters; serious modern writers prefer to give the results of their analysis and to leave the work of analysis to their readers. In the latter instance, the writer is making demands on his reader that the earlier writer did not always make; he is asking of his reader a capacity for analysis that is roughly equivalent to his own. The reader's ability to meet the responsibility means that he, like the writer, is unusually able to observe and analyze human beings, collect evidence from their appearance, speech, manners, and conduct, and weigh accurately the significance of that evidence. On occasions when the reader coöperates happily with the author in discovering the personality pattern of a character, he is experiencing the special psychological value that we have called analytical.

TECHNICAL VALUES

Since most of the chapters in this book have been devoted to the technical elements of the drama, it will be sufficient here to define this value and differentiate it from "factual," psychological, symbolical, and ideational values. The technical values of a drama are those that belong to its formal aspects, to the properties it has as a result of the fusion of a particular subject matter and a particular form, or, to put it differently, as a result of giving a particular subject matter the form that will express most satisfactorily its potential values. Any reader who is at all conscious of the pattern of action or the characterization of a play, is responding, however modestly, to the technical values of the literary work he is reading. It is the purpose of this book to make the reader intensely conscious of the technical values of the drama and of the functional relationship between the subject matter of a work of art and its technique—in other words, of the use of a particular technique as a means to the end of giving maximum expressiveness to a particular subject matter.

SYMBOLICAL VALUES

Through the elements the writer treats as symbols, a drama achieves a significance for its readers beyond the merely "factual" and literal. The words of which drama is composed are technically called *signs*. Words are combinations of sounds that point to an actual or an absent or an imagined person, action, object, or idea. The omnipresence of verbal signs—words—needs no illustration, although the creation of language is perhaps man's most spectacular achievement. But the world of nature is no less full of signs than the mind of man is full of verbal signs. Certainly no dweller in the country passes a day without attempting to interpret the signs that point to the weather for the rest of the day or the next day. So, birds flying high, smoke rising straight in the air, and a clear sunset are commonly regarded as signs pointing to clear weather, whereas leaves blown wrong-side out or smoke hanging low are commonly regarded as signs pointing to bad weather. But these are, as Mrs. Langer shows in *Philosophy in a New Key,* "natural signs," and, just as nature produces natural signs, man seems to have an uncontrollable impulse to produce artificial signs. Thus, a wedding ring is a sign of a particular personal and social relationship, just as a black band on the coat sleeve is a sign of a particular emotional state. But both the wedding ring and the black band are not only signs but symbols; that is to say, they not only *point to* something fairly specific, but they *stand for* a wide range of significant acts or attitudes. The wedding ring is intrinsically of very slight value; extrinsically, it takes on the values of the relationship toward which it points. Certainly we all know of persons whose overvaluation of a wedding ring is so great that they would hesitate to remove it from the finger, and who would regard the loss of a wedding ring as at least ominous and possibly disastrous.[2]

[2] One of the most exquisite literary uses of symbolism that occurs to me involves the loss of a wedding ring. In Maeterlinck's *Pelléas and Mélisande,* Mélisande is sitting by a pool with her husband's brother, Pelléas. She takes off her wedding ring and tosses it into the air above the pool. Suddenly, it slips through her fingers, and is lost. She is distressed, and her husband, when he learns of the loss, is very angry. A portion

The fact of the matter is that man finds it impossible to express the values that he finds most significant except through tangible physical symbols or relatively intangible verbal symbols. Intrinsically, many of these symbols may be valueless; extrinsically, they are beyond price. Two sticks crossed or a pattern of colored bunting cost little or nothing; actually, they may stand for values for which men have died the most painful of deaths.[3]

The artist, like man generally, must, if he is to precipitate and communicate his most precious values, choose and present symbols that will convey to the reader the values he holds dear. The symbols may be national or racial or universal; what he attempts to do is to present them in such a way, arrange them in such a pattern that the reader will catch the particular values that he attaches to them. Psychoanalysts have shown through the analysis of dreams that certain symbols are almost universal, and such symbols, if the artist uses them, are likely to make the deepest—because sometimes unconscious—appeal to the reader. But the artist, on the other hand, may reject universal or even common symbols, and create his own symbols. In the use of such symbols, his task is indeed difficult, because he must persuade the reader to accept the symbolical significance he attaches to persons, actions, objects, or words.[4]

---

of her distress and of her husband's anger is, as the psychoanalyst would say, due to the awareness of both of them that Mélisande would not have "lost" the ring if she had not "wanted"—perhaps unconsciously—to lose it. Another famous literary "loss" is that of Desdemona's handkerchief in Shakespeare's *Othello*. Othello's elaborate explanation of the magical powers of this particular bit of embroidered cloth is probably pure "rationalization." Othello is furiously angry with Desdemona for losing the handkerchief, not because it has any intrinsic value but because he thinks her loss of it implies that she does not treasure it, that is to say, his gift to her, that is to say, *him*. And when Othello sees the handkerchief in the hands of Cassio, he is sure not only that he has lost Desdemona's love but that she is unfaithful to him.

[3] Of course, there is a common tendency to increase the intrinsic value of a symbol in order to suggest its great extrinsic value. Thus, we may explain the creation of monetarily very valuable (and incidentally very beautiful) religious symbolic objects, and of engagement rings that are intended to suggest by their size and brilliance the "overvaluation" of the beloved person that is implied in the bestowal of the ring.

[4] A symbol may be compared profitably and contrasted with a simile on the one hand and a metaphor on the other. All three—simile, metaphor, and symbol—resemble each other in that they indicate a kind of relationship between one object, entity, or concept and another object, entity, or concept, of a different sort. They differ

The significance of symbols in the drama may now become apparent. It is possible for a drama to take on a greater significance than a non-imaginative work like an encyclopedia article on Borneo or a demonstration of a geometrical proposition, largely because the artist utilizes words not only as signs but also as symbols. In fact, if he wishes the work to have a wide significance, he embodies in it a pattern of symbols that points to the meaning that he wishes to communicate.

Let us see, for example, what the symbols are in Yeats's play, *Cathleen ni Houlihan*, and what meaning arises out of the way in which Yeats arranges them. In a literary work, as in life, a symbol may take the form of a person, an object, an act, or even a term, like *mother*, *home*, *kiss*, or *integrity*. There are three major symbols in Yeats's play: the bridegroom, the young bride, and the old woman. Of the first two the significance is immediately obvious. The young bridegroom "stands for" a young man on the verge of entering into the most meaningful of personal relations, and the prospective bride, who is the least stressed of the symbols, stands for this most meaningful relationship, marriage. The significance of the old woman is least apparent. As a matter of fact, on the literal level, she is meaningless; what sense could one pos-

---

from each other in the nature of the relationship. The simplest of these relationships is that of the simile, the verbal form of which—"like" or "as"—indicates that the relationship is that of comparison. A slightly more complex type of relationship is the metaphor which involves a momentary identification of the two elements in the comparison; thus, the metaphor "dripping wistaria" suggests a momentary but imaginatively illuminating identification between the pendant flowers of the wistaria and a little shower of raindrops. The symbol represents the most potentially complicated kind of comparison; it may be indicated by the phrase "stands for." This loose phrase makes it clear why a symbol is capable of an almost indefinite expansion of meaning, since the symbol may be made by a man or a race to stand for a very considerable variety of significances. Thus, a nation's flag is a symbol that "stands for" the whole range of emotions and ideas that are associated by an individual or a people with the country to which they belong. Since it admits of a wide variety of significances, it is easy to see why the symbolic significance of a flag ranges from the casually to the tragically meaningful. In wartime this particular symbol is most potent, as one realizes when he recalls the great emotion stirred in the American people by the photograph of the flag being planted by a group of Marines on Iwo Jima. Similarly, the symbol of the national anthem permits of varying significances. When it is played at the beginning of a concert or the performance of a play in wartime, only the most insensitive person remains quite unmoved by patriotic emotion. It is astonishing that the habit of playing the national anthem under such circumstances should lapse rapidly after the end of a war.

sibly make of a young man's leaving his young bride-to-be to follow an old woman who at first has the aspect of a beggar? One can easily imagine an Oriental student reading this play for the first time and quite failing to see the significance of the old woman and, therefore, any meaning in the play. It is only when we see what the old woman symbolizes that this particular play takes on meaning. The old woman's speeches, the song she sings, her aspect after she has left the house are all means by which the poet suggests that this woman is not a mad beggar wandering the roads, but "stands for" Ireland herself. And the pattern of symbols that Yeats builds points to the idea that for some men, if not for all, love of country will take precedence over love of woman. But Yeats refrains from turning this statement into dogma by presenting the case without explicit comment, although the way in which he weights the symbols—since the bride-to-be is hardly given a chance to exert her influence upon the young man—indicates on which side Yeats's feelings are in this particular play.

It is the symbols that make the play meaningful. The symbol of the old woman, Cathleen ni Houlihan, brings home to the reader the problem, particularly acute in some countries and in some periods, of what direction his major loyalty is to take, whether the focus is to be on his personal or his political relationships. "The arts are our storehouse of recorded values," as I. A. Richards says, because artists are especially skilled in the use of symbols to express the values they find most significant.

IDEATIONAL VALUES

The somewhat formidable term "ideational" is used to suggest the philosophical or ethical values in the drama. Every play implicitly, and many plays explicitly, express the philosophical, ethical, or religious attitudes of the writer. He chooses and presents his subject in the light of, and against the background of, his total intellectual experience. The attitude he takes toward his subject is part and parcel of his general attitude toward the world and the values or absence of values in that world.

It may be well to indicate as simply and specifically as possible the meaning of philosophical, ethical, or religious views. Philosophical views

are ideas of the nature of reality, the nature of the world, the nature
of man, and the relationship between man and the universe in which
he finds himself. Ethical views are ideas as to what constitutes good
and what constitutes evil. Religious views are ideas concerning the
nature of the power behind the universe, whether that power be a
personal deity, immanent or transcendant, or an impersonal force,
and man's relationship to the power or force. If in a short play the
reader is unable to see ideas relevant to these great intellectual problems, he should remember that the writer's choice of a subject implies
that he feels that the subject is worth treating, and his preference for
this subject implies his rejection of other subjects as less important. And
almost no work is so brief as not to suggest what the writer regards as
good and what he regards as less good, or evil. A writer's views of the
world often change, however, and he should not be expected to express
or suggest the same ethical or philosophical views in every work he
produces during his lifetime.

The attentive reader will watch for the ideational overtones in any
drama and will not be satisfied until he has grasped and understood
them, particularly when they are antithetical to his own philosophical,
ethical, or religious views.[5]

Imaginative literature is the embodiment by the artist in alluring and
enduring words, of substances that have for him explicit or implicit
values. The substance thus alluringly embodied may vivify, clarify, and
make meaningful experiences that the reader has had, or make compelling and illuminating experiences he has not had. Literature may
stimulate and enrich the reader's imaginative experience on its sensory
and emotional planes. Literature may, by its presentation of the author's
philosophical, ethical, or religious views, clarify and order the reader's
views or may give him the temporary experience of philosophical, ethical, or religious views that are not his own. The reader's temporary.

[5] The distinction between the philosophical-ethical approach to literature and the discrimination of the ideational values in a literary work may be difficult to keep in mind,
but it nevertheless exists. Quite simply, the philosophical-ethical approach removes the
ideas from their context and considers their validity in a philosophical framework. The
discrimination of the ideational values in a literary work does not divorce the ideas
from their context, does not concern itself with their validity, and weighs them as only
one—and often not the most important—of the aesthetic values of the work.

acceptance of unfamiliar views may deepen and broaden the whole stream of his ideas, may encourage him continually to modify his own view of life in the light of views that he only partially accepts, and may —in the long run—increase the store of wisdom he may garner from the insights of greater and more penetrating intellects. Literature in its technical aspects may give the reader an intense experience of the infinite variety and wonder of human creativity, of the artist's godlike power to give a peculiar permanence to fleeting and transitory experience through the immensely evocative patterns made by words.

Index

INDEX

Page references to the texts of plays and to commentaries and questions on the plays are in italics.